The Shaman From Elko

The Shaman From Elko

PAPERS IN HONOR OF JOSEPH L. HENDERSON
ON HIS SEVENTY-FIFTH BIRTHDAY

EDITORIAL COMMITTEE

Gareth Hill, *chairman*
Virginia Detloff
Thomas Kirsch
William McGuire
Louis Stewart

SIGO PRESS

Printing History
Originally published by the C.G. Jung Institute of San Francisco, Inc. 1978

SIGO PRESS
25 New Chardon Street, #8748
Boston, Massachusetts 02114

Publisher and General Editor: Sisa Sternback

Grateful acknowledgement is made to the following for permission to reprint copyrighted material: Princeton University Press for quotations from the *Collected Works of C. G. Jung* edited by G. Adler, M. Fordham, H. Read, translated by R. F. C. Hull, Bollingen Series XX. Copyright © 1953, 1954, 1955, 1956, 1957, 1958, 1959, 1960, 1961, 1963, 1964, 1966, 1967, 1968, 1969, 1970, 1971, 1972, 1976.

Beacon Press for quotations from *The Psychoanalysis of Fire* by Gaston Bachelard. Copyright © 1964 by Alan C. M. Ross, French edition © 1938 by Librairie Gallimard.

From *The Poetics of Reverie* by Gaston Bachelard, a translation Copyright © 1969 by Grossman Publishers, Inc. Reprinted by permission of Viking Penguin, Inc.

Walter-Verlag, Olten, for quotations from *Bewusstsein* by C. A. Meier. Copyright © 1977.

Abbreviations of Principal References
B. S. = Bollingen Series
CW = *The Collected Works of C. G. Jung*. Edited by Gerhard Adler, Michael Fordham, and Herbert Read; William McGuire, Executive Editor; translated by R. F. C. Hull. New York and Princeton (Bollingen Series XX) and London, 1953-1978, 20 vols.
JAP = *The Journal of Analytic Psychology*

Library of Congress Cataloging-in-Publication Data

The Shaman from Elko : papers in honor of Joseph L. Henderson on his
  seventy-fifth birthday / editorial committee, Gareth Hill, chairman
  [... et al.].
    p. cm.
  Originally published: San Francisco : C. G. Jung Institute, 1978.
  Includes bibliographical references.
  ISBN 0-938-434-80-2. -- ISBN 0-938434-79-9 (pbk.)
    1. Psychoanalysis and culture. 2. Shamanism–North America-
-Psychological aspects. 3. Indians of North America–Religion and
mythology. 4. Psychoanalysis and literature. 5. Psychotherapy.
6. Jung, C. G. (Carl Gustav), 1875-1961. 7. Henderson, Joseph L.
L. (Joseph Lewis), 1903-   . I. Hill, Gareth. II. Henderson, Joseph
  L. (Joseph Lewis), 1903-
[BF175.4.C84S42 1991]   90-8814
150.19'54–dc20   CIP

Printed in Korea
∞

Contents

Part Three

Foreword

THE IDEA OF A FESTSCHRIFT for Joseph Henderson was perhaps first suggested two or three years ago by William McGuire, who has had a genuine interest in the history of analytical psychology in the United States. The idea began to germinate in the minds of those who heard the suggestion, notably Louis Stewart, Melvin Kettner, and James Yandell. In the meantime, in keeping with a desire to honor venerable members of our Institute community, the idea of a Festschrift for Joe had also occurred to me, but I had put it in reserve somewhere in my mind. In April 1977, Joe gave a public lecture on an aspect of his work on the archetype of culture. I found the lecture useful in relation to certain clinical situations in my practice at the time, and I was moved to write Joe a word of appreciation. I wrote the letter on April 30th but somehow dated it August 31. On May 8, Joe wrote back, "I was especially intrigued by the date on which your letter was written, *August 31, 1977*, which happens to be my birthday when I will be 74, I hope a favorable anticipation." I was flabbergasted, because I had no conscious knowledge that August 31 was Joe's birth date. I quickly surmised that the unconscious was speaking to my thoughts about a Festschrift, and after consulting the *I Ching*, I felt the courage and resolve to approach Joe with the idea.

The response of the *I Ching* was "(8) *Pi*/Holding Together (Union)," which changed to "(47) *K'un*/Oppression (Exhaustion)." Encouraged and chastened, I followed the instructions given in "8" and consulted the oracle again to determine whether I possessed the qualities needed for the task. The *I Ching* yielded "(13) *T'ung Jên*/Fellowship with Men." It is hard to imagine more auspicious hexagrams considering the nature of the project at issue, the sobering warning of exhaustion notwithstanding. I wrote to Joe, and he graciously gave his approval to the project. Soon after, through Thomas Kirsch,

I became aware of the thoughts and interest of others. As Tom said, "It's an idea whose time has come." A Festschrift Committee was formed consisting of three analysts, Louis Stewart, Thomas Kirsch, and myself, and we invited William McGuire to join in recognition of his early, seminal idea and in quest of his editorial experience. Virginia Detloff graciously volunteered her editorial services, most fittingly, not only in the light of her expertise but because she had done bibliographical work and prepared the index for Joe's *Thresholds of Initiation.* The skills and services of John Levy, Barbara McClintock, Paul Anderson, and Helen Dunham were also enlisted toward production of the book. For the Festschrift Committee, it has been a labor of love, but special recognition and thanks are due Virginia Detloff and William McGuire for their many hours of editorial attention.

This volume of papers by his friends and colleagues, presented in honor of his seventy-fifth birthday, August 31, 1978, is a celebration which flows from the respect, gratitude, and love felt by many for Joe Henderson for his enormous contribution to our personal and professional lives—as analyst, teacher, model, and friend. Papers have been contributed by members of the San Francisco Institute community, analyst members, candidates, and Board members-at-large, and by certain of Joe's especially long-time colleagues from the international Jungian community.

The contributions fell naturally into three categories, which reflect interests Joe has had throughout his long career. In Part One are selections which relate closely to his interest in native American cultures and shamanism. Papers on culture, philosophy, and literary themes of psychological interest, including initiation, are grouped in Part Two. And, in Part Three are clinically oriented papers.

G. S. H.

J. L. H.
His Life and His Work

GARETH S. HILL

JOSEPH LEWIS HENDERSON WAS BORN on August 31, 1903, in Elko, Nevada, and he grew up there. His relation to native Americans —a principal theme of the present volume—dates back to his earliest life. As a child, he took Indians for granted as "part of the landscape." From a village just outside Elko, Indians came to town to market, and as a boy, Joe was looked after by an old Indian woman. But, it was not until he was in analysis with Jung, beginning in the fall of 1929, when he was twenty-six, that Joe became conscious of the psychological importance of his early experiences with Indians.

In 1927, the British psychiatrist H. Godwin Baynes, called "Peter" by his close associates, suggested to Joe, when they first met in Carmel, California, that he "belonged" in Europe and would feel at home there. Dr. Baynes was right; Joe found the comfortable homogeneity and security of his social milieu in Europe entirely compatible. He said to Thomas Kirsch, in an interview recorded by the Film Archive Project of the C. G. Jung Institute of Los Angeles, "Living in Europe, I was in danger of becoming too European for my own good, and the Indian kept coming into my dreams to remind me that I was American." In a talk to the Analytical Psychology Club of San Francisco in 1976, he recalled his skepticism about Jung's assertion that Americans are all possessed by an Indian soul. When he expressed his doubts in one of his hours with Jung, Jung brought the conversation around to Joe's latest dream, asking for his associations. A clear association to a childhood image of the Indian women of Elko and their papooses arose in Joe, and

Jung's laughter in response convinced him that Jung was right, that the American psyche does contain an Indian component.

Later, in 1931, while home on holiday from his premedical studies in London, Joe was invited by his aunt on a trip to the Southwest to witness various Indian dances. His aunt, Ethel Smith Henderson, had been his "second mother" and a formative influence in his early education and intellectual development. She, her friend Leslie Denman, Noel Sullivan, a nephew of Senator Phelan of California, and others planned the trip. They traveled to Gallup, New Mexico, a center from which they would visit the Zuñi and Sia to see the corn dances and Hopi country to see the snake dance. Following this trip, Joe was "quite obsessed" with Indians, and his study of their cultures broadened and deepened. The Hopi snake dance became the subject of his first paper read to the Analytical Psychology Club of London in 1932.

In the meantime, the initiation archetype assumed increasing importance in his continuing analytic work with Jung in early and late summer between years of medical school in London. In 1933, he met the family of Professor Francis M. Cornford, the famous scholar of Greek philosophy and mythology, at Cambridge University. His wife Frances was a poet of distinction. Professor Cornford, later to become his father-in-law, introduced him to the work of Jane Harrison and other Greek scholars of the period. During these years of medical school at Saint Bartholomew's Hospital, his evenings were often spent in study which brought together his analysis, his study of native American cultures, and his increasing knowledge of cultural parallels flowing from the initiation archetype. His study, reflection, and research culminated in the book *Thresholds of Initiation*, published in 1967.

In spite of the eruption of Indian imagery during the European period, it is difficult to imagine origins more thoroughly pioneer American than Joe's. Both sides of his family possessed the spirit of the old West. His great grandfather, Lewis Rice Bradley, left Virginia in 1845 and settled in Missouri, where he farmed for seven years. He had one son and three daughters. In 1852, pushing farther westwards, he settled in Stockton, California, where he was successful as a cattleman. In the wagon train, he met Jefferson Henderson, a young pharmacist from

Missouri, and they struck up a friendship. Bradley fell ill on the trip, and the young pharmacist successfully treated him. His health restored, the grateful Bradley suggested that, after they had found a place to settle in the West, they return to Missouri, where Henderson could meet his daughters. In the pragmatic and expedient spirit of the times, the plan made by the two men was a complete success, and Henderson was married to Sarah Bradley. Bradley returned to Stockton, but Jefferson and Sarah Henderson remained in Missouri, where John Henderson, Joe's father, was born in 1864.

Bradley was very successful in Stockton and was elected to the California legislature in 1860. In 1866, however, he sold out and moved to Elko, Nevada, where he again established himself in the cattle business. Opportunities abounded for him in Nevada, and gradually raising cattle gave way to other interests. In 1870, Bradley was elected the second governor of Nevada, and he was re-elected by a greater majority in 1874. In the meantime, Jefferson Henderson brought his family to Elko in 1872 but soon moved on to San Jose, California, where Joe's uncle, Charles Belknap Henderson, was born in 1873. Their start in San Jose, however, was a false one, and they returned to Elko, where Jefferson Henderson founded the house of J. Henderson, Banker, in 1880, succeeding a defunct banking operation. He was the only banker in that part of the state, and, because of his acumen and his connections in the livestock business, he was enormously successful where others had failed. In 1889, his banking house was incorporated into the Henderson Banking Company, and its presidency eventually passed to John Henderson, Joe's father. Members of the family held stock in the bank as well as in the Henderson-Griswold Live Stock Company, which had extensive ranching interests. The family member for whom Joe was named was his uncle, Joseph Jefferson Henderson, M.D., an ophthalmologist in San Francisco.

Joe's mother, Maud Henley Henderson, was born in Red Bluff, California, where her father, William N. Henley, was a mining engineer. The Henley family originally had come from Kentucky and her mother's family from New Orleans. Left an orphan at an early age, she was reared by two maiden aunts. She studied at a normal school in San Jose, California, and after finishing her training in 1891, she took her first teaching job in Elko. She soon met John Henderson, and six months later, they were married. A strikingly beautiful woman, she was characterized by great warmth of feeling and was loved by everyone. She devoted her life entirely to her family.

Joe was one of three children; a sister, Marjorie, is eight years his senior and a brother, John, Jr., nine years younger. He spent his boyhood in the local public school and worked on a family ranch during the summers. His father cherished the wish that Joe, the scion of a well-to-do and influential family, would follow in his footsteps, as he had in his father's, and assume a position in the family bank and the management of the family's interests. In fact, he made a certain effort to train Joe for a role in the bank in the period of his early adolescence. Though he outwardly cooperated, Joe was so profoundly and benignly uninterested that he was never able to find anything to say to his father about it. Gradually his father realized the futility of his wish, and he genuinely supported Joe in his own aspirations.

Ethel Smith Henderson, married to Joe's uncle, Charles Henderson, and a woman of considerable intellectual ability, was determined that her own sons and their cousins should have good educations. Joe's older sister was educated in Switzerland as a result of Aunt Ethel's guidance, and her influence prevailed in the decision that Joe should go to preparatory school at Lawrenceville, New Jersey. In 1919, at age sixteen, released from his father's aspirations for him, Joe started four years of schooling at Lawrenceville. In 1918, on the death of Senator Francis G. Newlands, Charles Henderson had been appointed to fulfill his term; he had moved to Washington and was elected for a second term. Joe spent considerable time with his Aunt Ethel and Uncle Charles in Washington during his holidays, and a stimulating new intellectual and social world opened up to him.

At Lawrenceville, he came under the tutelage of Thornton Wilder, who was a young assistant housemaster teaching French. Joe found him an inspired teacher at all levels of culture; he awakened in Joe an interest in literature, the arts, and psychology. Wilder was already reading such authors as Proust, Joyce, and Freud and he introduced their writings to his friends and students. Joyce had then published only *Dubliners* and *A Portrait of the Artist as a Young Man.* In 1919, Proust was just becoming known following the publication of the second of the seven parts of *À la recherche du temps perdu.* Not until the twenties did very much psychoanalytic literature become accessible in English. Joe's friendship with Wilder continued at Princeton, where Joe was an undergraduate and Wilder was taking a master's degree in French literature. It was Wilder who introduced him to the psychological perspective, but psychology was not to emerge as the proper direction for his career until later.

In this period, he was also greatly influenced by his reading of Henry Adams. Adam's delicate sensibilities and refined taste, reflected in *The Education of Henry Adams*, provided a model for his own development. *Mont-Saint-Michel and Chartres* awakened a sustained interest in the cathedrals of Europe and in the animating spirit behind their construction in the medieval period—the feminine (Virgin), a force Joe would only later come to know as the *anima.* During the thirties, he shared his interest in Gothic cathedrals with Joseph Wheelwright, whom he met in London in 1932. They took a motor trip together to study the cathedrals of France, and Wheelwright today reports, "Joe knew everything!"

In his filmed interview with Thomas Kirsch, Joe recalled that as a youth he held a predominantly aesthetic attitude toward his cultural experience. He said, "Later it became a more philosophic attitude, and the big thing that happened in my analysis was the discovery of a religious attitude. The social attitude is probably at the bottom of the list." It was not until 1944, in "The Problem of Maturity," an unpublished paper presented to The Analytical Psychology Club of San Francisco, that he first outlined the four attitudes which he later brought together into his theory of the archetype of culture. The aesthetic attitude had been greatly stimulated by the influence of Wilder and Adams, and it was carried into his somewhat vague aspirations to be a writer. We might surmise that his differentiated experience of a single cultural attitude as a young man served him later in his identification of other discrete attitudes.

He graduated from Princeton in 1927, with a degree in French literature, and then joined his parents in Oakland,

California, taking an apartment in the building where they lived, overlooking Lake Merritt. His father had suffered paralysis of the legs as a complication of pernicious anemia, for which there was no treatment at that time, and he and his wife had moved to Oakland to be near Joe's sister, who lived with her husband in Piedmont. His father remained a bedridden invalid until he died in 1933.

Joe's Aunt Ethel and Uncle Charles, who had left Washington for San Francisco, helped him get jobs as book reviewer and drama critic and introduced him into the salon of Elizabeth (Mrs. Ralph) Ellis. He wrote for two San Francisco journals, *The Argonaut*, a conservative weekly, and *The San Franciscan*, a weak imitation of *The New Yorker* which had just begun publication at that time. It was a difficult period because it gradually became clear to Joe that he was not really motivated to become a writer. He felt lost concerning his future; it was as if a new attitude was pushing up from within him.

In the meantime, he was a regular participant in the salon which Mrs. Ellis held in her large house in Berkeley. She brought together University of California professors and their wives, mostly from the English and philosophy departments, and interesting people from San Francisco. It was lively and stimulating company. Joe was first introduced to the work of C. G. Jung by Dr. Elizabeth Whitney and her husband Dr. James Whitney and by Andrew and Helen Gibb, Berkeleyans who had only recently returned from analysis and study with Jung in Zurich. Professor William Durham, of the English Department, and Henriette Goodrich, who later became Mrs. Durham, also had a memorable influence on Joe, and it was in Mrs. Ellis's salon that he first met Margaret Schevill, who was the wife of Rudolph Schevill, of the Spanish Department, and for whose *Pollen Path: a Collection of Navajo Myths* he wrote a psychological commentary in 1956.

Joe felt more and more at sea about his future, and he was urged by his friends in the salon to begin analysis with Elizabeth Whitney, the first analyst of any persuasion in the entire area. He started in the spring of 1928. That year the Whitneys as usual went to Carmel for the summer, and Dr. Whitney urged Joe to join them and continue his analysis. In the meantime, Peter Baynes, who was at that time Jung's assistant, and his wife, Cary, had come to California for the year and were dividing their time between Berkeley and Carmel. Dr. Whitney urged Joe to add an hour with Dr. Baynes while he was in Carmel.

Peter Baynes was a generous man who enthusiastically responded to Joe in their meetings in Carmel. He felt strongly that Joe should go to Europe and work with Jung himself if he were serious about analysis. He was thoroughly unimpressed with Joe's protestations that he could not possibly afford to do that; Joe would work it out somehow if he wanted to. He showed Joe a reproduction of Jung's painting, "Mandala of a Modern Man" (see the frontispiece of *The Archetypes and the Collective Unconscious*) and gave Joe *The Seven Sermons to the Dead* to read. Joe has said, "That absolutely bowled me over; I decided right there and then that, if I possibly could, I would have to go and meet the man who had written this."

In the meantime, he realized through his analysis that his continuing financial dependence on his family was interfering with his development. His writing was not sufficient to support him, and the problem of funding a period of work with Jung was a serious one. In the fall of 1928, one of the magazines for which he was writing sent him to New York to survey the coming theater season, and on a visit to Lawrenceville, he was offered a job as an assistant housemaster for the immediate academic year. He arranged through Baynes to begin work with Jung the following fall and spent the academic year at Lawrenceville, saving his money in preparation.

In the fall of 1929, Joe installed himself in the Hotel Sonne in Küsnacht, where Esther Harding and several other analysands of Jung were lodging, and began his analysis. He participated in the seminar on Dream Analysis during that academic year, 1929-30. His own dreams soon revealed his movement toward analytical psychology as a career, for which he would need to become a physician or doctoral psychologist. The central theme in his analysis was his own initiation experience, but he noticed, among those who were in Zurich for either analysis or the seminars, the operation of differing attitudes toward and differing expectations of Jung's psychology, which he would later differentiate into four cultural attitudes. He recalled, in his filmed interview with Thomas Kirsch, "Many of them had cultural attitudes that were very different from each other's, and they tended to project into analysis what they expected to find rather than what was actually there. What they expected to find was [determined by] whatever cultural pattern they favored." It is remarkable that Henderson's first year of analysis saw the germination of the two principal subjects of his research in the nearly fifty years since: initiation and culture.

By June, 1930, he had formulated a clear plan to go to London to study medicine, and Peter Baynes, who had returned to Zurich, offered him guidance and help. Joe enrolled in the University of London where he began his premedical studies, and with Baynes' help, he was admitted to Saint Bartholomew's Hospital as a premedical student in 1931. The following year he received a letter from Cary Baynes introducing Jane and Joseph Wheelwright; they were going to London so that Jo might also attend Bart's. That introduction, of course, began a lifetime association as friends and colleagues.

Wheelwright, an inveterate raconteur, enjoys telling stories of their difficulties in getting through their medical education. In one, Joe spent most of the allotted time of the final examination in premedical physics jotting down notes on his dream of the previous night, which meant a great deal more to him than physics, his least favorite subject. Of course, he failed the exam. Joe had indeed had trouble with physics, and it appeared to him that perhaps the dream was telling him that medical education was not the proper direction. He had dreamed about a white horse running over a dark sea. A black eagle came out of the sky and severed an artery at the back of the horse's neck, and the blood came gushing out. He knew that was the end of the horse.

It was a very frightening archetypal dream which captured most of the libido meant for the physics examination. The night following the failed exam, he had a companion dream in which, at the bottom of the sea, a snake with a red head came up and bit a flat, ray-like, black fish, just as the eagle had bitten the horse in the first dream. But, the feeling tone of this image was life-giving, because the black fish needed to be killed. Joe was haunted by these dreams for some time to come. It was the end of the term, and he went to Zurich to see Dr. Jung, but Jung left almost immediately for his summer vacation. Joe spent the summer alone in his hotel working with his dreams on his own.

His friendship with the Bayneses had deepened considerably by this time, and although their marriage had dissolved and Peter had moved to London, Joe maintained his relationship with both of them. That summer, Cary Baynes was the only person in Zurich to whom Joe could talk about his psychological material. Cary had always maintained that she had no personal experience of the unconscious; she was mainly identified as a student of German and was translating some of Jung's works. But she was a wonderful listener. Joe worked on through the summer analyzing his own material and had his first real experience of being able to do so successfully. His confidence was greatly strengthened. By the time Jung returned from vacation, the material had come together into a clear indication that he should resume his medical studies, and he returned to London. There, on the second try, he passed physics and was admitted to medical school at Bart's. Later in his medical education, he was to have another psychological eruption in response to the final examination in surgery, a problem shared in common with Jo Wheelwright. A special mid-year trip to Zurich for work with Jung led to the resolution of that obstacle too, and he completed his medical studies in 1938.

When Joe had been in London a little over two years, a sense of isolation from stimulating social contact led him to complain in a letter to Cary Baynes that none of the British he had met seemed to have enthusiasm for anything. She responded with a letter of introduction to a Cambridge family she said was full of enthusiasm, the Cornfords. At the time, Joe was seeing a young actress in whom he was somewhat interested, and she invited him to join her for a weekend at her parents' home in Cambridge. Her parents turned out to be heavy and dull, and the actress was so adversely affected by being with them that Joe sought diversion by calling the Cornfords. Mrs. Cornford asked him to tea. Cary Baynes was right in her judgment that they would like one another, and Joe was soon invited for a weekend. At their mother's insistence, Helena and her brothers met him at the train. They all seemed rather young to Joe; Helena is ten years his junior, which must have seemed a great gap at age twenty-eight. After that, Joe saw the Cornfords frequently at their country house, a converted mill on the coast of Norfolk, where they had big house parties. He began to see more of Helena, because he would drive her back to the Ballet Club in London after these weekends. The gap gradually narrowed, and they became engaged.

During his first three years in London, Joe lived in Landsdowne Place. He was so comfortable in his digs there and in such harmony with the "inner wife" that Cary Baynes suggested that, if he didn't move, he would never get married. Joe decided she was right and took a room in Gower Street, a relatively dreary street in Bloomsbury, from which he was forced to go out for meals. Another of Wheelwright's stories about those early days is of asking Joe why he lived in such a Godforsaken street. Joe said, "Why, because it reminds me of Nevada." "Nevada?" Wheelwright retorted. "Yes, don't you see, I can look up this vista and visualize the Ruby Mountains in the distance." Gower Street was, perhaps, the longest straight street in London, running from Bedford Square to Hampstead Heath, and in those days, the vista was clear: one could see the Heath.

After their engagement, Joe and Helena decided that, if she were to be married to an analyst, she had better know something about analysis; besides, she had a problem with her mother. Helena went off to Zurich for a couple of months and worked with Toni Wolff, attended the seminars, and saw something of Dr. Jung socially. Joe's own relationship with Jung gradually took on a social dimension. This was initiated at the time of Jung's lecture at Saint Bartholomew's Hospital in 1936. Peter Baynes introduced Dr. Jung. After the lecture, Joe left the hall and went home. Later, Jung asked him why he hadn't joined them for a beer afterward, and Joe asked how he could have known he was welcome; from that time forward, he knew that he was.

Joe and Helena were married on September 18, 1934, when Joe was thirty-one and Helena twenty-one. The wedding was simple; it was held in the small, local church, the rectory of which was now lived in by Helena's cousin. Her cousin called it an "amateur wedding." The Wheelwrights and the wife of a Princeton friend were the only guests from Joe's side other than Peter Baynes, his best man. Joe has joked that he chose

Peter Baynes to be his best man because Baynes was in his fourth marriage at the time and obviously knew a great deal about weddings. Wheelwright delights in remembering that Joe, in the American tradition, had had the letters "H. C. H." engraved on his gift to Helena. When her cousin saw it, she couldn't imagine what the "C" stood for. Helena's middle name, she fussed, is Darwin in memory of her illustrious great grandfather, Charles Darwin, and she would be known as Helena Darwin Henderson. Of course, the gift had to be re-engraved. After their marriage, the Hendersons took two rooms upstairs in the Gower Street building. In 1936, their only daughter, Elizabeth, was born.

Both Joe and Helena worked in analysis from time to time with Erna Rosenbaum, a German analyst who had come to London to escape the Nazis, and Joe continued to go to Zurich for his summertime contact with Jung. The last period of analysis with Jung was in 1938, following graduation from Bart's, when the Hendersons spent about two months in Zurich before leaving, together with Elizabeth's nanny, to make their life in the United States.

Though his earliest aspiration was to become a writer, Joe's major writing as an analyst developed slowly. His research had been fertilized in the early thirties by his relationship with the Cornfords and his reading of the works of Jane Harrison, together with his analysis and early study of native American cultures. Before leaving London, in 1938, he had read two papers to the Analytical Psychology Club there: one on the Hopi snake dance and another on his own dream material, neither of which he is currently willing to have anyone see. During the two years he spent in New York before coming to San Francisco, he presented two papers to the Analytical Psychology Club there: "Initiation Rites," in 1939, and "Historical Factor of the European War," in 1940, both of which were published in the Club *Papers*. Another paper, "The Drama of Love and Death," appeared in 1944, but there was nothing more for the next ten years beyond certain unpublished presentations.

In 1948, Joe took his first postwar trip to Europe. He saw Dr. Jung, of course, but no longer as analysand, since Jung had stopped seeing patients as a result of his heart attack in 1944.

On this trip and on a subsequent trip to Europe in 1952, a year before her death, Joe had two periods of analysis with Toni Wolff. One summer, Miss Wolff went to a spa in England to get relief for her arthritis. From there she went to Devonshire, where she and the Hendersons stayed in the same hotel. Both Joe and Helena had sessions with her every morning. During that stay, Joe first met Irene de Castillejo, who was a great friend of Miss Wolff and whose son was a close friend of a nephew of Helena. Miss Wolff encouraged Joe to write and found in his dreams evidence that he had an important contribution to make on the subject of initiation. But for many years Joe found that, whenever he set about the project which became *Thresholds of Initiation*, new material would present itself requiring further study and revision.

During the fifties, the Hendersons usually went to Europe every two years. In 1954, the trip was occasioned by Joe's presenting a major paper on transference, "Resolution of the Transference in the Light of C. G. Jung's Psychology," at the International Congress for Psychotherapy. On these trips, Joe always spent some time with Jung. They usually had a formal appointment, and then Jung would invite Joe for a meal. These meetings were typically dominated by whatever subject Dr. Jung was interested in at the time. The most enjoyable visit was the last one, in 1958, while Jung was still in good health. This was after Mrs. Jung's death; Dr. Jung was being cared for by Ruth Bailey at that time, and Joe was invited to stay for lunch. Jung was mainly interested in what Joe was doing, particularly in his work on the psychology of culture; he encouraged Joe's interest in this area, which he felt had been somewhat neglected in his own work. After lunch, they retired to the sun porch, where Dr. Jung spent his afternoons, and chatted freely about many things. Jung was at that time taken up by his research on flying saucers as psychological phenomena, and he excitedly shared his latest findings with Joe. Later, they walked in the garden, where Jung showed him the bas relief he had carved in memory of Miss Wolff. He had placed it under the ginkgo tree the students of the Institute had given him. Two years after that visit, Jung invited Joe to contribute a paper to *Man and His Symbols*, and Joe recalls that that invitation really stimulated his own writing, beyond the miscellaneous papers he had published during the fifties. He traveled to Zurich for a planning session in 1960, but Dr. Jung was already too weak even to attend. Joe's last meeting with him was simply a greeting and a handshake.

Soon after *Man and His Symbols* appeared, in 1961, Joe was invited by Alan Watts to write *The Wisdom of the Serpent* together with Maud Oakes, in a series Watts was editing. It was published in 1963. His collaboration with Maud had begun when Jung suggested to her that Joe could help her with some writing she was doing about the stone Jung had carved at Bollingen. They met at her house in Big Sur. Sometime after that, Maud consulted Joe about a dream, and this led to their collaboration on *Wisdom of the Serpent*. By now, *Thresholds* had been germinating for a long time, and, after many revisions, it appeared in 1967. Though his work on the archetype of culture had begun in the forties, his first paper on the subject was not presented until 1962, at the second International Congress for Analytical Psychology. It was published in 1964. Joe worked from that time until about 1974 on the manuscript of his most important opus, which still awaits publication. He presented an introductory piece of that manuscript at Panarion in 1976, and he gave another portion of it in a public lecture in San Francisco in the spring of 1977.

On their return to the United States, in 1938, the Hendersons had settled in New York because Joe was reluctant to return to California. To go back at the time seemed regressive, and he was not eager to be near members of his family, with whom he felt little in common. He soon found New York stifling, however, both professionally and as a place to rear a child. It was difficult to get a practice going, partially because the Jungians were isolated from the larger psychotherapeutic community and maintained an orientation primarily to Zurich. This atmosphere did not suit his needs, but Joe was unable to come to a clear realization of where he might best settle. He asked his dreams for guidance, and they produced repeated images of train trips back and forth across the continent and names of midwestern places as well as of Princeton. Gradually, he realized the issue was not a geographical one, but an inner one. He could see that Princeton was "prince" town, the place of the self, and all the rest pointed to the middle way. He realized that his strongest Jungian ties in America were with the Whitneys, in Berkeley, and the Wheelwrights, who had since come back and settled in San Francisco.

The Hendersons moved to Berkeley in 1941, and Joe set up practice in their garden cottage on Spruce Street. Soon Jo Wheelwright suggested that he join him in his offices at 450 Sutter Street in San Francisco two afternoons a week, and he innocently proceeded to add Joe's name below his on the office door. One afternoon a man appeared at the office asking for an appointment with Dr. Henderson. That was not Henderson's afternoon, but Wheelwright was in and offered the man an appointment the following day with Joe, whose schedule was not very full at the time. The man, a police official, kept the appointment, arrested Joe for practicing medicine without a license, and booked him at City Hall, where he was incarcerated. Joe had passed his licensing examination in New York State and had assumed that was sufficient sanction for practice throughout the country. He was behind bars for about an hour before Jo Wheelwright and Elizabeth Whitney bailed him out.

Pressure was brought to bear upon the Board of Medical Examiners, including the intervention of Jane Wheelwright's father, a California State Assemblyman, to drop its charges against Joe and grant him a license to practice. The Board compromised—it dropped any prosecution for illegal practice but insisted he complete a medical internship in California before it granted a license, because he had a foreign medical degree. Joe borrowed money from a friend to support his family for the year, and the Hendersons moved to the Mission District to be near Joe's internship at San Francisco General Hospital. He recalls it as a nightmare for Helena and Elizabeth but a good experience for him. After a few months, he became the admitting officer for the acute psychiatric service and obtained invaluable experience in psychiatry.

Joe Henderson has, of course, been a central figure in the evolution of the Society of Jungian Analysts of Northern California and the C. G. Jung Institute of San Francisco. In 1939, Jo and Jane Wheelwright, Elizabeth Whitney, and Lucile Elliott had founded the Analytical Psychology Club of San Francisco. In 1940, when Heinrich Zimmer lectured in San Francisco, Joe came from New York to hear him. The impression made by the

RICHARD SCHOENBRUN

Joe, Helena and Neptune in their garden, March 1978.

local group clearly influenced Henderson's decision to move to the Bay Area a year later. After Joe had arrived and joined the group, movement began toward a professional society separate from the Club. The earliest "training seminars" were held in Margaret Tilly's house, next door to Wheelwright's famous red house at 2206 Steiner Street. They were attended by James Whitney, Elizabeth's son and the first analyst trained by the San Francisco group. In 1943, they founded the Medical Society for Analytical Psychology. In 1950, MSAP united with its counterpart group for doctoral psychologists, which Clare Thompson had founded in 1949, to become the Society of Jungian Analysts of Northern California.

Unlike its sister societies in Los Angeles and New York, the San Francisco group has had a profound commitment to being an active part of the larger psychotherapeutic community. Following the early example of Jo Wheelwright, Horace Gray, and later John Weir Perry, many members have held teaching positions in the Area's universities and hospitals. Because of his introverted nature and his devotion to his own writing and research, Joe Henderson might have shied away from such involvement. But Horace Gray and Jo Wheelwright saw to it that he accepted an assistant clincial professorship at Stanford Lane Hospital, where Gray was a faculty member. For many years, Joe conducted a Friday morning dream seminar for psychiatric residents, stopping only when Stanford moved its medical school to Palo Alto. After the move, Joe went down to the new medical school for a series of three seminars on dreams. But he was soon dropped from further seminars as Stanford's psychiatric training program moved away from depth psychology toward a more behavioral approach. Presently, Joe holds emeritus status at Stanford.

Over the years, Joe has been notable among his colleagues for his steady and devoted involvement in the affairs of the Society and the Institute. Seeming never to tire, he comes faithfully to the dinner meetings and the Executive Committee meetings, and he has continuously sat on committees. He was Librarian of the Institute until the appointment of a Library Committee in 1961; Chairman of the Institute Committee through 1965; a member of the Candidates' Review Board since 1961; liaison to the Analytical Psychology Club through

1967; Chairman of the Education and Training Fund Committee, 1961-63; member of the Clinic and Research Committee, 1963-64; delegate to the International Association for Analytical Psychology in 1961-62 and 1965-66; member of the Curriculum Committee, 1965-67; on the Certifying Board, 1967-71; on the Publications Committee, 1970-78; and a member of the Transition Committee, 1977-78. Joe was President of the Society of Jungian Analysts and the C. G. Jung Institute of San Francisco in 1967-68 and in 1972-73. And, he was American Vice President of the International Association for Analytical Psychology from 1962 to 1965. Following that term of office he was proposed as nominee for the presidency. He did not want the post, however, fearing that it would take him too far afield from his writing and research. In a moment of temptation he consulted the *I Ching*, and it said unequivocally, "No!"

Of all that Joe has done in and for the Institute, perhaps what has meant most to him and may come to have the most lasting significance is his advocacy of the Archive for Research in Archetypal Symbolism (ARAS) and his chairmanship of the ARAS Committee. In 1962, Jung and the Bollingen Foundation asked Joe to edit the four-hour film in which Professor Richard I. Evans interviewed Jung. Jung had been disappointed with the interviews and wrote Joe asking him to do whatever he could to improve their presentation. In New York, Joe worked with a professional film editor. The result was a condensed and more effective film. While in New York, he became acquainted with the work that Jessie Fraser was doing with ARAS at the Bollingen Foundation. She had carried on the original Eranos Archive of symbolic pictures, methodizing, cataloguing, and expanding it. In 1967, as the Foundation was bringing its program to an end, the question arose, what to do with ARAS? The Foundation could not continue support, the C. G. Jung Foundation of New York had not the means to carry it on, and John D. Barrett, President of the Foundation, was considering giving it to the Yale University Library or a similar disposition. Joe recognized the great potential of ARAS and immediately put in a bid that it be given to the San Francisco Institute. This, of course, sparked the interest of the New York group, and funds were raised so that the Archive would be carried on in New York. At that time, Joe was the West Coast delegate to the

Jung Foundation of New York, and he was present for the ensuing discussions of the disposition of ARAS. It emerged that it was possible to make a photographic copy, so that the collection could be lodged in both San Francisco and New York. Over a period of years Paul Anderson, with the assistance of Joan Reynolds, organized the preparation of the copy for San Francisco. Since then, of course, ARAS has grown, and with the appointment of Harry Prochaska to work on its development at the San Francisco Institute, it will continue to grow in an orderly way.

On the occasion of a Sunday afternoon gathering in honor of his retirement as Director of Development of the Institute, Maurits van Löben Sels called attention to another of Joe Henderson's remarkable contributions to the San Francisco Institute. Maury referred to "Joe's stable"—his remarkable resourcefulness in producing the right person for whatever job had to be filled at the Institute or just the right service for whatever needed to be done. Maury himself is, of course, one of the outstanding products of "Joe's stable." Joe's quiet and reliable presence and his unerring sense of what is right for the Institute have so often tempered unwise passions or produced suggestions necessary to the Institute's creative and orderly development.

When Maud Oakes consulted Jung about her long-pondered book on his stone at Bollingen, Jung realized that she needed help with it beyond what he could offer. He said, "I have a great friend in California I suggest you see. He's one of the best." We, of course, know that he is and have come to call him the Dean of San Francisco analysts.

Publications of Joseph L. Henderson

1939
"Initiation Rites." *Papers of the Analytical Psychology Club of New York*, 3 (1939). 16 pp.

1940
"An Historical Factor of the European War." *Papers of the Analytical Psychology Club of New York*, 4 (1940), pp. 8-9.
"Picasso's Minotaur." *Bulletin, Analytical Psychology Club of New York*, 2 (Mar. 1940), p. 5.

1941
Review of H. G. Baynes: *Germany Possessed. Bulletin, Analytical Psychology Club of New York*, 3 (Dec. 1941), pp. 9-12.

1943
"Transcendent Function in Gibb's *In Search of Sanity.*" *Bulletin, Analytical Psychology Club of New York*, 5 (Oct. 1943), pp. 7-8.

1944
"The Drama of Love and Death." *Spring*, (1944), pp. 62-74.

1954
"Resolution of the Transference in the Light of C. G. Jung's Psychology." *Acta Psychotherapeutica, Psychosomatica et Orthopaedagogica*, 2 (1954), pp. 267-83.

1955
"Analysis of Transference in Analytical Psychology." *American Journal of Psychotherapy*, 9 (1955), pp. 640-56.

"The Inferior Function." In *Studien zur Analytischen Psychologie C. G. Jungs. Festschrift zum 80. Geburtstag von C. G. Jung.* Zurich: Rascher, 1955. Vol. 1: *Beiträge aus Theorie und Praxis,* pp. 134-40.

"Jungian Psychology in San Francisco." *Bulletin, Analytical Psychology Club of New York,* 17 (June, 1955), pp. 14-6.

1956

"Psychological Commentary." In *The Pollen Path: A Collection of Navajo Myths,* retold by Margaret Schevill Link. Stanford, Calif.: Stanford University Press, 1956. pp. 125-40.

"Stages of Psychological Development Exemplified in the Poetical Works of T. S. Eliot." *JAP* 1 (1956), pp. 133-44.

1957

"Stages of Psychological Development Exemplified in the Poetical Works of T. S. Eliot" (continued). *JAP* 2 (1957), pp. 33-50.

1963

"C. G. Jung: a Personal Evaluation." In *Contact with Jung: Essays on the Influence of His Work and Personality.* Ed. by Michael Fordham. London: Tavistock, 1963. pp. 221-3.

Review of Alan Watts: *Psychotherapy East and West* and *The Glorious Cosmology. JAP* 8 (1963), pp. 186-7.

With Maud Oakes. *The Wisdom of the Serpent: The Myths of Death, Rebirth, and Resurrection.* Patterns of Myth Series, ed. by Alan Watts, New York: George Braziller, 1963.

1964

"Ancient Myths and Modern Man." In *Man and His Symbols,* by C. G. Jung et al. London: Aldus Books; New York: Doubleday, 1964. pp. 104-57.

"The Archetype of Culture." In *Der Archetyp/The Archetype* (Proceedings of the 2nd International Congress for Analytical Psychology, Zurich, 1962). Edited by Adolf Guggenbühl-Craig. Basel and New York: S. Karger, 1964. pp. 3-14.

1967

Thresholds of Initiation. Middletown, Conn.: Wesleyan University Press, 1967. pp. xi-260.

1968

"Der moderne Mensch und die Mythen." In *Der Mensch und seine Symbole*, by C. G. Jung et al. Olten: Walter, 1968. pp. 104-57.

Review of C. Kerényi: *Eleusis: Archetypal Image of Mother and Daughter. JAP* 13 (1968), pp. 171-2.

"Unity of the Psyche: a Philosopy of Analysis." In *Papers from the Second Bailey Island Conference, Held in Honor of Dr. Esther Harding's Eightieth Birthday, August, 1968*. Mimeographed. pp. 95-108.

1969

Review of C. G. Jung: *Alchemical Studies* (CW 13). *JAP* 14 (1969), pp. 189-92.

Review of C. G. Jung: *Analytical Psychology: Its Theory and Practice. Quadrant*, No. 3 (1969), pp. 7-8.

Review of Joseph Campbell: *Creative Mythology. JAP* 14 (1969), pp. 193-4.

1970

"An Archetypal Theme in Three Films: 'Easy Rider'; 'Midnight Cowboy'; and 'Butch Cassidy and the Sundance Kid.' " *Psychological Perspectives* 1 (1970), pp. 69-73.

"Inner Perception in Terms of Depth Psychology." *Annals of the New York Academy of Sciences* 169 (1970), pp. 664-72.

Editor, *News Bulletin*. San Francisco: C. G. Jung Institute of San Francisco. Vol. 1, nos. 1 and 2, 1970.

"Transcendence: Symbols of Man's Search for Self." *Psychological Perspectives* 1 (1970), pp. 34-42.

1971

"The Artist's Relation to the Unconscious." In *The Analytic Process: Aims, Analysis, Training* (Proceedings of the 4th International Congress for Analytical Psychology, Zurich, 1968). Edited by Joseph B. Wheelwright. New York: G. P. Putnam's Sons for the C. G. Jung Foundation, 1971. pp. 309-16.

"Symbolism of the Unconscious in Two Plays of Shakespeare." In *The Well-tended Tree: Essays into the Spirit of Our Time*. Edited by Hilde Kirsch. [Festschrift for James Kirsch's 70th birthday.] New York: G. P. Putnam's Sons for the C. G. Jung Foundation, 1971. pp. 284-99.

1972

"M. Esther Harding: Obituary Notice." *JAP* 17 (1972), pp. 66-9.

"Nostalgia" (review of the film "Cabaret"), *Psychological Perspectives* 3 (1972), pp. 194-6.

"The Psychic Activity of Dreaming." *Psychological Perspectives* 3 (1972), pp. 99-111.

1973

"A Change in the Model for Depth Analysis." In Conference of the Societies of Jungian Analysts of Northern and Southern California: *Professional Reports, 19th, 20th, and 21st, 1971-73*. San Francisco: C. G. Jung Institute, 1973. pp. 148-51.

"Persona Triumphant" (review of the film "Cries and Whispers"), *Psychological Perspectives* 4 (1973), pp. 96-101.

"The Picture Method in Jungian Psychotherapy." *Art Psychotherapy* 1 (1973), pp. 135-40.

1974

With Joseph B. Wheelwright. "Analytical Psychology." In *American Handbook of Psychiatry*, 2nd ed. New York: Basic Books, 1974. Vol. 1, pp. 809-18.

"Films of Social History" (review of "A Doll's House" and "Upstairs, Downstairs"). *Psychological Perspectives* 5 (1974), pp. 81-5.

1975

"Analytical Psychology in England." *Psychological Perspectives* 6 (1975), pp. 197-203.

"C. G. Jung: A Reminiscent Picture of His Method." *JAP* 20 (1975), pp. 114-21.

"The Land of the Free" (review of the film "Nashville"). *Psychological Perspectives* 6 (1975), pp. 207-9.

Review of Joseph Campbell: *The Mythic Image. Quadrant* 8:1 (1975), pp. 69-70.

1976

"Pueri Aeterni" (review of the films "Barry Lyndon" and "The Magic Flute"), *Psychological Perspectives* 7 (1976), pp. 117-21.

"T. S. Eliot's Poetry and the Life of Man." *Psychological Perspectives* 7 (1976), pp. 23-51.

1977

Articles in *International Encyclopedia of Psychiatry, Psychology, Psychonanalysis, and Neurology*. New York: Aesculapius Publishers, 1977. ("Archetype: Father," Vol. 2, pp. 98-101; "Self and Individuation: Jung's View," Vol. 10, pp. 118-22. "Transference: Jung's View," Vol. 11, pp. 249-53.)

"Filmland Anti-heroes." *Psychological Perspectives* 8 (1977), pp. 111-5.

"Individual Lives in a Changing Society." *Psychological Perspectives* 8 (1977), pp. 126-42.

1978

"Dreams of Nazi Germany." *Psychological Perspectives* 9 (1978), pp. 7-12.

"Oh, UFO" (review of the film "Close Encounters of the Third Kind"). *Psychological Perspectives* 9 (1978), pp. 85-9.

G. S. H.
V. D.

Part One

The Navaho
Prayer of Blessing

DONALD F. SANDNER

NAVAHO HEALING CONSISTS OF A GREAT NUMBER of chants (also called sings or ways), such as Beauty Way, Night Way, Mountain Top Way, Blessing Way, etc., which are given for the individual patient to bring him into harmony with himself and the surrounding social and physical environment. At the heart of these chants are the sandpaintings and prayers, both used to bring the patient into close contact and finally actual identification with the supernatural power.

The prayers are recited by the medicine man at various important points during the ceremonies, and often a prayer is repeated line for line by the patient in the form of a litany. Such is the prayer of blessing given by a Navaho medicine man as part of Big Star Way, an evil-chasing chant lasting five days and nights. But after the evil has been removed, the world has to be restored once more to a harmonious balance. That is the purpose of this prayer. In the context of the ceremony it is really used as a part of a much longer prayer which is concerned with obtaining supernatural power and using it to destroy evil.

It is well known that Navaho sandpaintings are often in mandalic form, but it is not often noted that the prayers also have a mandalic structure. In the case of the prayer given here, the patient and the medicine man are in the center of the mandala. Special emphasis is placed on the four cardinal directions and their ordering and symbolic functions. A sacred mountain, tutelary deity, and symbolic color are associated with each direction. Around the patient and within the boundaries of the four sacred mountains which mark the limits of the traditional Navaho homeland, all the forces of nature are turned toward the patient in blessing and good will. He is their grandchild.

Of the deities mentioned in the prayer, Talking God and Calling God are spiritual directors of the Navaho chant heroes in times of danger and guardians of the Navaho people. They are associated respectively with the rising and setting sun. Changing Woman is the great Navaho earth goddess, whose form changes with the seasons of the year and the phases of human life, yet remains ever the same. She goes from youthful springtime to full summer maturity, fall ripeness, and then wintery old age, only to renew herself again and again. This periodic renewal has been seen as one of the central secrets of the Navaho healing chants. First Man and First Woman are the original Navaho beings who came up from the four underworlds. Pollen Boy and Corn Tassel Girl are fertility deities associated with the growth and ripening of the life-giving corn. The Man of Long Life and the Woman of the Good Way are symbols of the Navaho way of life, called the pollen path, which holds the ideal of a long and balanced life based on the healing and rejuvenating power evoked in the chants.

The prayer was given by Natani Tso, a Navaho medicine man, at Rock Point on the Navaho reservation in the summer of 1969. The translation was made with the help of Albert Sandoval, Jr.

As a last note, before the prayer is allowed to speak for itself: it is fitting that this prayer should be presented as a tribute to Joe Henderson, who, it seems to me, has attained in his life a harmony and peace that come close to the Navaho ideal of one who has walked the pollen path.

From the horizon of the East, from the Sun's house,
  everything will bless me.
From the horizon of the South, from Agate's house,
  everything will bless me.
From the horizon of the West, from Changing Woman's house,
  everything will bless me.
From the horizon of the North, from Cold People's house,
  everything will bless me.
From the East where the Sun rises,
  everything will bless me.
From the South where the blue light rises,
  everything will bless me.

From the West where the yellow light rises,
       everything will bless me.
From the North where the darkness rises,
       everything will bless me.
From the summit of the sacred mountain of the East
              where Talking God lives,
       everything will bless me.
From the summit of the sacred mountain of the South
              where Calling God lives,
       everything will bless me.
From the summit of the sacred mountain of the West where
       Talking God lives,
       everything will bless me.
From the summit of the sacred mountain of the North
              where Calling God lives,
       everything will bless me.
From the Mountain-around-which-moving-was-done
              at the center of the Earth where First Man lives,
       everything will bless me.
From the sacred mountain at the center of the Earth
              where First Woman lives,
       everything will bless me.
From the Place of Emergence,
              blessings will come to me.
From the surface of the Earth,
              blessings will come to me.
From all growing things,
              blessings will come to me.
From the homes of the Rainbow People,
              blessings will come to me.
From the homes of the Air People, from the homes
              of the Black Cloud People,
              blessings will come to me.
From the summits of the mountains where sunlight strikes first,
              blessings will come to me.
From the mountain trails where the people walk,
              blessings will come to me.
From the foot of the mountains where the spruce trees grow,
              where water runs under the trees,
              blessings will come to me.

From the overhanging cliffs and the cliff walls,
　　　　　blessings will come to me.
From the open land where the bushes grow,
　　　　　above them and around them,
　　　　　blessings will come to me.
From the high, rocky walls where the rocks speak,
　　　　　blessings will come to me.
From the overhanging cliffs where the Rock People live,
　　　　　blessings will come to me.
From the sacred springs where water comes out of the rock,
　　　　　blessings will come to me.
From all beings will come respect for me;
　　　　　they will think of me as their grandson;
　　　　　they will watch over me.
From everywhere, all beings will know me;
　　　　　I will live in harmony with them.
Talking God will walk before me,
　　　　　I'll be joyful.
Calling God will walk behind me,
　　　　　I'll be joyful.
Pollen Boy will walk before me,
　　　　　I'll be joyful.
Corn Tassel Girl will walk behind me,
　　　　　I'll be joyful.
The Man of Long Life will walk before me,
　　　　　I'll be joyful.
The Woman of the Good Way will walk behind me,
　　　　　I'll be joyful.
Everyone will be happy; all beings will be happy;
　　　　　from this day all will be in harmony.
We will be like those who live in harmony for a long time.
　　　　　Everything will be beautiful.
　　　　　Everything will be beautiful.
　　　　　Everything is beautiful.
　　　　　Everything is beautiful.
　　　　　Everything is beautiful.
　　　　　Everything is beautiful.

Shamanist Principles of Initiation and Power

WILLIAM REED

FOR THOSE STANDING ON THE PRECIPICE of true and enduring personality change, the view is everywhere and always the same. To the frightened fourteen-year-old thrust by his elders into the mystery theater of an Australian jungle, and to the overwrought business executive falling apart under the stress of macabre and irrepressible nightmares, the same sequence of imaginal events unfolds—estrangement from family and friends, grueling ordeal, solitary odyssey into the cradle of the world mother, disintegration, world's end, and birth of a new identity. In some cultures, vivid ritual enactment of these themes is as institutionalized as birthday cake. But where this is not so and where rites of passage have become insipid, the same images spontaneously occur in the dreams, fantasies, and visions of certain people as though to narrate the course of their personal upheavals. Rarely is such a consecration of new personality consciously sought. Rather it seems to choose its victim, and the reluctant novice must, for a successful outcome, submit to the process, rolling with its punches. As one analyst colleague put it, "No one ever wants to change, but it hurts too damn much to stand still."

What can be said of this "it" that selects the who and when of significant change and choreographs the images so ubiquitously encountered? What is the "it" that hurts us when we stand still? Analytical psychologists call "it" the death and rebirth or initiation archetype. It is an instinctual force, and one with a form, the imaginal sequence described above. The archetype resides in each individual, inert until it is activated by maladaptation to the environment, in short, until survival of the organism demands a change. At these times it shows its face and nudges the individual into a new perspective vis-à-vis his culture. Indeed, the initiation archetype sometimes seems like a sleeping giant whose repose is broken by an alarm clock preset to certain points in the life cycle. At these times new tasks face the individual and the old personality no longer suffices. The giant awakens, overwhelms and extinguishes the old, and points the direction toward a new order of adaptation.

Like all metaphors for the unknowable, this one seems to capture only one of the giant's many faces. With it we bring the enigmatic appearance of death-rebirth imagery into relation with the external environment. We can begin to fathom its elusive nature by reference to the time and circumstance under which it appears. In short, we are reassured when we recognize that the psyche begins to speak its very strange language of change at predictable moments, i.e., when a new external adaptation is required for survival. But surely the stimulus to initiation does not come exclusively from external relations, nor is it really like an alarm clock that sounds at one time or another for each and every one of us. Only a few people experience upheavals replete with death and rebirth imagery and fewer still experience them with an intensity that would mark them as truly twice-born. We are left wondering why some and not others, why now and not later?

The problem is well known to the shamanist clan societies of Eurasia, the Americas, and elsewhere. For them death-rebirth imagery is the first manifestation of the mystic vocation and conveys the initiant's potential for marshaling sacral power. The following pages are intended to explicate these notions of the initiation archetype and the power it confers. I do not intend to equate the shaman's initiatory illness with the syndrome so often encountered in the consulting room. Not all analysands are bound for a visionary calling. Nor for that matter are all Siberian or Eskimo initiates destined to become fully acclaimed healers. However, I think the reader will find considerable wisdom in the shamanist paradigm that is applicable to initiatory experiences whatever their intensity and wherever encountered.

Why initiation? In the shamanist conception, because a particular spirit would have it so. Initiatory symptoms are the stirrings of a spirit who has chosen the neophyte for a relation to it. To the shaman the initiator is not only the cause but also the goal of initiation. From our own frenetic, technological perspective, we can hardly appreciate this conception of election by spirit. For us, the figure of an ancestral, animal, or part-animal initiation master and guardian spirit is atrophic. We would hardly consider the horse, the butterfly, or the peal of thunder in a patient's dream to be a central and archaic re-organizer of his psyche. And, even if we recognized one of these as a radical of transformation, an initiation master, we would be inclined to consider it as more of a catalyst than a power source to be reckoned with for the rest of our patient's life. Yet, this would be the attitude of the shaman *qua* dream analyst toward the spirit variously called the helper, guardian, ally, tutelary, or double. It is a troublesome conception and must be set in the context of the "animistic" consciousness of shamanist cultures.

In the animist world view, spirits may intrude upon man from a variety of sources: from the pool of ancestral souls, from animals or trees, or indeed from transistor radios or telephone poles. All of these, and in fact all things animate and inanimate, living and dead, have inner faces, essences, person-alities, and reactivity to man. It is this inner face which appears in dreams or visions and is a harbinger of change.

The primitive conceives himself to be a late-comer to a uni-verse where mountains, moon, ancestors, and animals are al-ready on the scene, elaborately interrelated. With more wisdom than modern man, the primitive is aware of his intrusion into the balanced ecosystem and feels himself unwelcome. He must therefore negotiate the terms of his occupancy on earth with its landlords and must practice ritual coercion, propitiation, or intimidation of the spirits involved. Thus throughout Central Asia, travelers will still stack stones and tie little ribbons at especially hazardous places to request safe passage from the resident spirits. Ground-breaking ceremonies attend the con-struction of new homes in order to assuage the spirits whose land is being poached.[1] The Burmese have traditionally made

[1]Laurence A. Waddell, "Lamaism in Sikkim," in *Gazetteer of Sikkim* (Bengal, 1894), and his *Tibetan Buddhism* (repr., New York, 1972).

human sacrifices to the same end. In doing so they conscript the soul of the sacrificial victim to guard new edifices against resentful spirits.[2] This same consciousness extends as well to products of man's own hand each of which becomes imbued with the spirit of its creator. One therefore sees, for example, the "spirit line" in exceptionally fine Navajo rugs. The weaver, feeling a particular rug is unusually endowed with her spirit, allows a tiny line of its pattern to cut through the margin thus releasing the spirit to pass out and into her next creation.

Against this backdrop of a universe teeming with potentially resentful powers, man's diseases and injuries are quite naturally imputed to them. Unseen by all but the keenest visionaries, the spirits work their quiet revenge for disregard of the environment. Greed on the hunt or disrespect for the prey is punished with illness inflicted by an animal mother. Violation of tribal taboo is vindicated by that spirit whose will and morality are reflected in the taboo.

However, not all illness is retributive, and the mere touch by a spirit spells illness or catastrophe, even if inadvertent. Souls of the departed, reluctant to take their leave for the next world, may, by their continued presence, harm the living. Or, for that matter, those who have spirits at their bidding, i.e., shamans, may hire them out to settle interpersonal disputes or use them against their own adversaries.

In this compendium of pathology we encounter many of the essential ingredients of our own pathologies—guilt over violation of the conceived natural order, unresolved grief (lingering ancestors), interpersonal conflict (sorcery), and abasement of cultural integrity. This last will be very important later and requires additional explanation. Our term "shaman" derives from "šaman," in the Tungusic language of Siberia, denoting (1) teller of epic or legend, and (2) conductor of the ecstatic seance.[3] These in a nutshell are the shaman's most fundamental duties. In the first capacity, he is archivist of the tribal lore and therefore the custodian of its highest values. In the second, he animates these for the laymen in public seances and

[2]Melford E. Spiro, *Burmese Supernaturalism: A Study in the Explanation and Reduction of Suffering* (Englewood Cliffs, N.J., 1967).
[3]G. M. Vasilevich, "Early Concepts about the Universe among the Evenks," in *Studies in Siberian Shamanism*, ed. Henry N. Michael (Toronto, 1963), pp. 46-83.

seasonal ritual. During ecstasy he incarnates the relevant spirits and dramatizes their relationship to man using an impressive repertoire of theatrical skills.[4]

The aims of his seances are manifold: healing, weather control, divination, retrieving lost articles, witch hunting, and, perhaps most important, protecting his fold against attack by other shamans. Amongst the Siberian Evenks each shaman presides over one tributary of the river "Engdekit" which courses through all the spirit realms. Each clan's deceased go to reside along the backwaters of one tributary and are prohibited access to the other worlds by the shaman's helpers posted at the mouth of the tributary. The helpers which guard one tributary are under constant attack by those guarding the adjacent tributaries in the service of other shamans. Each defends its own holdings while trying to penetrate the rival's.[5]

In the performance of these roles, each shaman becomes a locus of culture to be defended against neighboring influences. Should his defenses break down, his own constituency becomes vulnerable to alien helping spirits or cultural contamination.

With this overview of animistic consciousness and shamanistic cosmology in mind, we can return to the initiation paradigm so highly developed amongst these peoples. As it occurs amongst Siberian, Arctic, and most American aboriginals, initiation devolves from the will of a particular spirit who needs a human partner for its fullest expression. Whatever its own character, when a spirit visits a potential human host, it makes him physically ill, psychologically morbid or hysteroid. At this point, the Eskimos would say the spirit possesses the elected man and, as the drama of his illness with its death and rebirth imagery unfolds, the man gradually possesses the spirit. A human shaman catalyzes the process of upheaval by helping to extract the possessing spirit from his patient and putting it at the latter's disposal as a helper.[6]

---

[4]Waldemar Bogoras, "The Chukchee," in *American Museum of Natural History Memoirs*, XI (Jesup North Pacific Expedition, vol. 7; New York, 1904); A. A. Popov, "Consecration Ritual for a Blacksmith Novice among the Yakuts," *Journal of American Folk-lore* 46 (1933) 257-71; B. D. Shimkin, "A Sketch of the Ket, or Yenisei 'Ostyak,'" *Ethnos* 4 (1940), 147-76.

[5]Vasilevich, op. cit.

[6]Asen Balikci, "Shamanistic Behavior among the Netsilik Eskimos," *Southwestern Journal of Anthropology* 19 (1963), 380-96.

In Tibet, the initiating lama requires his protégé to seek out the scene of a recent death, disaster, or interment. There, alone and at night, the youngster calls upon the hungry infernal demons with a drum and trumpet made of human bone and commits psychological suicide, chanting, "For ages, in the course of renewed births I have borrowed from countless living beings—at the cost of their welfare and life. . . . Today, I pay my debt. . . . I give my flesh to the hungry, my blood to the thirsty. . . ." Only those spirits who have eaten of it can subsequently be mastered by him.[7] By the same token, the Hungarian shaman, who is summoned by the power of dog, wolf, or bear, is considered most unfortunate since these are the most voracious helping spirits and exact the greatest payment from their earthly master, "gnawing at his heart" during ecstatic ritual.[8] In this light, "helping spirit" seems to be a naïve translation of the tutelary's role. As it initiates and confers power, so does *it* also derive nourishment from the student. Whatever its counterpart in our own conceptions of the psyche, the helping spirit has a psychoid character and needs the ego's cooperation in its destiny.

The notion of a spirit ally or double has found currency in societies as remote in time and space as the ancient Egyptian, Nigerian Yoruba, and Siberian Chukchee, as well as in the world of European alchemy. Yet the very idea sits poorly with contemporary Western consciousness. Our nearest counterpart, the guardian angel, is a heady theological abstraction unconnected to daily emotional life. The average man can hardly admit that his fantasies are not his own creation but instead happen to him and must therefore have something like a will of their own. Much less could he acknowledge that anything in his subjective world could become so developed and materialized that it could serve his ends in relation to other people without his own intervention. The notion seems absurd that, by relating properly to autonomous fantasies, one could dispatch *them* to work on the external world, unseen and immeasurable by it. Nonetheless, this is precisely the shaman's experience of the ally.

[7]Alexandra David-Neel, *Magic and Mystery in Tibet* (reprint, New Hyde Park, N.Y., 1965), pp. 150-51.
[8]Géza Roheim, "Hungarian Shamanism," *Psychoanalysis and the Social Sciences* 3 (1951), 131-69.

The relationship between shaman and spirit helper some-times has the quality of an armed truce. Helpers are commonly considered by their owners to be dangerous liabilities as well as the source of supramundane powers. One Eskimo shaman complained bitterly of his helper's habit of sneaking up behind him and stealing his genitalia. The forlorn shaman could then recover his lost parts only during self-induced trance.[9] In order to keep the mischievous spirit in check, he had to resubmit to the eclipse of ego consciousness that attended his original ini-tiation. The point is even more clearly illustrated by the Balahi shaman of northern India who must make an annual pilgrim-age in tribute to his helper. Death and decay are dramatized during nine days of sleeplessness, fire-walking, and self-mortification, and at the same time the shaman celebrates new birth by planting and tending seedlings in a basket, which he ultimately casts into a lake. Should he fail to stage this yearly passion play, he would be killed by his own helping spirit.[10] Continued rapport with the images of death and annual sub-mission to its ravages are the tribute exacted by the spirit familiar for the loan of its power. More precisely, from the shaman's perspective, he must live with death to avoid being struck down, and, if he does so, he is invested with the super-natural abilities of the helper.

In view of the fact that the whole idea of a mystic vocation was not the shaman's in the first place, his initiation is not completely enviable. The dues are high, but the attitude afoot in most shamanistic cultures is that one may not refuse. If the electing spirit be denied its prerogative, it will kill the prospec-tive initiate.[11]

The shamanist slant on growth, then, is not unlike that pro-posed by the analyst quoted earlier; i.e., it is not especially desired or sought. For those who feel its not so gentle persua-

---

[9]Balikci, op. cit.

[10]Stephen Fuchs, "Magic Healing Techniques among the Balahis in Central India," in *Magic, Faith and Healing*, ed. Ari Kiev (New York, 1964), pp. 121-38; Rudolf Rhamann, "Shamanistic and Related Phenomena in Northern and Middle India," *Anthropos* 54 (1959), 681-760.

[11]Such is the case in Siberia and the Arctic and over much of North America. Amongst the tribes of North American Indians and in Tibet as well, the phenomenon of mystic election has become so culturally determined that the quest for spirit helpers begins to look like a religion. Even in this case, sacrifice of the ego's ascendancy and submission to death are fundamental.

sion, standing still can occasion not only pain but, indeed, physical deterioration and death.

We could regard growth and its subjective counterpart, initiation, as a realignment of the individual to environmental demands, and to this extent it is an adaptive function. One anthropological interpretation holds that shamans are essentially madmen who have carved, from the substance of their illness, an ecological niche.[12] Given a delusion, they manage to convince others of its authenticity and market it as divine inspiration. Predisposed to episodes of dissociation, they make of these episodes healing seances and sell tickets to their tribesmen; adaptation *par excellence*! But, as we have seen, the individual shaman feels heavily taxed by his spirit helper and shamanizes only because he must.

While in one sense he is highly adapted to his community and cherished by it, in another the shaman lives on its fringes. Far from being enveloped and warmed by secure relations with his fellows, the shaman is feared, respected, despised, loved, and occasionally murdered. We are wont to consider the twice-born, the initiated, and especially the initiated healer as kindly disposed and incorruptible, paradigms of beneficent fatherhood. To the tribal mind, however, initiation confers power and power is bivalent. Thus, for example, no Netsilik Eskimo shaman is considered exclusively "white," i.e., healer, or "black," i.e., warlock. All vacillate between these dispositions.[13] The most surreptitious black magician may at times perform miraculous cures, and the most reliable healer may resort to fierce supernatural combat with competitors, casting love spells and hiring himself out as a spiritual assassin.

The choice of these paths is not even necessarily decided in the shaman's own moral fiber. For example, the tunraq, or spirit ally of the Eskimo shaman, is capable of *either* healing or destruction and is responsive to the dictates of its human master. If the shaman deploys his spirit as an assassin, he must be utterly confident of his mastery over it or be himself in jeopardy. For, should the helper fail in such a mission, the spirit is

[12]L. Bryce Boyer, "Remarks on the Personality of Shamans; with Special Reference to the Apache of the Mescalero Indian Reservation," *Psychoanalytic Study of Society* 2 (1962) 233-54; Julian Silverman, "Shamans and Acute Schizophrenia," *American Anthropologist* 69 (1967), 21-31.
[13]Balikci, op. cit.

transformed instantly into a murderous beast that turns upon its master and his family. Only other shamans' allies are then capable of restraining the miscreant spirit. No specifically moral injunction, no Hippocratic oath, exists against the malicious use of healing power. The shaman is free to steal the souls of his clansmen and inflict illness or death upon them if he dares to do so. The more developed his mastery and the more fully initiated he is, the less he needs to fear retribution for doing mischief.

Amongst Jivaro shamans of the Amazon basin, a similar situation exists. During a long and arduous initiation, the neophyte incubates within his stomach a *tsentsak,* or spirit familiar, with which he has been impregnated by a senior shaman. Cultivation of the relationship with the *tsentsak* and the novice's ultimate mastery over it invest him with the power to cure or kill. Which direction he takes is due more to the inclination of the *tsentsak* than of the shaman himself. If the power has been previously billeted in a sorcerer's stomach, it will tend toward malice. The initiant is not without choice in the matter, however. About a month after its acquisition, the *tsentsak* emerges from the neophyte's mouth and can be dispatched on supernatural missions. At this early stage of its career with the new master, it is capable only of mischief. If the shaman can restrain its eagerness to wreak havoc and can reswallow it for further incubation, he will later be able to heal with the *tsentsak,* or, for that matter, to kill with it.[14] In the Jivaro world-view, initiation confers a talent for doing harm. The more evolved the superordinary faculties, the greater this talent will be, and this is true also of the power to heal. The choice resides as much in the will of the spirit familiar as in the shaman's. How candid is this simple admission of the healer's shadow, of the underside of initiation. And how well it undermines a purely adaptive conception of initiation.

To summarize a few points in the shamanist notion of initiation and power:

(1) Profound initiatory upheaval is neither a response to maladaptation nor to stage of life; instead it represents a particular spirit's need for actualization through a human partner.

(2) Initiation, the spontaneous occurrence of death-rebirth

---

[14] Michael J. Harner, "The Sound of Rushing Water," in *Hallucinogens and Shamanism,* ed. Michael J. Harner (New York, 1973), pp. 15-27.

imagery with its attendant illness, is the first act in a lifelong subjective relationship to a specific, spiritual principle or agency called the "helping spirit." The figure of initiation master appears not simply to effect transformation, but to assert its identity and demand affirmation.

(3) The ego's hegemony is overturned by the helping spirit on the occasion of its first manifestation. Living in close quarters with death is the ineluctable demand of the ally upon the shaman *for the rest of his life.*

(4) Although the human subject of all this upheaval has no choice in the matter, his consolation prize is power. He is not better, more kindly, or more accepting but simply more powerful, though the choice to do good or evil is not fully his to make. As a friend put it in more contemporary context, "Analysis" (he might have said initiation) "does not teach people not to fart in elevators."

There are several variations on the theme of spirit election that should be mentioned for the sake of faithfulness to the anthropological field work. Shamans commonly survey the children of their clan for signs of inspiration and begin to tutor them in advance of any profound initiatory upheaval. To this end, the Kwakiutl shaman of the Northwest Pacific coast employs "spies," presumably spirit allies, who ferret out prospects for apprenticeship. The shaman throws a quartz crystal into the chosen novice's abdomen and thereby begins his ritual initiation with a symbolic wound.[15] Even in this case, it is not properly the shaman who has chosen the new candidate, but indeed a spirit. It is the shaman's special vision that enables him to detect the earliest signs of election and to foster it.

Sometimes the shamanic vocation is hereditary. Again, the youngster's chromosomes usually do not suffice, and he must also receive the call of a spirit in order to claim his birthright.

In some cultures where the visionary quest is highly developed, shamanism is in a relatively debased state. Initiation is no longer purely a prerogative of the spirit but is instead usurped by men bent on accruing superordinary power. Initiatory illness is self-inflicted, and the initiant seeks out a spirit helper rather than vice versa. The Plains Indians are especially given to this version of inspiration, and amongst them the more dis-

---

[12]Franz Boas, Kwahiutl Ethnography, ed. Helen Codere (Chicago, 1966).

tinctive features of ecstatic healing are much less vivid.[16] Eliade
has called attention to the use of psychotropic drugs in various
shamanist cultures as another sign of corruption in the art.[17]

The last significant exception to the principle of election by
spirit is the commerce in helpers so commonly conducted
amongst shamans. Even where immediate inspiration is the
cause of initiation, additional spirit helpers may be received as
gifts or even purchased from other shamans. Usually many
helpers are acquired during the shaman's career, and one received from another shaman seems to have the same significance to its owner as the spontaneous variant.

Perhaps a few examples of spirit helpers will clear up some
of the ambiguity that surrounds them. Three shamans from
different cultures have been selected and their allies listed in
order of acquisition:

SHAMAN A: Henry Rupert (1885-   ), Washo (California-
Nevada) Indian.[18] ALLIES: (1) A horned buck, "Boss of the
Rain," appeared in a dream punctuated by a nosebleed, the
usual indicator of power dreams. (2) A young Hindu male
whose skeleton Henry had seen in a high school he attended.
The spirit of the man "got on" Henry. (3) A Hawaiian spirit
helper named "George" who resided in a volcano in Hawaii.
George had been presented by a Hawaiian healer, a relative by
marriage, who was successfully treated by Henry.

SHAMAN B: Chief of the Salara tribe, residing in the Nuba
Mountains of southern Sudan.[19] ALLIES: (1) A gentle and
friendly red horse with white legs; an ancestral spirit previously
incarnated by this shaman's father. (2) An enormous telegraph
pole which spoke to the shaman in a dream he had during a
severe illness. It identified itself as "li" which translates as "all
that is uncontrollable and evil." (3) A small motorcar like the
British commissioner's; the shaman dreamed he was driving
the car through dark mountains heaped with iron.

[16]J. Gilbert McAllister, "The Four Quartz Rocks Medicine Bundle of the Kiowa-
Apache," *Ethnology* 4 (1965), 210-24.
[17]Mircea Eliade, *Shamanism: Archaic Techniques of Ecstasy* (B. S. LXXVI, New York,
1964), p. 401.
[18]Don Handelman, "The Development of a Washo Shaman," *Ethnology* 6 (1967),
444-64.
[19]Siegfried F. Nadel, "A Study of Shamanism in the Nuba Mountains," *Journal of the
Royal Anthropological Institute* 76 (1946), 25-37.

SHAMAN C: Very ancient member of the St. Lawrence Eskimos.[20] ALLIES: (1) Walrus. (2) Polar bear. (Both 1 and 2 acquired before World War II.) (3) The souls of four Communists shipwrecked and presumably drowned near the island in the postwar period.

The most impressive thing about these helpers is, not surprisingly, their weirdness. The least idiosyncratic in each list is the first, the initiating spirit. It indeed is the most culturally determined: the red and white horse is a totem well known to Salara shamans; the horned buck seems somehow more Indian than do Henry Rupert's subsequent helpers, a Hindu and a Hawaiian. Certainly walrus and polar bears are favorite subjects of Eskimo stone sculpture, but—four Communists?

Anthropologists readily discern two classes of totems: (1) collective (clan or tribal) totems, which are shared by the group and reflect its heritage, and (2) personal totems which belong to the individual's unique experience. The initiating spirit in each of the examples is more a clan or cultural emblem than the subsequent spirits. It carries the mark of the ancestors, or, perhaps we should say, it conveys their call to greater "Salara-ness" or "Washo-ness." Without a very complete understanding of a group's history and common experience, we cannot say why, for example, it should be a red and white horse. Even if we had the needed information, we would probably be left only with a feeling for the symbol much as we have for our own stars and stripes or eagle. But in this feeling we would capture the mystery of group identity, its *esprit de corps*. We would, like the shaman-initiant, experience greater continuity with our kind, and each would thereby experience himself as more of a person.

In the second and subsequent helpers on each list resides the real clue to their *raison d'être*. Through the eyes of an African chieftain, what could be more alien and threatening than an automobile or telegraph pole? To an American Indian raised in rural Nevada, what could be more otherworldly than the skull of another supposed mystic who lived and died on the other side of the world? And, for the Eskimo subject of the

[20]Jane M. Murphy, "Psychotherapeutic Aspects of Shamanism on the St. Lawrence Island, Alaska," in *Magic, Faith and Healing*, ed. Ari Kiev (New York, 1964), pp. 53-83

United States, what more chilling threat than the Communist hordes of the 1950s, virtually knocking at his door from across the Bering Strait? These helping spirits carry the most bewildering qualities and feared contagion from cultures other than the shaman's own. If the initiating spirit causes an increased psychological participation in the smaller tribal group, the later spirits demand attention to a larger, virtually global culture. From what has already been said about the insistence of spirits and the inadvisability of running from them, these alien cultural influences must be embraced once they have intruded. The point is even more clearly made in a mythical power quest recorded by the Kiowa Apache.

It tells of a magical lake called "Kutizze," Medicine Water, that lies somewhere in the hills of the Apache country. Many men sought its powers but were frightened off by the apparitions the lake spewed forth to discourage them. As a very young boy, the hero of our story had heard about these exploits and determined to undertake the quest himself when he came of age.

The boy grew up, fathered children of his own, and, while still a young man, was reminded of his vow by a tribal elder. Compliantly, he trekked into the wilderness with only a breech-clout and peace pipe. As he drew near the secluded lake, he lay down to await inspiration or understanding. And as he was lying motionless on the ground, he heard sounds from the lake, which became louder and louder. Patiently he continued his vigil. One day stretched into the next and still he persevered. From the fifth day on, he was assailed nightly by all manner of demons sent by the lake to discourage him. Following an inner voice each time, he lit his pipe, calmly blew four puffs of smoke at his pursuers, and thereby dissipated them. On the ninth night the last assault came from an insane boy who emerged from the lake, knife in hand. He also was rendered harmless and, transformed by the smoke, became the hero's guide. Together they descended into the depths of the lake, where a party of old men were waiting in a teepee to confer their powers on the indomitable pilgrim. Each one was the soul of a dead Apache. When the young man entered the teepee, the elders began to sing, and each rose in turn to proffer his gift of power. One gave meat and the power to hunt, another seeds and the power to cultivate. The list of precious gifts went on and on, and the young man received each with gratitude, thinking, "This is good." Finally one old man arose to dance. He was deeply pitted with smallpox scars and heavily scabbed. The hero thought, "This is not good," and the old man said, "All right, I will not give it to you." The old man possessed the power to heal and had intended to confer it upon the hero. But, in his aversion to the old man's ugliness, he could not think "this is good" as he had with the others. Instead he had lost the most precious power to cure illness.

This little legend is the central mystery of the Four Quartz Rocks medicine bundle.[21] It speaks in no uncertain terms about the attitude necessary to tap the electing spirit's power. In view of what is known about the insistence of spirits, we might expect the scarred old man to return in a sequel and haunt the reticent hero.

The Four Quartz Rocks tale helps to explain the bizarre aspect of personal helping spirits. We can infer by now that helpers are images of the most alien and repulsive phenomena imaginable to the subject. They demand that he embrace what is newest and least known.

Harkening back to what was said earlier about the shaman being protector and preserver of tribal tradition, it appears that he alone is the testing ground for departure from it. While he organizes the uninitiated around an "old way," he is in his own mind assailed by new possibilities. The Salara shaman instructs his following in how to be Salara, while he himself is put upon by the vision of being British and surrounded by telegraph poles and motorcars. He is, as it were, a conduit through which these new cultural influences reach the tribe modulated by him. The shaman is in a real sense the fashioner of his culture.

The three shamans chosen to illustrate this point were all natives of acculturating civilizations. All were subject to political and technologic pressures. Quite naturally then, at the leading edge of their awareness, we would find the symbols and products of the oppressor cultures with which they were having to contend.

Where these alien cultural influences are lacking, personal helping spirits are even more macabre. In this case, they are

[21]McAllister, op. cit.

not simply culturally foreign, like automobiles and telephone poles, but biologically aberrant—black dogs with three legs and one eye, dwarfs with gigantic mouths and a single large hair, and beings with every conceivable distortion of form. Unlike the griffin, centaur, or unicorn, the grotesque creatures which serve as *personal* helpers in sequestered shamanist cultures look like caprices of nature.

To try to tie a neat philosophical ribbon around the idea of helping spirits, we might draw a metaphor from the theory of evolution. The initiating and especially the personal helping spirits can be thought of as the psyche's genetic material. The appearance of a helper is a mutation of the basic theme and, as such, it is bizarre. Certainly the first possessor of an opposable thumb must have been appalled and bewildered by it. Only with his acceptance did it begin to act in his service and confer upon him power previously unknown. With it he could more effectively club his fellows or, on the contrary, show them the use of tools. Such is the power conferred by the spirit ally, the terrifying and often belligerent figure who will not desist from tormenting the shaman or, for that matter, modern man in the process of transformation. It is the substance of evolution, not simply of adaptation but of hitherto unknown ways of being.[22]

[22]General references: Joseph Campbell, *The Masks of God: Primitive Mythology* (New York, 1970); I. M. Lewis, *Ecstatic Religion* (Harmondsworth, England, 1971).

The Shaman from Elko

C. JESS GROESBECK

WHEN I FIRST LEARNED Joe Henderson had been born and raised in Elko, Nevada, I hesitated to mention it to him for fear it would embarrass him. He was associated with other places important for experiences to which he could relate his life, such as Eastern United States, England, and Zurich. It seemed to me the town of his birth and early life would be of least importance to him, especially since it was such an obscure place. To my surprise, I found just the opposite was true. He told me his Elko heritage was so significant to him that it came up frequently in his dreams while in analysis with Jung. And, as the years of my own early life have unfolded in analysis with Joe, I have felt the connection to my Western Mormon roots in Utah and Washington via the image I have of his connection to his roots in Elko. In fact, I think of him as the Shaman from Elko. I'd like to honor him on his seventy-fifth birthday by amplifying that theme.

In Joe's writings concerning the process of analysis, he noted that, at the core of real analysis, "the analysand *himself* was to be amplified as well as his dream material; that is, his own *symbolic origin*, life-style and purpose are to be determined to the widest extent possible."[1] Applying that criterion to Joseph Henderson, I sense overwhelmingly the symbolic image of the ancient shaman, the medicine-man-healer among the Indian tribes who inhabited Nevada and the neighboring West long before Joe's ancestors settled there.

It is interesting to note that one important image Joe had of Jung was that of the shaman. He stated, in recalling the impact of Jung on his life:

[1]Joseph Henderson, "C. G. Jung: A Reminiscent Picture of His Method," *Journal of Analytical Psychology* 20 (1975), 116.

There was, however, another aspect of Jung's character which refused to conform to European cultural patterns because it seemed to come totally from outside any culture. It seemed to burst upon him from an absolutely foreign but absolutely compelling primitive level of being. I think of it today (thanks to some of his own formulations) as the shaman which made Jung at times into a man of uncanny perception and frightening unpredictability of behavior.

This same shamanistic tendency, freed from any tricksterism, was an essential part of the psychological doctor who came to the rescue over and over again during analysis, placing the healing fingers of his intuition upon our symptoms. He diagnosed and cured them frequently before we ever had a chance to describe them or even to complain of them.[2]

When Joe left Zurich in 1935 after six years of intense analysis with Jung, he dreamed, "Jung had died, and everyone was upset. People close to Jung were asking, 'What will we do?' Then, some Chinese in a group came and beat drums to accompany Jung's spirit to the other side in the manner of the passing of a great shaman to the other world." The shamanic archetype was being activated as Joe was beginning to go his own way in separation from Jung.

Somehow, I think Joe experienced Jung's shamanic qualities because those same qualities and symbolic imagery were emerging from his own psychic life and rootedness, which went back in time and place to his origin, to Elko, Nevada, and the spirit of shamanism inhabiting that land.

Surely Joe Henderson must have been among those referred to by Jung when he commented that, in the dreams of his American patients, "in the course of very thorough and deep analyses . . . I came upon symbols relating to the Indian. The progressive tendency of the unconscious, as expressed . . . in the hero-motif, chooses the Indian as its symbol."[3] Jung points out that a man finds his highest aspirations in the hero-motif:

The hero-motif affects not only the general attitude to life but also the problems of religion. Any absolutist attitude is always a religious attitude, and in whatever respect a man becomes absolute, there you see his religion. I have found in my American patients that their hero-figure possesses traits derived from the religion of the Indians. The most important figure in their religion is the shaman, the medicine-man or conjurer of spirits.[4]

[2]Joseph Henderson, "C. G. Jung: A Personal Evaluation," in *Contact with Jung*, ed. Michael Fordham (London, 1963), pp. 222-3.
[3]"Mind and Earth," CW 10, par. 99.
[4]*Ibid.*, par. 101.

It was Jung's contention that there seemed to be a psychological law that strange ancestral spirits of former inhabitants are reincarnated in the souls of conquerors who settle on foreign soil.[5] He further elaborated this thesis by noting that, since in America the image of the healer was the Indian shaman, the quality of healing experience expressed by Americanized religions, such as Christian Science, Spiritualism (Pentecostalism?, Mormonism?, Shakerism?), had "more to do with the shaman's mental healing than with any recognizable kind of science."[6]

Joe Henderson, in making his own connections with his roots in his native soil of Elko, Nevada, touched the Indian roots of those ancestral peoples who had come before him. He has often related early life impressions of and contacts with the Indians of the West. He has told of significant dreams involving Indians in his later analytical work and development with Jung.

His writings have included description of shamanic initiation patterns seen in his book, *The Wisdom of the Serpent*, and his lectures on American Indian mythology featuring the Sioux, Pueblo, and Navajo. And, since Joe, in his early years, was set apart to be a healer through a number of deep personal experiences, what more natural development could have occurred than a connection with the powerful shaman-healer archetype? Apparently, Jung in his analysis of Joe was able to mediate that connection for him. It can be no wonder that he has presented himself primarily as analyst and friend, the shaman-healer.

In my experience of the "Henderson way of analysis," he often functioned as the Symbolic Shaman. First, he seemingly "broke all the rules" of neutrality and anonymity by talking about himself, his life, and his attitudes, much like the shamans of old. Whenever I was in a tight place, in an impossible, irreconcilable position, he would characterize an experience he had had so as to mediate for me the way out. Second, like the shaman of old, he seemed to have a *direct living* relation to the unconscious and to the spirit realities of "the other world." Often he discussed an experience that seemed totally unrelated to the one with which I was struggling, and then uncannily the realization would dawn on me that he was speaking directly to

[5]*Ibid.*, par. 102-3.
[6]"The Complications of American Psychology," CW 10, par. 977.

my unconscious psychic needs of the moment, but from a different perspective. I've continually marveled at his simple, direct, and clear way of reading the meaning of a dream without recourse to some external basis for its validity—ability to get at the heart of the dream without being caught up in details. The shaman is best defined as that ancient form of medicine man who, through his *direct* connections and experiences with the spirit world, could function as a mediator of healing in finding the lost soul of the patient and restoring him to a whole life.[7] The Henderson method of analysis and, most importantly, Joe's whole personal being and demeanor are best described by that image.

One striking example of that shamanic quality of Joe occurred when a patient who had been analyzed by him moved to another part of the country and had unforeseen difficulties. He finally went to another analyst, but with great resistance because he couldn't conceive of working with anyone but Joe. The analyst he saw wisely said, "Let us go ahead and work on your problem by asking Dr. Henderson questions and seeing what he would answer, *as though he were here in spirit!*" The second analysis was conducted in that manner quite successfully.

I'd like to relate a dream I had that was part of my own development and initiation in becoming an analyst. I was at a very difficult point, trying to separate out my childhood world and young adult attachments. Then I dreamed:

I was in my home town of Seattle. I was on my way to the medical school I had attended, but this time it was for an operation. The operation was to prepare me to be a better physician and healer. It was done in my nose, a rhinoplasty, and then my appendix was removed. Finally, preparations were made for the "big operation" on my head by a neurosurgeon. However, when he came in, it turned out he did not operate like a modern neurosurgeon, but was, in fact, an Indian medicine man with the secrets of Indian healing lore and early English history. Strangely, the secrets of this old Indian medicine were known to George Albert Smith, an early Mormon pioneer in Utah.

Interpretation of the dream foretold a shift in my own direction as a healer, from a more compartmentalized, technique-oriented, modern medical approach to a more ancient, shamanistic way of symbolic healing. The image of the Indian

[7]Willard Z. Park, *Shamanism in Western North America* (New York, 1975), pp. 8-10.

healer, who had knowledge of English history, connected directly to Joe Henderson. The image of George Albert Smith expressed my Mormon roots. Thus Joe, having himself experienced his own rootedness in the shamanic archetype, was mediating this experience, via the transference, for me. The dream motif suggested a shamanic initiatory rite in becoming a healer.

An experience Joe described is that of a recurrent dream he had until recently that summarizes all that has been attempted in this paper. Here are his dream and comments:

I was back in my home town of Elko, Nevada, living there and practicing analysis. Everything seemed right and in harmony. I awoke, puzzled by the dream, especially when it recurred on several consecutive nights. What was puzzling was that I knew it could not be taken literally, i.e., that I ought to be living in Elko. There would not be any use for an analyst there, and I have had no family connections there for many years.

At the time, I'd been wrestling with certain problems of my patients in analysis and wondering if I were seeing things just right. Finally, the meaning of the dream came as an answer to my conscious concern. It was saying, "things are just right and in harmony because you are doing it *as though* you were practicing analysis in Elko."

The unconscious was confirming Joe in his analytical work by showing him that his symbol of inner harmony and balance as an analyst was "practicing in Elko" where his roots were.

The greatest task of the shaman in all cultures has always been to help his patients and/or community stay in balance, and Joe did this by getting himself in balance first. This experience of his suggests how he fulfills that shamanic task in his work. No wonder he has helped so many of us find our way!

The Blessing Way Ceremony

MAUD OAKES

NEAR A TOWERING RED MESA on the Navajo Reservation, in New Mexico, stood the hogan (house) where a Blessing Way rite, a purifying ceremony, was to be given that evening. My friend Wilito, a well-known blind medicine man, had offered to give this ceremony over me. He said it would drive the white man's poison out of me, enabling the medicine men to give me their prayers, songs, and paintings without endangering themselves or me. I accepted with eagerness and timidity.

That morning Charlie, my Navajo interpreter, and I had gone to Gallup, twenty-two miles away, to buy all the food for the ceremony, including a huge watermelon, and also the medicine basket and two yards of material on which the medicine man would lay his equipment. We gave all of this to Jo Brown, Charlie's father-in-law. He was tall and handsome and a famous Yebitsai dancer. His wife, White Eye, was a well-known Hand-Trembling Diagnostician. They offered me the use of their hogan without charge, even though the entire family had to move out with their belongings.

The Blessing Way rite is considered to be the most important of all ceremonies. It is a private family affair, for the purpose of blessing the initiate's possessions, his animals, and his crops. Its songs and prayers cover every aspect of life. It protects against war and witches, and it purifies. No medicine is given, only corn pollen, which is the food of the gods. Every Blessing Way rite commences with a hogan song, since for the Navajo the hogan is the center of their world and a symbol of their soul. Late in the afternoon I returned to the hogan with my bedroll under my arm. I was wearing a long Navajo skirt, a gay velvet blouse, moccasins, and plenty of borrowed silver and turquoise jewelry. I also had a duplicate skirt and blouse with me.

It was strange to realize that this time I was to be the initiate and not the observer. Yet it was also not strange, as I had always thought my path in life was the path of initiation. I visualized it as spiral in form with many tests on the way, similar to the ancient initiations.

Entering the door of the hogan, which always faces east, I walked sun-wise to my place on the west side. Old Wilito, the medicine man, sat in the southwest corner with his medicine pouch at his side. He wore a scarf around his gray hair, a patched blue pajama top, and plenty of beautiful old jewelry, including the silver buttons on his earth-red moccasins.

When the men's dinner came, I went out to join the women and children and animals in an open kitchen with a kerosene barrel stove. After the men's empty plates were brought out and darkness enveloped us, I entered the hogan and the women followed.

I noticed that the possessions of mine that were to be blessed had been put behind my seat against the wall. Wilito picked up his large two-sided medicine pouch; it was made of the skin of a fawn that had been suffocated in pollen. Down the middle of the pouch was sewn a strip that stood for the Milky Way. All this and more he told me as he laid the things in the pouch on the material between us. From each side of the pouch he took seven sacks and bundles. Inside these were many objects, such as prayer sticks, stones, shells, arrowheads, and one squat, fat buckskin bag the size of a grapefruit. Inside this were four little sacks of sand; each had come from one of the four holy mountains and was designated by a bead of the mountain's symbolic color.

A bowl of yellow, female corn meal was handed to Charlie; he represented me, since I had no family there. He sprinkled the walls of the hogan and the objects to be blessed with the corn meal; this ritual purified and blessed them.

Wilito then rubbed pollen from his pollen bag on the soles of my feet, my knees, and my hands. He put it down my neck and back, on my shoulders, in my mouth, on my temples, and on top of my head. And he made an upward mark with pollen on my cheek. He followed this procedure every time he gave me pollen, which was often. Then he took some himself, blessed the objects in his medicine equipment, and the hogan behind me, and then passed the pollen bag so that all present could partake of the pollen. At the same time he sang out his power. Then he gave me the bag of the holy mountains and two talking prayer sticks to hold. He prayed over me for at least an hour. It was most impressive—the mixture of facial expressions, his tone of voice, and the feeling that came from him and the others in the hogan. I felt wrapped up in all this pure energy. Later Wilito told me that the prayers were of the twelve Holy People, the holy mountains, the sun, and especially the dawn, for the Holy Dawn People would guard me from harm and bad dreams. He pressed me all over with the mountain sands, and I breathed in deeply of the sands and ate pollen. Then I walked out into the night with the new moon over the hogan and all the friendly stars blinking down. With deep humility I said a prayer, and then I went back into the hogan. So ended the evening ceremony.

Wilito told me to sleep in my place, and he slept in his. Charlie and Mary, his wife, and his children were my chaperones. The room was so hot that I could hardly stand it. At the first streak of light I took the pollen bag and walked out into the cold dawn. Beauty was everywhere. I put pollen on top of my head and in my mouth and I threw the rest to the dawn and its beauty.

Charlie left to gather four leaves of yucca (soap weed) and three herbs, one of which was sage. Before picking them he sprinkled pollen on them. Wilito pressed the Talking Prayer Sticks and the holy sands all over me, and then I went out in the sun.

After Charlie returned, he called me into the hogan, and this is what I saw. A path of sand led from the door up to a round platform made of sand from the corn fields, so that I would think straight. The ceremonial basket symbolizing the hogan had been placed in the center of the platform, which was almost in the center of the hogan. Charlie had made four steps of pollen up the path to the basket. A line of corn meal went up the middle of the sand path, through the pollen steps, and around the basket to the north, ending in a cross which symbolized female lightning. The line of corn meal and the sand platform symbolized the universe. As the medicine man sang, he mashed the ends of the yucca leaves with a rock and swished them in the water in the basket, making suds for my bath. Wilito held the yucca leaves over the basket, pointing them in the four directions. With the pollen in his bag he made many different symbolic lines around and on the basket. The herbs were laid in front of my seat. Two pollen crosses had been made where I would kneel, and two more were made for my hands, one on each side of the basket. These symbolized strength of thought for the patient and good thoughts in the four directions.

The medicine man took the bag of holy sands that I had been holding and continued singing. At a certain place he signaled, and I commenced walking on the path, being careful to step in each footstep, and in this way I returned to my place. Mary helped me remove my jewelry, moccasins, and blouse. Wilito sprinkled pollen on me and put yucca suds on my knees. I knelt on two crosses and put my hands on the other two crosses, bringing my head over the basket. Mary washed my hair and put suds on my body from the waist up. A blanket was then held in front of me, and Mary washed my body from the waist down as I stood in the basket. The jewelry was washed, and Wilito rubbed corn meal over my body as he sang. I sprinkled my legs with corn meal. Pollen from Corn Bug Girl was put in my moccasins. This would make me strong and able to walk straight in life. I breathed out, not in, on the holy mountain sands. Then I put on my other clean blouse and skirt and jewelry. Later Wilito told me the songs he had sung were those sung over their great goddess Changing Woman, she who is born in the spring and dies in the winter and then is reborn.

I went out to comb my hair and, since I had no comb with me, I was given the community wire hair brush. I had to use it or hurt their feelings, even though I knew it had been used on rugs and the animals. I was sure it was alive with lice. I returned to my place, and again Wilito pressed me all over with the holy mountain sands and sprinkled me with pollen. So ended the ceremonial bath.

After lunch, Wilito went for a sweat bath, and I remained in the hogan with a million flies. When he returned, he came to me and pressed hard with two fingers on each temple, under my arms, on my solar plexus, and under my knees. Then he returned to his seat, saying in Navajo "all right" and "beautiful."

At sundown the guests began to arrive on horse or on foot. The men were served dinner at nine o'clock, and I joined the women outside. An hour later the women and I were called into the hogan. There were fifteen men and five women. I recognized four medicine men who had given me paintings. They were all Navajo. The men sat on the south side and the women on the north side. I was pollen-blessed and mountain-pressed altogether eight times until dawn. The singing of Wilito and the other men went on all night. The women are never allowed to sing. The men stopped only for food and water, to smoke, or to spit. Before midnight no one was allowed to leave the hogan until I had gone out and returned. By 2 a.m. most of the elderly people were asleep. One old man sang in his sleep; it was half chant and half snore and amused everyone except Wilito. He sat cross-legged with his left hand cupped to his left ear, his back straight and supple. He never faltered; he just kept on singing out his power. It took all my will to keep awake, for the singing was hypnotic. Navajo singing is unlike any singing I have ever heard. It is strange and beautiful and full of nature sounds.

When the cool dawn finally came, I went out into it with the pollen bag in my right hand. There was just a streak of light, and to this I said my prayers. With arms outspread I brought the pollen bag up to my face four times, breathing in of its strength and purity, and then entered the hogan. The Blessing Way Ceremony was over. When the sun was well up, Wilito gave me my new name, Glenniba, she who walks with her friends.

I returned to the Newcombs, where I had my own hogan-studio. I felt awed and humble and not the Maud Oakes I had always known. Laughing to myself, I thought, I have enough pollen lining my intestinal tract to make me so holy that wings might sprout any second.

Part Two

Romeo and Juliet:
A *Coniunctio* Drama

EDWARD F. EDINGER

SHAKESPEARE'S ROMEO AND JULIET OFFERS ITSELF for many different interpretations. Perhaps on the deepest level it can be seen as a drama of the mystery of *coniunctio*. Its major themes—love, war, beauty, marriage, death, and the union of opposites—are all related to this archetype. The interplay and paradoxical union of opposites is a particularly prominent motif, appearing for instance in Romeo's first speech.

> *Here's much to do with hate, but more with love:*
> *Why then, O brawling love! O loving hate!*
> *O any thing! of nothing first create.*
> *O heavy lightness! serious vanity!*
> *Mis-shapen chaos of well-seeming forms!*
> *Feather of lead, bright smoke, cold fire, sick health!*
> *Still-waking sleep, that is not what it is!* (I, i, 180-186)[1]

This passage is reminiscent of the quotation that Jung chose as a motto for his study of *coniunctio* symbolism, in *The Psychology of the Transference*: "Bellica pax, vulnus dulce, suave malum. (A warring peace, a sweet wound, a mild evil.)"[2] The parallel does not end there. As we shall see, in still other respects *Romeo and Juliet* corresponds symbolically with the series of pictures from the *Rosarium Philosophorum* which Jung discusses in that essay.

The play begins with a prologue which outlines the plot with brevity and beauty.

> *Two households, both alike in dignity,*
> *In fair Verona, where we lay our scene,*

[1]Quotations are from the Oxford edition of Shakespeare, ed. W. J. Craig.
[2]CW 16, preceding par. 353.

> *From ancient grudge break to new mutiny,*
> *Where civil blood makes civil hands unclean.*
> *From forth the fatal loins of these two foes*
> *A pair of star-cross'd lovers take their life;*
> *Whose misadventur'd piteous overthrows*
> *Do with their death bury their parents' strife.*
> *The fearful passage of their death-mark'd love,*
> *And the continuance of their parents' rage,*
> *Which, but their children's end nought could remove,*
> *Is now the two hours' traffick of our stage.*

The play concerns, we are told, a new outbreak of an "ancient grudge." It is as though the conflict between the houses of Montague and Capulet represents a current, personal version of the archetypal strife between the opposites. The created world began with a separation of opposites. ("God divided the light from the darkness." Gen. 1:4) That initial *separatio*, the tearing apart of the united opposites, was a crime, and hence Anaximander can speak of the "injustice" incurred by the existence of separate things.[3] The existence of the ego is based on the separation and perpetual conflict of the opposites. This is the original sin, the ancient grudge that breaks out again and again in new forms.

Every major increase of consciousness involves a reawakening of that ancient grudge. It corresponds to the condition that Jung speaks of which "occurs when the analysis has constellated the opposites so powerfully that a union or synthesis of the personality becomes an imperative necessity. . . . [A conflict is generated that] requires a real solution and necessitates a third thing in which the opposites can unite. . . . In nature the resolution of opposites is always an energic process."[4] Romeo and Juliet are personifications of the constellated opposites, and the third thing which arises between them, the energic process that resolves the conflict, is love. This corresponds to the dove descending between the king and queen in first of the *Rosarium* pictures (figure 1†).

---

[3]"The Non-Limited (Apeiron) is the original material of existing things, further, the source from which existing things derive their existence is also that to which they return at their destruction, according to necessity; for they give justice and make reparation to one another for their injustice, according to the arrangement of Time." Kathleen Freeman, *Ancilla to the Pre-Socratic Philosophers* (Cambridge, Mass., 1948), p. 19.
[4]CW 14, par. 705.
†Woodcuts reproduced from CW 16.

Figure 1

Romeo and Juliet concerns the *mysterium amoris*. Since this is a manifestation of the *numinosum* it defies rational description. As Jung says,

I falter before the task of finding the language which might adequately express the incalculable paradoxes of love. Eros is a *kosmogonos*, a creator and father-mother of all higher consciousness. . . . I have again and again been faced with the mystery of love, and have never been able to explain what it is. Like Job, I had to "lay my hand on my mouth. I have spoken once, and I will not answer." (Job 40:4f). . . . For we are in the deepest sense the victims and the instruments of cosmogonic "love."[5]

[5]*Memories*, pp. 353-4.

The encounter with Eros, the mighty daimon, occurs early in the play. For Romeo, love was generated by beauty, which might be defined as the aesthetic aspect of the *numinosum*. Rilke's lines are relevant here.

> *For beauty is nothing*
> *but the beginning of terror we can just barely endure,*
> *and we admire it so because it calmly disdains*
> *to destroy us. Every angel is terrible.*[6]

The passage describing Romeo's first reaction to Juliet's beauty is itself exquisitely beautiful, a magnificent wedding of form and content. Beauty is described by beauty.

> *What lady is that which doth enrich the hand of yonder knight?* . . .
> *O! she doth teach the torches to burn bright.*
> *It seems she hangs upon the cheek of night*
> *Like a rich jewel in an Ethiop's ear;*
> *Beauty too rich for use, for earth too dear!* (I, v, 45-51)

Love and beauty are transpersonal factors, evoking a sense of the divine. Thus, at their first meeting, Romeo and Juliet speak to each other in religious terms.

> Romeo: *If I profane with my unworthiest hand*
> *This holy shrine, the gentle sin is this;*
> *My lips, two blushing pilgrims, ready stand*
> *To smooth that rough touch with a tender kiss.* (I, v, 97-100)

But transpersonal factors are dangerous; a holy shrine is charged with mana. Like the tabernacle of Yahweh, it has destructive effects if approached carelessly. A meeting between the lesser (the ego) and the greater (the Self) is indeed a "fearful passage." The risk is that the lesser will be dissolved by the greater. This accounts for the symbolic connection between love and death. *Romeo and Juliet* is a rich study in this linkage. Love threatens one with loss of identity. If love is based on the projection of an archetypal image, perhaps the Self, to unite with the loved one threatens dissolution. In one dialogue Romeo's identity, i.e., his name, is specifically at issue. Juliet is speaking.

> *'Tis but thy name that is my enemy;*
> *Thou art thyself though, not a Montague.*

[6]Rainer Maria Rilke, *Duino Elegies*, tr. C. F. MacIntyre (Berkeley and Los Angeles, 1961), First Elegy, p. 3.

> *What's Montague? it is nor hand, nor foot,*
> *Nor arm, nor face, nor any other part*
> *Belonging to a man. O! be some other name:*
> *What's in a name? that which we call a rose*
> *By any other name would smell as sweet;*
> . . .
>
>   *Romeo, doff thy name;*
> *And for that name, which is no part of thee,*
> *Take all myself.*
>
> Romeo: *I take thee at thy word.*
> *Call me but love, and I'll be new baptiz'd;*
> *Henceforth I never will be Romeo.* (II, ii, 38-51)

This willingness to relinquish his identity is dubious, at least from the standpoint of the ego. Romeo asks to be called love; i.e., he identifies with the archetype. As Jung tells us, this leads to dismemberment.

> When the *spiritus phantasticus* in man, his creative phantasy, reaches beyond man in any respect, below or above, he really becomes divine. Then Synesius says an extraordinary thing: he says, "And being divine, he has, as such, to undergo the divine punishment." And the divine punishment is dismemberment: he will be torn in pieces, he will be sacrificed like a sacrificial animal that is cut asunder upon the altar.[7]

Romeo and Juliet are both sacrificial victims. They fall into identification with the archetype of *coniunctio* and are thus fated for dismemberment. At the conclusion of the play Capulet calls them, "Poor sacrifices of our enmity!" (V, iii, 304)

At one point, Romeo's rage against his name takes on the proportions of madness. After he has killed Tybalt and hears from the nurse how Juliet is weeping and calling out his name, he vents his despair.

>   *As if that name,*
> *Shot from the deadly level of a gun,*
> *Did murder her; as that name's cursed hand*
> *Murder'd her kinsman. O! tell me, friar, tell me,*
> *In what vile part of this anatomy*
> *Doth my name lodge? tell me that I may sack*
> *The hateful mansion.* [Drawing his sword.] (III, iii, 101-107)

Romeo has been inundated by more self-knowledge than he can stand. He would annihilate his identity, the hateful mansion of his name. As Jung has said,

[7]Jung, *The Visions Seminars* (Zurich, 1976), vol. 1, p. 85.

The way to yourself is the longest way and the hardest way. Everybody would pay anything, his whole fortune, to avoid going to himself. Most people hate themselves, despise themselves, and for nothing in the world would they go where they are, where their native town is, because it is just hell![8]

Romeo's loss of his name also has a positive side. He is no longer confined to a narrow, one-sided identity. His love for Juliet has released him from the Montague-Capulet conflict. He is no longer identified with one side of a pair of warring opposites. However, his friend Mercutio (his shadow) is not so released. Mercutio is an aggressive, high-spirited figure who plays at shadow projection and stirs up dissension wherever he goes. In II, iv, Mercutio, in his usual manner, fences with Romeo intellectually, engaging in the thrust and parry of witticisms. At one point he exclaims, "Come between us, good Benvolio; my wit faints." (73) This theme of "coming between" the warring opposites occurs again in graver form in III, i, where Tybalt tries to provoke Romeo to fight. Romeo will not be baited by Tybalt's insults. His love for Juliet lets him see Tybalt as a brother. For the moment, he is beyond the conflict of the opposites. Mercutio is incensed at Romeo's composure. As the one-sided partisan characteristically does, Mercutio interprets Romeo's position beyond the opposites as weakness and exclaims scornfully, "O calm, dishonourable, vile submission." Mercutio provokes Tybalt and they fight. Romeo comes between them in an effort to stop the fight. Instead, Mercutio is mortally wounded under Romeo's arm.

It is a fearful thing to come between the warring opposites. Romeo had gotten a glimpse of a wholeness beyond the opposites but had overestimated the strength of his position. His insight was not yet effectively realized. When Mercutio is dying, he and Romeo exchange standpoints. Mercutio achieves an attitude beyond the opposites, expressed negatively in the words, "a plague on both your houses." Romeo, however, regresses to Mercutio's earlier state of identification with the conflict. Such a regression is a typical, transient phenomenon during the integration of the shadow. Having been indirectly responsible for the death of Mercutio by stepping between the opposites, Romeo must now assume the responsibility for cor-

[8]Ibid., vol. 1, p. 30.

recting the balance. Coming between the opposites makes one
the carrier of wholeness, a divine burden, which, if shouldered
unconsciously, has tragic consequences. Thus could Romeo
well exclaim after killing Tybalt, "O! I am Fortune's fool."
(III, i, 142)

Romeo is caught in the coils of a tragic process. Significantly,
the theme of dismemberment now makes its first appearance.
Just before the nurse announces Tybalt's death to Juliet, the
latter, in the midst of an apostrophe to night, exclaims,

> *Give me my Romeo: and, when he shall die,*
> *Take him and cut him out in little stars,*
> *And he will make the face of heaven so fine*
> *That all the world will be in love with night,*
> *And pay no worship to the garish sun.* (III, ii, 21-25)

When Romeo pours out his suicidal despair to Friar Lawrence, the friar replies,

> *Fie, fie! thou sham'st thy shape, thy love, thy wit*
> . . .
> *Thy wit, that ornament to shape and love,*
> *Misshapen in the conduct of them both,*
> *Like powder in a skilless soldier's flask,*
> *To set a-fire by thine own ignorance,*
> *And thou dismember'd with thine own defence.* (III, iii, 121-133)

And finally Romeo, in the last stage of his desperation, about
to enter Juliet's tomb, warns Balthasar not to spy on him.

> *But, if thou, jealous, dost return to pry*
> *In what I further shall intend to do,*
> *By heaven, I will tear thee joint by joint,*
> *And strew this hungry churchyard with thy limbs.*
> *The time and my intents are savage-wild,*
> *More fierce and more inexorable far*
> *Than empty tigers or the roaring sea.* (V, ii, 33-39)

Romeo is the dismembered one. He has been rent asunder by
his desires and their frustration, the yea and nay of the archetypal opposites. This is the consequence of identifying with
archetypal love, coming between the opposites and carelessly
entering the divine region of wholeness. Like Actaeon, Romeo
encountered the transpersonal unexpectedly and was dismembered by his own hounds (instinctual passions). Dismemberment is one of the consequences of the alchemical *coniunctio*.
Jung writes,

[Speaking of the "Arisleus Vision," which says:] "With so much love did Beya embrace Gabricus that she absorbed him wholly into her own nature and dissolved him into indivisible particles." Ripley says that at the death of the king all his limbs were torn into "atoms." This is the motif of dismemberment which is well known in alchemy. The atoms are or become "white sparks" shining in the *terra foetida* (stench of the graves). They are also called the "fishes' eyes."[9]

Analogous to dismemberment is the theme of igniting gunpowder, which is used several times. In addition to the friar's reference to "powder in a skilless soldier's flask," he had earlier cautioned Romeo to mitigate his urgent desires in these words:

> These violent delights have violent ends
> And in their triumph die, like fire and powder,
> Which, as they kiss consume. (II, vi, 9-11)

Again, when Romeo is buying poison from the apothecary, he says,

> Let me have
> A dram of poison, such soon-speeding gear
> As will disperse itself through all the veins
> That the life-weary taker may fall dead,
> And that the trunk may be discharg'd of breath
> As violently as hasty powder fir'd
> Doth hurry from the fatal cannon's womb. (V, i, 59-65)

Gunpowder represents the explosive energy charge contained in an archetype. No sooner does an immature ego touch the archetype than it becomes inflated and in danger of being exploded by its transpersonal energy. Both Romeo and Juliet have fallen into the archetypal image of *coniunctio* and, in their immaturity, are cruelly ground between the opposites. When Juliet first learns that Romeo has killed her cousin, Tybalt, she is burdened with a load of opposites beyond her ability to bear. She expresses her agony in these lines:

> O serpent heart, hid with a flowering face!
> Did ever dragon keep so fair a cave?
> Beautiful tyrant! fiend angelical!
> Dove-feather'd raven! wolvish-ravening lamb!
> Despised substance of divinest show!
> Just opposite to what thou justly seem'st;
> A damned saint, an honourable villain!

[9]CW 14, par. 64.

> *O, nature! what hadst thou to do in hell*
> *When thou didst bower the spirit of a fiend*
> *In mortal paradise of such sweet flesh?*
> *Was ever book containing such vile matter*
> *So fairly bound? O! that deceit should dwell*
> *In such a gorgeous palace.* (III, ii, 73-84)

Juliet awakens quickly from this frantic state and recovers her personal feelings for Romeo. However, she had momentarily projected onto Romeo the paradoxical and awesome qualities of the *coniunctio*. Similiarly, Romeo falls into a frenzy upon learning of his banishment. Fate has tossed him violently back and forth between the opposites. Heaven is where Juliet is; hell is her absence.

> *. There is no world without Verona walls, .*
> *But purgatory, torture, hell itself.*
> *Hence banished is banish'd from the world,*
> *And world's exile is death; then "banished,"*
> *Is death mis-term'd. Calling death "banished,"*
> *Thou cutt'st my head off with a golden axe,*
> *And smil'st upon the stroke that murders me.*
>
> *. . .*
>
>   *"Banished!"*
> *O friar! the damned use that word in hell;*
> *Howlings attend it.* (III, iii, 17-47)

For the once-born ego, encounter with the *coniunctio* appears first as heaven and then as death. *Romeo and Juliet* is one of our most explicit literary expressions of that fact. The equation "marriage equals death" runs like a black thread through the entire play. When Romeo first urges Friar Lawrence to marry them, he says,

> *Do thou but close our hands with holy words,*
> *Then love-devouring death do what he dare;*
> *It is enough I may but call her mine.* (II, vi, 6-8)

When Juliet is found apparently dead, Capulet exclaims to Paris,

> *O Son! the night before thy wedding-day*
> *Hath Death lain with thy wife. There she lies,*
> *Flower as she was, deflowered by him.*
> *Death is my son-in-law, Death is my heir;*
> *My daughter he hath wedded: I will die,*
> *And leave him all; life, living, all is Death's!* (IV, v, 35-40)

The wedding has turned into a funeral.

> *All things that we ordained festival,*
> *Turn from their office to black funeral;*
> *Our instruments to melancholy bells,*
> *Our wedding cheer to a sad burial feast,*
> *Our solemn hymns to sullen dirges change,*
> *Our bridal flowers serve for a buried corse,*
> *And all things change them to the contrary.* (IV, v, 84-90)

Finally, in the last scene of the play, Romeo wonders at Juliet's beauty in the tomb.

> *Ah! dear Juliet,*
> *Why art thou yet so fair? Shall I believe*
> *That unsubstantial Death is amorous,*
> *And that the lean abhorred monster keeps*
> *Thee here in dark to be his paramour?* (V, iii, 101-105)

The theme of marriage to death is widespread in myth and folklore, for instance, Persephone's abduction by Hades and the tale of Amor and Psyche. Alchemical imagery also connects marriage or sexual union with death. An example is the series of pictures from the *Rosarium Philosophorum*. In this series, the picture following sexual union shows the king and queen, merged into one figure, lying dead in the tomb (figure 2). Concerning this symbolism Jung says,

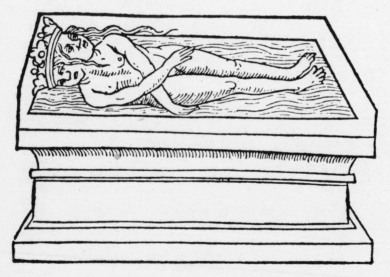

Figure 2

The integration of contents that were always unconscious and projected involves a serious lesion of the ego. Alchemy expresses this through the symbols of death, mutilation, or poisoning.[10]

We have seen how both Romeo and Juliet were "poisoned" by their encounter with the united opposites. But yet the ultimate meaning is not negative. During a process that unites the opposites, i.e., individuation, good and evil can often be paradoxically reversed. Friar Lawrence sounded this theme explicitly in his panegyric to the herbs and minerals of the earth.

> *For nought so vile that on the earth doth live*
> *But to the earth some special good doth give,*
> *Nor aught so good but strain'd from that fair use*
> *Revolts from true birth, stumbling on abuse:*
> *Virtue itself turns vice, being misapplied,*
> *And vice sometime's by action dignified.*
> *Within the infant rind of this weak flower*
> *Poison hath residence and medicine power;*
> *. . .*
> *Two such opposed foes encamp them still*
> *In man as well as herbs, grace and rude will.* (II, iii, 17-28)

Grace and rude will correspond to the two basic modes of psychic being, power and love. As Jung says, "Where love reigns, there is no will to power; and where the will to power is paramount, love is lacking. The one is but the shadow of the other."[11] Each of these modes can be lived at different levels, from the most primitive to the most differentiated. They are a pair of opposites, equal in value and importance. Power promotes differentiation, separateness, knowledge, and the individualized ego. Love promotes union, togetherness, social interest, and relation to the transpersonal. As a pair of opposites they contradict one another. The truth of one is the falsehood of the other. To win in the power mode is to lose in love. Thus Juliet says, while waiting for her lover,

> *Come, civil night,*
> *Thou sober-suited matron, all in black,*
> *And learn me how to lose a winning match,*
> *Play'd for a pair of stainless maidenhoods.* (III, ii, 10-13)

Romeo and Juliet both lose a winning match. In ego-power terms they are defeated by death. However, in transpersonal-

---

[10]Ibid., par. 472.   [11]CW 7, par. 78.

Figure 3

love terms they are victorious. Symbolically, death is the prelude to rebirth. "The alchemists assert that death is at once the
conception of the *filius philosophorum*,"[12] i.e., the realization of
the Self is born out of the death of the ego. The *Rosarium*
pictures show death followed by resurrection (figure 3). Rebirth
following death is also suggested in *Romeo and Juliet*. The rec-
onciliation of Capulet and Montague is an expression of life

[12]CW 16, par. 473.

reborn from the deaths of their children, "poor sacrifices [of their] enmity." (304) Also, there is Romeo's rebirth dream which pictures the coming events from the standpoint of the unconscious.

> *My dreams presage some joyful news at hand:*
> *My bosom's lord sits lightly in his throne;*
> *And all this day an unaccustom'd spirit*
> *Lifts me above the ground with cheerful thoughts.*
> *I dreamt my lady came and found me dead;—*
> *Strange dream, that gives a dead man leave to think,—*
> *And breath'd such life with kisses in my lips,*
> *That I reviv'd, and was an emperor.* (V, i, 2-9)

The play leaves one with the definite sense of life and love triumphant over death. Donald Stauffer, the Shakespearian scholar, notes this fact.

The intensity of their single-souled impulse has turned their passion into a death-devouring love. . . . Man's deeper instincts play strange juggleries in attaining truth beyond the reach of metaphysics, so that there is a mysterious authenticity in Romeo's phrase "a triumphant grave." . . . The sense of triumph descends upon the play from a love so straight, so simple, and so certain that its very bravery transforms death and time and hatred—yes, and the accidents of fate—into insubstantial shadows. The quick bright things remain shining and alive.[13]

The "triumphant grave" passage occurs as Romeo lays dead Paris in Juliet's tomb.

> *O! give me thy hand,*
> *One writ with me in sour misfortune's book:*
> *I'll bury thee in a triumphant grave;*
> *A grave? O, no! a lanthorn, slaughter'd youth,*
> *For here lies Juliet, and her beauty makes*
> *This vault a feasting presence full of light.* (V, iii, 81-86)

It has been noted[14] that *Romeo and Juliet* is unusual among Shakespeare's plays for the number of references it makes to light. And almost all of these link light to beauty as occurs here where Juliet's beauty is described as "a feasting presence full of light." Keats has taught us that beauty is truth. For Shakespeare, beauty is light. If light refers to consciousness, then consciousness is beautiful. And also we can say, beauty pro-

[13]Donald A. Stauffer, *Shakespeare's World of Images* (New York, 1949), p. 59.
[14]Caroline F. E. Spurgeon, *Shakespeare's Imagery and What It Tells Us* (Cambridge, Eng., 1952), p. 312.

motes consciousness. The fine arts can thus be seen as great collective carriers of consciousness.[15] Certainly this play, in its beauty, is a bringer of consciousness.

If there was an historical Romeo and Juliet, they did not die in vain. Their lives have bodied forth an archetype for the benefit of all. These lines of Juliet, modified to apply to both, picture their translation to eternity and their eternal witness to the light that shines in the darkness.

> *And, when they shall die,*
> *Take them and cut them out in little stars,*
> *And they will make the face of heaven so fine*
> *That all the world will be in love with night,*
> *And pay no worship to the garish sun.*

[15]Strictly speaking, only individuals carry consciousness. Works of art *transmit* consciousness from the artist to the perceiver if the latter is ready to receive it.

Some Comments about the Masque in Shakespeare's *Tempest*

JAMES KIRSCH

IN 1971 DR. JOSEPH HENDERSON was gracious enough to contribute an insightful article to a Festschrift for me. In it he discussed two of Shakespeare's plays. *A Midsummer Night's Dream* and *The Tempest.* In his analysis of *The Tempest* he paid particular attention to Prospero, whom he considers "not merely a personality," but a human being who has a "typical psychological problem." The other "figures" are, in his opinion, "mere personalities." Based on his comprehensive knowledge of psychology and anthropology, he saw this play as essentially a drama of initiation.

In *The Tempest* the initiation prefigures the way of individuation as we understand this term in modern analytical psychology.[1]

In response to his perspective overview of *The Tempest*, I take the opportunity of honoring him on his seventy-fifth birthday by making some comments about one scene in the same play, the Masque.

Dr. Henderson describes Prospero as a man of power, a Duke who had been the ruler of a city state (a "signiorie"), but one who had turned over the reins of government to his brother. As a result, he was expelled by his brother and after many dangers, landed on an island. When the play opens, he and his daughter have been living on the island for twelve years. Then, through a strange event—a tempest—his treacherous brother, together with the King of Naples and a group of courtiers, also find themselves on the island. By Prospero's

[1] Joseph Henderson, "Symbolism of the Unconscious in Two Plays of Shakespeare," in *The Well-Tended Tree*, ed. Hilde Kirsch (New York, 1971), p. 297.

magic, Ferdinand, the King of Naples' son, and Prospero's daughter, Miranda, have fallen in love and a marriage is planned. Prospero, who is the hierophant, has promised the lovers a particular gift. This turns out to be the Masque.

While Prospero as Duke of Milan was a man of worldly power, we see him in *The Tempest* as the great magician who has power over the world of spirits. It is his servant, Ariel, through whom all the tasks in the spirit world are performed. The Masque is perhaps the most puzzling of Ariel's magical achievements. In Elizabethan times the masque was frequently inserted in a play as a special scene, as a form of entertainment in which music played a particular role. But for Shakespeare the masque had a purpose far transcending entertainment. As a play within a play it becomes an integral part of the initiation.

As in every initiation in primitive societies, an encounter with supernatural forces is enacted. Prospero arranges such an encounter for the lovers. The Masque occurs after Ferdinand has performed all the tasks imposed upon him by Prospero, and Prospero has to admit to Ferdinand:

> All thy vexations
> Were but my trials of thy love, and thou
> Hast strangely stood the test. (IV, i, 5)[2]

As Prospero's gift, Ferdinand receives Miranda "worthily purchased." She is Prospero's "rich gift," and Ferdinand will find that "she will outstrip all praise." Shakespeare chose Miranda's name for its symbolic significance. It is derived from the Latin *mirari*, to wonder, to find wonderful. Our word "miracle" also has its roots in the Latin *mirari*. One can compare "Miranda," the wonderful one, whom Ferdinand calls a goddess and addresses with "O you wonder," with the Indian Shakti or with Chochma of biblical literature.

The audience for the Masque consists of only Prospero, Ferdinand, and Miranda. Prospero calls his Spirits to enact the supernatural performance. He asks them to

> Bestow upon the eyes of this young couple
> Some vanity of mine art. (IV, i, 40)

He then commands Ariel to "bring the rabble," that is, the "meaner fellows," and a "corollary" (which means many more

---

[2]Quotations are from the Arden edn. of Shakespeare, ed. W. J. Craig.

Spirits). In so doing Shakespeare lifts the Masque to a purpose far beyond the conventional uses of it in the Elizabethan theatre. It becomes a show of goddesses. Shakespeare knows a great deal of Greek mythology and presents it in exquisite poetry, verses in which rhyme and rhythm are totally different from all the rest of *The Tempest*.

As T. W. Baldwin proved in his classical book *William Shakespere's Small Latine and Lesse Greeke*,[3] Shakespeare knew Virgil's *Aeneid* well. In writing *The Tempest* he probably used the original Latin text as well as an English translation. His description of the three goddesses follows very closely the text in the *Aeneid*, as well as a text in which Ovid used the *Aeneid*. Colin Still pointed out that Shakespeare must also have been familiar with certain aspects of the Eleusinian mysteries. He refers to "dusky Dis" who "got his daughter," that is, to what we know as the Demeter and Persephone myth.[4] Here Demeter is called Ceres. Kerényi gives us the message:

A birth was possible in death. . . . The ear of corn could express everything that Demeter and Persephone had given to mankind: the daughter gave new birth below the earth, the mother gave nourishment and wealth above the earth. For whoever had seen the Kore (Persephone) this was not a simple parable which did not prove anything but was a memory of a meeting in which the goddess of death did not destroy herself but showed herself a mother.[5]

As Dr. Henderson emphasizes:

The Tempest, like *The Winter's Tale* before it, contains unmistakable references to the interrelation of death and rebirth, which we know is the heart and soul of any initiation ritual.[6]

It is, therefore, of great importance for the understanding of the whole play that just this scene, which is so strongly mythological, contains the myth of death and rebirth, of Demeter and Persephone.

Iris is the goddess who introduces and calls the other two goddesses. She is, as Jung describes her in *Mysterium Coniunctionis*, the *nuncia Dei*, the messenger of the gods. She is also a

---

[3]Thomas W. Baldwin, *William Shakspere's Small Latine and Lesse Greeke* (Urbana, Ill., 1944).
[4]Colin Still, *The Timeless Theme* (London, 1936).
[5]Kerényi, *Die Mysterien von Eleusis* (Zurich, 1962), p. 100 (my translation).
[6]Henderson, op. cit., p. 291.

synonym for the *cauda pavonis*, the peacock's tail. The more frequent synonym is that of the rainbow. In the Masque, Iris speaks of herself as the "wat'ry arch" and "messenger" of Juno, i.e., as the rainbow and the messenger of the gods, while Ceres (Demeter) addresses her as "many-coloured messenger." Jung comments in regard to the colors:

The exquisite display of colours in the peacock's fan heralds the imminent synthesis of all qualities and elements, which are united in the "rotundity" of the philosophical stone.[7]

He further comments:

The peacock is an attribute of Juno, and one of the cognomens of Iris is Junonia.[8]

In the Masque it is Iris who acquaints us with Juno's constant companions: "her peacocks fly amain."

Ceres is described as the goddess of agriculture. As Iris says in addressing her:

> Rich leas
> Of wheat, rye, barley, vetches, oats, and pease (IV, i, 60)

while Juno's blessings refer to personal and social joys.

> Honour, riches, marriage-blessing,
> Long continuance, and increasing,
> Hourly joys be still upon you!
> Juno sings her blessings on you. (IV, i, 106)

The three goddesses all indicate that the *coniunctio* is soon going to take place, and so it is said several times that they had been summoned there "a contract of true love to celebrate." There is also a brief dialogue between Ceres and Iris in which Ceres addresses Iris as "heavenly bow" and asks if

> Venus or her son . . .
> Do now attend the queen? (IV, i, 87)

because they might represent a danger. But Iris assures her that Eros, "her waspish-headed son has broke his arrows" and "swears he will shoot no more."

For Ferdinand this has been a most majestic vision and has made a tremendous impression. Prospero agrees with Ferdinand that they are spirits.

[7]CW 14, par. 397.   [8]Ibid., par. 398.

Spirits, which by mine art
I have from their confines call'd to enact
My present fancies. (IV, i, 120)

As we see occasionally in our practice, the fascination with the spirit world can occasionally be so intense that the one having the visionary experience wishes to remain in it forever and does not want to return to real life.

Certain other spirits enter whom Shakespeare calls "Reapers" and "Nymphs." They now perform a graceful dance, which Colin Still considers a Reaping Rite comparable to the one "that Hippolytus declares to have been the most solemn and sacred feature in the Eleusinian Third Degree."[9] They are characteristic of a preponderantly agricultural society, as Greece was in antiquity and Shakespeare's England was in Jacobean times.

Reality breaks in with the threat of Caliban's mischievous plans, and Prospero announces to Ferdinand that "our revels now are ended"—"revels" in the sense of the rites of antiquity. Ferdinand remains in a "moved sort."

It appears improbable to me that Shakespeare wanted to present nothing more than a repetition of antique rites even though his poetry far transcended that of Virgil's. It is more probable that he used his knowledge of the Eleusinian mysteries, of the *Aeneid*, and of antique lore to describe his own initiation into the mysteries of spiritual reality. Since he knew alchemy through his playwright friend Ben Jonson, who wrote *The Alchemist*, and through John Dee, the famous author of *Monas Hieroglyphica*, my impression is rather that Shakespeare put upon the stage the imagery of philosophical alchemy, which made use of antique mythology. In this way he became the first modern man to free himself from the concretistic projection the alchemists made upon matter. He understood his poetry and all his plays as a means of finding himself. The theatre became a place in which his growing self-knowledge could incarnate. There is no play of his in which the question of self-knowledge is not raised—for example, in *Macbeth*:

Alas! poor country
Almost afraid to know itself. (V, iii, 164)

It is clearly stated in *The Tempest* in Gonzalo's final statement:

[9]Still, op. cit., p. 185.

> *In one voyage*
> *Did Claribel her husband find at Tunis,*
> *And Ferdinand, her brother, found a wife*
> *Where he himself was lost. Prospero his dukedom*
> *In a poor isle, and all of us ourselves*
> *When no man was his own.* (V, i, 208)

In *The Tempest*, the most objective of all poets found his *anima mundi*, his royal self, his totality.

Reflections on "Chance" and "Fate"

GERHARD ADLER

Aller Zufall ist wunderbar, Berührung eines höheren Wesens, ein Problem,
Datum des tätig religiösen Sinns.

Novalis, Fragmente†

I FIRST MET JOE HENDERSON in London over forty years ago.
Since then we have been together in many places and on many
occasions: at congresses and on private visits in Zurich, London,
and Rome, to mention only a few. Two memories of our association are especially strong: for one, the hospitality he and
Helena extended to us when I lectured in San Francisco in
1959. We spent many serious and hilarious hours together on
that occasion. The other episode was a Greek holiday that we
shared, with a memorable Delphic birthday night. And last
year we met again in Rome, where Joe delivered a delightful
gem of a lecture on the clinical use of alchemy. So, when I
contemplated my contribution to this volume, it occurred to me
quite spontaneously that a friendship of over forty years did
not need another detached, "scientific" offering but something
very much more personal and intimate. I decided on a paper
that was quite "unorthodox," utterly personal, even to the point
of including very intimate experiences about which I had never
talked in public.

I feel I have to put at the beginning a *captatio benevolentiae*
and a warning to the unwary reader of my paper: my essay is a
completely "unscientific" bit of writing, extremely personal,
possibly boring to some, and even embarrassing to others. It is
something one dares expose to the daylight of white paper only
with great misgivings but which perhaps can be excused by the
fact that my own age is only slightly less than that of the friend
for whom this essay is written as a birthday gift.

---

†All chance is miraculous, the touch of a higher being, a problem, evidence of the
active religious essence.

Most of what I shall say in this paper concerns the part that "fate" has played in my own life. I would like to begin with a very early recollection. I started school in Berlin at the age of six and quickly formed a close friendship with two other boys, who were also six. We became inseparable, with the intensity and immediacy typical of boys of that age. About nine months later my parents decided to move to a different part of Berlin, almost diametrically remote from our previous neighborhood. Inevitably I lost contact with my two friends; and I am sure I must have felt the loss strongly for at least some time. Several decades later, when I had been well established as an analyst, I met both friends separately. One had become a Jungian analyst; the other had undergone a Jungian analysis and was steeped in Jungian thought. In other words, all three of us, now adults, had made Analytical Psychology the crucial influence in our lives.

How explain this? There must have been a very decisive—unconscious—mutual understanding, a true and deep "sympathy" of being, a true "felix concordia" and meeting of souls, much stronger than one would usually connect with the friendship of three six-year-old boys. In short the self had played a crucial part in our relationship. I don't know what this says about children's friendships in general, but, at least in the case described, I find it impossible to attribute it to "chance" or accident. Did fate have a hand in it? Were we somehow "predestined," inescapably linked in our young relationship? (Only in parentheses do I want to mention that another boy in my new school, with whom I struck up a close friendship, became a professor of psychology at Swarthmore.)

Fate seemed pivotal, but what part do the *experiences* of youth play in one's life? What *is* the role of fate, and what of actual events? Here again I remember some incidents which, at least at first glance, seem to belong to a different order, to a different arrangement of one's life pattern. Before relating an experience of my own, which I believe has played a crucial part in my life, I should like to mention the experiences of two other people.

A grown man, a physician, told me of a traumatic event in his very early life. From various circumstances it could be estimated that this event had probably taken place when he was two or three years old. He had a canary in his nursery which he loved dearly. The cage had been on a stand in a corner of the room. One day, while riding his rockinghorse, he had accidentally upset the stand; the cage had fallen down, and the canary had died. He had no doubt about the influence of this accident on his life. From that point forward, he had decided on his future career. He simply *had* to become a doctor, a healer—to heal his own "illness," the guilt of his "murder." He had to atone for the killing by supporting life.

An analogous case was that of a lawyer who, as a child, had been unjustly accused of having stolen some money, a few pennies. His parents had not believed his protestations of innocence. For him there was no other way into life than to become a lawyer, not in this case to atone for his guilt, but to help innocent people establish their innocence.

My own case is more complex. As a small child I had attended the usual kindergarten. I do not remember my exact age, but I must have been under six when I started school. My own feeling is that I was considerably younger than that. We used to play in the courtyard of the kindergarten. One day while playing there, I noticed a strange object inside one of the apertures in the wall. It contained something that resembled a hydrant, and the opening was protected by a wire cover. When I inquired about it, I was told that it had been a caterpillar which had turned itself into the form that was hanging there and that one day it would turn into a beautiful butterfly. I accepted this but was frightened by the thought that this butterfly could never come out of the hole since there was a wire netting across it. The poor butterfly would certainly have to die. It was a deep shock to me, but being a highly introverted child, I kept it to myself instead of asking more about it.

The story has a redeeming sequence which seems to me highly significant. When I went to Zurich to analyze with Jung for the first time, in January, 1931, I spontaneously remembered this incident as one of the traumatic experiences of my childhood. But then and there I realized the little wire door could be opened, and the butterfly could fly out into the sun. This flash was a true *satori* experience—a sudden freeing of frozen feeling, a sudden opening up of life's possibilities. Here again I am convinced that it was the anxiety about this poor little imprisoned butterfly that led to my becoming an analyst; I wanted to help free souls which were captive. Needless to say, the first soul to be freed was my own, but what also had to be freed were the contents I had projected into life in general. And is it not rather a play of maya that the symbol of the psyche stood in the center of this experience?

Now the question is, how such actual experiences relate to the story of the three boys ending up in the orbit of Jung? Is there some destiny within us that preforms the pattern of our life, or is it the actual experiences which shape it? Are the experiences we encounter predestined, or do we feel them so intensely and remember them so well because of an inner need? Or is there a coincidence of inner needs and outer events, an interconnectedness of within and without, which makes this division into the two spheres irrelevant and even misleading? I hope to return to this question later on. But first I should like to relate some rather intimate experiences which may throw their own light on the problem of inner fate and outer events.

I have just mentioned the story of the captive butterfly which seems to have played such a decisive influence on the choice of my work and my whole future life. But how did this inner fateful destiny become concretized? How did I find my way into the actual career of an analyst and, first of all, into analysis? It is a strange and highly personal story.

As a young man I was very fond of dancing and especially of fancy-dress balls, which were in vogue in the Berlin of the twenties and early thirties. I think it was in 1928 that I had danced through two nights with hardly any sleep. On the following morning, a Sunday, I was pretty fagged out. So I was not at all pleased when the telephone call of a friend, actually the one who became a Swarthmore professor, woke me up, inviting me to a party he was going to throw that afternoon. I refused, but, in the end, the persuasive power of my friend won the day and I went. As I entered the room, my then very susceptible eye was immediately caught by the sight of a beautiful girl. When my friend introduced me to her, the introduction went like this: "Dr. Adler—Mrs. Adler." This kind of thing hits one; at least it hit me. It immediately created some unexpected interest and opened up a somewhat deeper level of communication than you expect to find at a cocktail party. We talked quite a bit and were both quite curious about each other. So we decided to continue our talk on another occasion. We met again, and several times after that. In short, this first meeting, if not yet of common souls but only of common names, led to a close and most fruitful friendship. But—and now comes the crunch—as it turned out, my namesake had seen Jung and was deeply steeped in his ideas. In true anima fashion, she kindled a considerable curiosity in me about this strange man and his Analytical Psychology; until then, I had been much more interested in Freud. (Reading Freud was the fashion among educated people in Berlin, in those days, particularly among Jewish intellectuals, so much so that psychoanalysis was frequently referred to jokingly as "Jewish Science."

But of greater significance is the fact that at that time I was a fairly mixed-up young man. I had taken my Ph.D., studied science, history, philosophy, and psychology for about ten years and had taken training in the field of psychiatric social work. There was one central point in my work: an interest in people. So I had worked with prisoners and blind children and was strongly interested in education and related fields. Part of my living was earned by writing scientific reports for newspapers, and I had even been to Darmstadt to report one of the meetings of Keyserling's Schule der Weisheit, where I had heard Jung speak without registering any particular reaction.

In short, I had not really found my professional way of life at all, except for a rather confused interest in human beings and the world of ideas. All this suddenly fell into place: my anima-lady suggested I start analysis with James Kirsch. He told me, after one year, to go to Zurich and analyze with Jung. For this I am eternally grateful to James. In January, 1931, I went to see Jung after he had written that he could give me *only* (sic) three weekly interviews, and, for that reason, I should also work with Toni Wolff. Jung's letter ended with the classical sentence, "In case these conditions do not suit you, I request your reply." He did get my reply. There is hardly any need to mention that I readily agreed to his conditions, and this is how my analytical career started.

"*This* is how it started"—but what is "this?" What role did my dear namesake anima play in it? Would I have gone the Freudian way without her, or no analytical way at all? Was she the instigator, or was she the inevitable trigger provided by fate? (Was I destined anyway, considering the early friendship with the two boys?) Would I ever have had this experience working with Jung if I had not arrived, tired and reluctantly, at the Sunday afternoon party? I can't help but feel that a God had arranged it all, or perhaps the self of which I was blissfully ignorant at that time.

If it were arranged for me in that or some other way, what did it all mean for the woman involved in this affair? How did *she* get into it? I have no doubt that she did not merely get into it as I did but also got something out of it. However that may be, here the fate of two people was deeply intertwined in a complex pattern because of what, in ordinary language, one can only call a chance meeting. Chance, fate, nurturing an inner preparedness for change and direction—how can one disentangle them? At any rate, here we can discern a "meaningful coincidence" of inner fate and external events.

The whole problem is thrown into relief by another strange experience of mine which happened early in my analysis with Jung. I had a dream, what one would call a "big" dream, full of numinous feeling. In the dream I seemed to go through my whole life, past, present, and most important and almost uncanny, through all my future life as well. In short, I experienced in the dream the course my life was going to take in great detail. Needless to say, it was a most impressive and stirring dream, but, when I woke up, I had "forgotten" every detail, and with it, of course, all knowledge of what was going to happen to me in the future. Still, there was the absolute conviction, the inner evidence, that the dream *had* described my whole life from beginning to end. This feeling was confirmed to me by Jung who said that I *had* to forget all details, because it would have been impossible for me to live a free and creative life with the knowledge of all that was going to happen to me.

This dream has always stayed with me, and it has always been a tremendous problem and enigma to me. If the dream really foretold my future, and I had no doubt it did, what about the vexing and eternal problem of freedom of will or predestination? Where lay my free decision when everything seemed fixed? Or were choices left to me in the dream rather as an intelligent astrologer might interpret a horoscope, not predicting inevitable events but pointing out nodal points in the curve of life—crises in which one still has one's own say by living them out in one way or another, accepting or rejecting, in a constructive or destructive way? At least this is how I have tried to come to terms with my dream. Still, the question arises, were not the people whom I met, to wit the encounter with my analytical anima, inevitable carriers of my fate, just as I was bound to be of theirs? Although choices were still left open, I wondered if there were not an interdependence of destinies which still presented me with these very choices as predestined and inevitable patterns. Thus I might have met all the people whom I had to meet, but my reaction and the mode of my relationship to them (and theirs to me) were open to choice—or were they? And the same would apply to life's situations, crises, and opportunities.

This interconnectedness manifests itself in so many ways that one has to accept it as undisputable reality. I should like to mention only two instances, meant only as selected examples for a general pattern: the one relates to the truly disturbing and enigmatic working of the *I Ching*, the other to the strange coincidence of patients' dreams and the analyst's unconscious intuition, a fact which I am sure most analysts have come across in their work. Let me talk first about this latter situation, illustrating it by one single instance which happened fairly recently.

One morning a woman patient talked about certain events in her daily life. Suddenly, completely unconnected with what the patient was telling me, there flashed through my mind the words "Cagnes-sur-Mer"—a place I had passed through several years ago and which had no importance to me whatsoever. There was not the slightest link to what my patient was reporting, and I dismissed the words as utterly irrelevant, and so they were to this particular patient. But then my next patient arrived. He told me about a dream which took place in the South of France, and Cagnes-sur-Mer played a part in it.

What happened here? I used the word "intuition" before to introduce such experiences between analyst and analysand, but I think this word begs the question. How could I have "intuited" my next patient's dream, without, at that moment, having any contact with him? But what else? Did my patient send an unconscious message to me before arrival? Was his thought of his analytical hour—to which at this time he was traveling in his car—strong enough for me to receive this message? Actually, even in his report, the place was not really of decisive importance, so the energy of this "thought transmission," if such it was, would hardly have been particularly high. How, then, did I pick it up? I have to leave this question open. But it seems to be another example of the psyche transcending time and space.

This brings me to another disturbing and enigmatic subject, the *I Ching*. Here we have perhaps the most remarkable illustration of the interdependence and intercommunication of psychic situations with archetypal (cosmic) patterns. How otherwise explain the efficaciousness of the oracle which at least to me is beyond doubt? I will give a relatively mundane, but nonetheless impressive, example.

When I returned to Berlin after my first term with Jung, I was invited to visit Mrs. Toni Sussmann. She was the first pupil of Jung to introduce his concepts in Berlin and was thus at the time the center of Jungian life there. We talked about many things, mostly psychological, and, in the course of our conversation, Mrs. Sussmann mentioned the *I Ching*, which was unknown to me. I was rather incredulous and expressed my reservations. The most marked characteristic of Mrs. Sussmann was her highly developed intuition, so she asked me if I might have a problem on which I might test the accuracy of the oracle. Indeed, I had a rather long-standing problem. At the time I was in love with a very attractive and intelligent girl whose whole background fitted mine extremely well. But she was as neurotic as she was attractive and intelligent, plagued by constant psychosomatic symptoms. I might have considered marriage, had it not been for her neurotic side, and so I was torn between these two extremes. Here quite clearly was my question for the *I Ching*: "Shall I marry her or not?" The answer was devastating: hexagram 44, "Kou/Coming to Meet," without a moving line. The Judgment says: "Coming to meet. The maiden is powerful. One should not marry such a maiden."[1] And the Commentary on the Decision adds: " 'One should not marry such a maiden.' This means that one cannot

---

[1] *The I Ching*, the Richard Wilhelm trans. rendered into English by Cary F. Baynes (B.S. XIX, 3rd edn., 1967), p. 171.

live with her permanently."[2] It is, of course, rare to receive such an unequivocal answer to one's question. I think this happened to me because it was necessary to break right through my rationalistic scepticism, to hit me with a hammer as it were.

But much more profound was another experience with the oracle which I shall try to describe. Our friends Erich and Julie Neumann had long expected us to visit them in Israel. But as we had two children, both too young to be left by themselves, we had never been able to arrange an Israel holiday. In 1953 we had found reliable help with whom we could trust the children. We decided at last to spend six weeks with our friends. But I was very tired and overworked, and most important, my contact with my unconscious had become rather rudimentary on account of this overwork. My wife, more perceptive than I, had all along expressed her doubts about the wisdom of the journey. I, being a true Aries, however, did not listen to her and went on with the preparations. When I was going to book the tickets, there was a final outburst of protest from my wife. She pointed out that Israel would mean more and more extraversion when, in fact, what we both needed was a period of quiet introversion.

So we decided to consult the *I Ching*. My hexagram was 38, "K'uei/Opposition," with no moving lines. The Judgment says "Opposition. In small matters, good fortune," but Wilhelm's commentary to the Judgment warns off brusque proceedings and advises one to produce "gradual effects in small matters."[3] Although this gave no clear answer to the Israel adventure, the feeling of the oracle was not particularly encouraging. Most important, it spoke of the divergence of will, of "two movements in direct contrast," of "opposition and estrangement"—words which I could not fail to acknowledge referred to my being too split off from my unconscious. The conscious and unconscious levels were not working in harmony. My wife threw her coins and received hexagram 6, "Sung/Conflict." There it says: "A cautious halt halfway brings good fortune. Going through to the end brings misfortune. It furthers one to see the great man. It does not further one to cross the great water."[4] To this Blofeld comments: "We can profit from the advice of someone truly wise, but a journey of any kind this

[2]Ibid., p. 609.   [3]Ibid., p. 147.   [4]Ibid., p. 29.

time would be disastrous."[5] Although Blofeld's version had not yet been published, we interpreted my wife's oracle exactly as he did at a later date. So the journey to Israel was off.

But what next? We had arranged everything for an absence of six weeks, and it seemed that such time should be put to good use. We meditated on this problem and both felt that "the wise man" from whose advice one would profit referred to Zurich. I consulted the *I Ching* once more, asking if a journey to Zurich would be advantageous. I got hexagram 46, "Shêng/ Pushing Upward," and The Judgment says: "Pushing upward has supreme success. One must see the great man. Fear not. Departure toward the south brings good fortune."[6] That clinched it: we were going to Zurich. My wife wrote that same day to Mrs. Jung and I to Toni Wolff, with whom I had worked very successfully during my first years in Zurich and with whom I had since kept in very friendly contact. Both ladies answered by return mail, expressing their willingness to work with us.

We arrived in Zurich on the 2nd of March, 1953, and the next day I started my analytical work with Toni, who had very kindly reserved a daily hour for me, including Saturdays. Our work went extremely well, and I immediately felt the great benefit of the renewed contact with my unconscious. This positive feeling grew all the time. On Friday, March 20, during my regular hour with Toni, I told her I felt that all the splintered bits of my psyche seemed to have come together, that conscious and unconscious, female and male, aspects seemed in a true *coniunctio*. It was one of those rare hours when everything seemed "in Tao." Toni was so near and warm and human, with a charming smile. We laughed a lot during this hour. Our relationship seemed closer than ever. When I left, Toni offered to see me on the following day, Saturday morning, but I felt that she needed the weekend and refused, fixing the next hour for Monday, the 23rd. I went home full of the radiance of that hour and with a profound sense of peace. When I met my wife, I told her of the experience, that I had now achieved all I had come to Zurich for, and that my work with Toni had now really

[5] John Blofeld, ed. and trans., *The Book of Change* (London and New York, 1965), p. 101.
[6] *The I Ching*, p. 178.

reached its true goal. We decided to celebrate it by taking a trip to the Rigi, something we had wanted to do for a long time. We left before dawn on Saturday, the 21st.

We spent a beautiful and harmonious day on the Rigi. When we returned to Zurich late in the evening we found three messages, each telling us of Toni's heart attack and death in the early hours of the night of the 20th. No need to describe our feelings. When my wife and I went to Toni's funeral, people were surprised to see us. How did it happen that we knew and were there? For we had lived a very withdrawn life while we had been in Zurich, in order to concentrate on our analytical work.

There are quite a few points which need clarification; they may lead to strange considerations and open up complex questions. When I heard the news of Toni's death, I felt I would never have forgiven myself if I had gone to Israel instead of to Zurich and missed seeing Toni and working with her for the last time. It seemed evident to me that all the hesitation about going to Israel was due to an unconscious knowledge and foreboding and that this had "forced" me to give up my journey to Israel. I knew then why I had had to go to Zurich. Of course, this may be an arbitrary interpretation of what happened, but can a feeling of inner evidence so easily be dismissed? And there were the other facts: my feeling that, with my talk on that last Friday, I had reached the proper goal of my work, and the wonderful harmony of that last interview. I was the last person to be given an analytical hour, as if everything had led up to that sad climax, which, from another angle was not sad at all but a complete fulfillment. At least I could express my deep feelings for and appreciation of Toni in a letter to Pfarrer Schär, which he found appropriate to include in his eulogy. It was a last expression of gratitude to a beloved person and something I could not have done if I had not been in Zurich at the time. Even this little detail seemed fated.

If my interpretation is right—and at least to me it is more than a mere "possibility"—how could my unconscious possibly have known what was going to happen? Was there a deeply hidden message of an event concerning Toni of which even she could not have been consciously aware? What could have been the nature and the secret of such communication? On what level does such rapport take place?[7]

Here we seem to be in the area of the deepest numinous mystery of the psyche, which, as Jung has pointed out so frequently, is beyond time and space. Here the secret interconnectedness of all life and its events shows through the veil of our daily existence with all its inherent blindness. All the experiences which I have tried to describe in this report lead up to the same conclusion: that we are all part of each other, that all life reaches out for all other life, even if we are almost always unaware of it or only very rarely notice it dimly. It is as if each of us is a stone thrown into a cosmic ocean, creating its circles, going outwards and, in its movement, meeting all other circles, some near and relatively clear in their interaction, others far away with meetings almost nonexistent and imperceptible.

But there are these rare moments when the meeting of two fates produces a miraculous illumination, when the veil is lifted and two destinies become visible in their interdependence. The three young boys, the meeting with my anima, the dream of my life, Cagnes-sur-Mer, the *I Ching* oracle, both of the unbelieving young man and of the adult, the events surrounding Toni's death—all contain and manifest the miracle and enigma of psychic existence. They point to what Jung has maintained: that there is a "transpsychic reality immediately underlying the psyche"[8] from which immediate bridges can be thrown to the latest findings of nuclear and subatomic research.

The connection lies chiefly in the concept of a space-time continuum which explains synchronistic phenomena as well as "the knowledge of future or spatially distant events."[9] For this my examples seem to give a relevant illustration. Here we are

---

[7] As I reread what I have written about Toni's death, another very tragic story comes to mind. It is of a Freudian patient whose analyst died during his analysis. He went to another analyst, and again this second analyst died during treatment. Then he started analysis with a third analyst, and he also died. (It was the widow of the last analyst, a well-known Freudian, who told this depressing story.) It is utterly baffling. Needless to say the patient could not find a fourth analyst! What happened here is beyond rational comprehension but seems to support the thesis of some strange unconscious rapport. I do not think the patient "killed" his analysts but rather that, in an incredibly morbid and destructive way, he was drawn towards analysts who carried premature death within themselves.

[8] "The Psychological Foundations of Belief in Spirits," CW 8, par. 600, n. 15.

[9] "Synchronicity," CW 8, par. 948.

in the realm of transcendental phenomena, in the realm of " 'absolute knowledge' . . . not mediated by the sense organs."[10] The space-time continuum of modern physics is irrepresent-able,[11] just as archetypes and synchronicity produce "a picture of the world so irrepresentable as to be completely baffling."[12]

And, indeed, the experiences described above are utterly baffling if not deeply disturbing, manifesting the connection between the enigma of the psyche and the irrepresentable space-time continuum. Here we find ourselves in the world of the archetypes which is " 'eternal,' i.e., outside time."[13] Pauli has said that they "function as the sought-for bridge between the sense perceptions and the ideas and are, accordingly, a necessary presupposition even for evolving a scientific theory of nature."[14] Jung himself has stated that the psychoid arche-type is "the bridge to matter in general,"[15] and that, on account of their psychoid nature, archetypes act as ordering factors in the physical space-time continuum.[16] In other words, here we are confronted with the reality of the *unus mundus*, the place of numinous experiences. It is the common transcendental back-ground to the microcosm of the psyche and the macrocosm of physics, the "transcendental background" on which "the world inside and outside ourselves rests."[17] In this *unus mundus* there is "no incommensurability between so-called matter and so-called psyche."[18]

Jung was deeply interested in the problem of the link be-tween psyche and matter. Modern physics has reached conclu-sions similar to his in the quantum theory, which "reveals a basic oneness of the universe,"[19] and its interconnectedness. Parenthetically I might mention that here we are also, perhaps surprisingly, in the territory of Eastern mysticism, which has always maintained the basic unity of the universe. Cápra, a sub-atomic physicist, gives numerous examples of this. He sums up as follows: "In the Eastern view, as in the view of modern

[10]Ibid.   [11]Ibid., par. 962.   [12]Ibid.
[13]Jung, *Letters*, vol. 2, p. 46.
[14]Jung and W. Pauli, *The Interpretation of Nature and the Psyche* (B.S. LI, 1955), p. 153.
[15]"On the Nature of the Psyche," CW 8, par. 420.
[16]Ibid., par. 439ff.
[17]*Mysterium*, CW 14, par. 787.
[18]Jung, *Letters*, vol. 2, p. 400.
[19]Fritjof Capra, *The Tao of Physics* (Boulder, Colorado, 1975), p. 68.

physics, everything in the universe is connected to everything else and no part of it is fundamental."[20] Perhaps this is how we can understand Krishna's words in the Bhagavad-Gita when he says of Brahman, "Undivided, He seems to divide into objects and creatures,"[21] or when Krishna teaches Arjuna, saying: "Who sees the separate lives of all creatures united in Brahman brought forth from Brahman, himself finds Brahman."[22]

All this seems to link up with the concept of "continuous creation" as "the eternal presence of the *one* creative act, in the sense that God 'was always the Father and always generated the Son' "—in other words, "what happens successively in time is simultaneous in the mind of God."[23] This we may understand again as the timelessness of the unconscious, which only in our empirical life is unfolded into time and causality. Indian philosophy has the concept of the *bindu*, the point which is the union of all opposites and contains all time in itself. The disciple of Zen similarly believes "all action occurs in an infinite present . . . all events occur simultaneously."[24] And in Dante, we find the Christian idea expressed as "il punto a cui tutti li tempi son presenti,"[25] or when he speaks of "là've s'appunta ogne *ubi* e ogne *quando.*"[26] These lines are reminscent of T. S. Eliot's words in "Burnt Norton": "At the still point of the turning world."[27]

Here we find ourselves also in the universe of the alchemists, whose "theoria" rested on the idea of a psychic cosmic unity as expressed in the famous words of Athanasius Kircher: "Heaven above/Heaven below/Stars above/Stars below/All that is above/ Also is below/Grasp this/And rejoice."[28] And the "ubi," the "everywhere" of Dante, is equally expressed in the words of the Buddhist teacher Ashvaghosha, "Be it clearly understood that space is nothing but a mode of particularization and that it has

[20]Ibid., p. 290.
[21]*The Song of God: Bhagavad-Gita*, trans. Swami Prabhavananda and Christopher Isherwood (New York, 1944; repr. 1954), p. 103.
[22]Ibid., p. 105.
[23]"Synchronicity," CW 8, par. 967, n. 17.
[24]Robert E. Ornstein, *The Psychology of Consciousness* (London, 1975), p. 107.
[25]Dante, *Paradiso*, XVII, 17-18. ("the point to which all times are present"—tr. C. C. Singleton, B.S. LXXX, 1975.)
[26]Ibid., XXIX, 12. ("where every *ubi* and every *quando* is centered"—ibid.)
[27]T. S. Eliot, *The Complete Poems and Plays* (New York, 1950), p. 119.
[28]"Psychology of the Transference," CW 16, par. 384.

no real existence of its own. . . . Space exists only in relation to our particularizing consciousness."[29]

Again, to modern relativistic physics, space-time is similarly a "timeless space of a higher dimension."[30] This higher dimension may correspond to the highest states of consciousness, to a "spiritual world [in which] there are no time divisions such as the past, present and future; for they have contracted themselves into a single moment of the present where life quivers in its true sense."[31]

I could go on for ever quoting from Jung, alchemy, Eastern mysticism, and even modern physics. Nor need I have stopped at my own experiences twenty-five years ago. But I shall end here, hoping to have made my point. It is quite simply (simply?) to express what has "made me tick" for most of my adult life: the profound experience of the miracle and enigma of the psyche, in the face of which awe and reverence are the only possible responses. It is the certainty that I find myself here on common ground with the friend for whom this is written that has given me the courage to include the very private experiences in my paper. I am sure he will know that only affection and friendship have enabled me to do so. It is in this certainty of mutual understanding, and with the memory of gay and serious hours spent together, that I wish him on this day and always the "preservation, and all blessings of this life."

[29]Capra, p. 164.   [30]Ibid., p. 186.
[31]Ibid., p. 179; cf. also Heinrich Zimmer, *Philosophies of India* (B.S. XXVI, 1951), p. 450f.

Localizations of Consciousness

C. A. MEIER

MANKIND HAS ALWAYS BEEN CONCERNED with the location of consciousness, although as often as not it was the soul or the psyche which was being referred to and not consciousness itself. Definitive assumptions have been made about their localization in different centuries or millennia and in various cultures. As we shall see, the Greeks debated for centuries about the location of the ruling principle. These century-long discussions about the seat of the Aristotelian *hegemonikon* are an especially striking example for us of this insecurity regarding the location of the psychic in general. Fortunately, M. Putscher[1] has gone to the trouble to research these transformations in accordance with this concept, so that we can refer here to her valuable book. With reference to Jung's four "orientation functions of consciousness," we should like to point out that Thomas Aquinas already sticks to a *quaternio*, as opposed to Avicenna, who postulated five psychic powers. With regard to the cerebral localization, we now have a lucid compilation recently published by Clarke and Dewhurst.[2]

From the standpoint of Complex Psychology, the available variants represent comparative material which makes possible an evaluation of the level of consciousness of each of the respective cultures and peoples. It should be said, however, that we do not suffer from hybris, which would lead us to assume that our contemporary level of consciousness, with its apparent localization of consciousness in the brain, is the highest step in this sequence. On the contrary. We are disposed to regard the

[1]M. Putscher, *Pneuma, Spiritus, Geist* (Wiesbaden, 1973).
[2]E. Clarke and K. Dewhurst, *An Illustrated History of Brain Function* (Oxford, 1972).

entire organism as the locus of the psyche and accordingly to accept specific organ locations as coordinates for special aspects of the psyche.

Certainly our scientific approach and methodology have shown us that by experimentally eliminating the cortex, consciousness is also extinguished. But the same empirical research shows that then the continuity of the psyche ceases as well. In addition, observations have been made in cases of accidents involving brain trauma, such as those which occur in war when the brain is pierced by a bullet: psychic processes continue which are no different from those in a normal state of consciousness but in an apparently unconscious state.[3] Along the same line are the well-documented cases of out-of-the-body experience such as those collected by Celia Green.[4] To be sure, they almost lie on a parapsychological plane, but that must not disturb us. We shall have to return to this later in another connection. The clinical observations of Jantz and Beringer throw an interesting light on Dunne's[5] observer of the observer. Also, the trivial fact that, in the final analysis, we have the most lively experiences every night in a state of almost total unconsciousness belongs to this problem. Thus it can be said that the matter of unconsciousness and indirectly of consciousness is not easily explained. Certain experiences at the bedside of the ill have shown every doctor that even with the most severely comatose patients not all consciousness and perception can be eliminated with certainty. Nevertheless, it has been established that the cortex has priority for processes of consciousness and that the subcortical processes have only a conditional influence on consciousness.

Inasmuch as the brain, like the skin, is of an ectodermal nature, it is, among other things, an organ of the senses and perceptions; its perceptions are for the most part of an optical and acoustic nature. This can be seen in sleep activity, that is, in the dream, where it is to a large degree shielded from external sensory stimulation. Thus, the brain is for the most part our psychic orientation system; it is by no means the psyche itself.

[3]H. Jantz and K. Beringer, "Das Syndrom des Schwebeerlebnisses unmittelbar nach Kopfverletzungen," *Der Nervenarzt* 17 (1944), 202, cited in CW 8, par. 949, n. 1.
[4]C. Green, *Out-of-the-Body Experiences* (London, 1968).
[5]J. W. Dunne, *The Serial Universe* (London, 1934).

Now we want to examine several of the older localization theories using the comparative approach referred to earlier.

(1) We know of the *bush soul* which is embraced by many "primitives." They believe that their soul and thus their most intimate identity—we would be inclined to say their conscious ego—can be found in a certain place in the bush, in a particular animal for instance, or a tree, or a stone. Its location would therefore be *extra corpus*. This is, of course, dangerous because the soul can easily get lost and then the owner becomes physically or psychically ill and can even die as the soul has a so-called *participation*[6] with him or he with it. The medicine man must get it back to him. This can be done, for example, as follows: the medicine man goes into the bush with his bird cage and captures several escaped "soul birds." When he returns, the patient lies on the ground and the cage is opened. The medicine man is situated some distance from the head of the patient, to which a row of seeds leads, the last one lying on the forehead of the patient. The birds, having been released, eat their way along the row of seeds, and the bird which picks the last seed from the forehead of the patient proves itself to be the escaped soul bird. In this manner it reintegrates itself with the sufferer. The "loss of soul," the illness, is cured. Examples of a similar kind are numerous. The location of the soul outside the body, typical of primitives, and the resulting *participation* give rise to many additional effects of the human being to the external objects and vice versa. In the primitive culture they are regarded as a matter of course, but it must be understood as purely parapsychological from our point of view, that is, as psychokinesis (PK). They also recall the old doctrine of sympathy, which, nonetheless, does not relieve us of the unsolved problem of the subject/object relationship. Especially difficult problems arise when both are separated spatially, and no known channels for the transmission of the effects are conceivable. By the way, during certain "mystical" moods, such sympathy-conceptions of significant poetic valency also easily befall us.

If we now want to pursue a comparative localization theory, only anatomy—that is, the body—remains as a frame of refer-

[6]L. Lévy-Bruhl, *How Natives Think*, tr. L. A. Clare (London, 1926).

ence. We shall have to proceed, then, from the lower to the higher segments.

(2) Localization in *bladder and rectum* would be the most primitive. And yet there are life phases (early childhood) in which these regions are of dominant importance or in which they more or less pathologically once again assume significance. Here, one is inclined to think of the "mentality" of the dog.

(3) For the next step, the *stomach* is the characteristic organ. I do not mean that class for whom the satisfaction of the stomach becomes the high point of existence and even less those peoples for whom almost everything else in life has fallen away in the face of satisfying hunger. And yet there were cultures in which there was not sufficient motivation, for example, to go hunting until the stomach growled so persistently that any further attempt to tighten the belt became futile.

It can also happen to us that we do not become conscious of certain facts until they begin to make us sick (to our stomach). The *plexus coeliacus* (also popularly called the solar plexus) which lies at this level on the aorta appears to be a kind of organ of expression for the various contents of the psyche. Especially impressive in this regard, as Laurens van der Post told me, are the Bushmen. They become aware of approaching strangers at enormous distances and thus can make predictions on the basis of an urgent, monitory tapping which, in all probability, comes from the *plexus coeliacus*.

(4) The *diaphragm*, from the Greek φρήν (phren), shows itself to be a psychic localization in the passage in the *Iliad* (XXII, 296) where Achilles kills Hector: "And Hector knew the truth inside his heart (ἐνὶ φρεσί) and spoke aloud." Today in psychiatry we speak of schizo*phrenia*, the illness which most severely impairs consciousness, although with this expression nothing is said about the location. For the Romans the diaphragm was the seat of thought and sensation. Another name for it is *praecordia*, from which the expression "intima praecordia movit" comes if something especially moving happens.

(5) Even for us today, the *heart* is the actual seat of the soul and not just a poetic metaphor, at least to the extent that it makes itself felt by strong feelings and passions. The corresponding Greek expression is θυμός (thymos) and actually means the breath of life, the Latin *passio, affectus,* or *perturbatio,*

that is, all emotions which belong in particular to our humanity. On the heart as the seat of the *koinon aistheterion,* of the central organ of sensation, see Aristotle, *De insomniis* (on dreams).

(6) As the highest level in this hierarchy, the *brain* is reserved to us moderns. This localization can hardly be contested, but it by no means eliminates the lower levels from also having their representation in the brain. There is even less possibility that the brain will ever manage completely to control or make ineffective the lower localizations. In that event we would have lost the direct contact with our biological and psychic prerequisites and have become a formidable super- or, more accurately, a non-human being. It can be said without compunction that the robot which is run with a pure brain computer is an absurd extrapolation. The *whole* person is the one who functions satisfactorily and in proportion on all these six levels: brain, heart, diaphragm, stomach, bowels and bladder and, finally, even *extra corpus.*

In a private seminar in 1930, C. G. Jung presented the case of a female patient who engaged in active imagination and produced drawings and pictures during the course of the analysis. These created the most extraordinary impression and were not understandable until Jung made the acquaintance of a book which had appeared for the first time in Madras in 1918: this was *The Serpent Power,* by Sir John Woodroffe, alias Arthur Avalon. This book presents the Sanskrit text, with an English translation, of the *Shat-Chakra-Nirupana* (in English, "Seven Circles Description") and is essentially a yoga meditation text. It is concerned with the special (for the most part Bengali-South Indian) Tantra yoga, also called Kundalini yoga. Tantra simply means "book," and this Tantrism comprises yoga sects which have their holy books just as we have the Bible. Kundalini (related to the Green χύλινδος equals round, cylinder) is conceived as a serpent and symbolizes, as is clearly evident from the text and the practice of meditation, psychic energy, that is, the libido *per se.* This is set in motion in the yoga process and circulates throughout the entire body, which in turn shows a striking similarity to the "Circulation of Light" in Chinese Taoism, as so cogently described by Erwin Rousselle.[7] The

---

[7]E. Rousselle, "Spiritual Guidance in Contemporary Taoism" (orig. 1933), in *Spiritual Disciplines* (Papers from the Eranos Yearbooks, 4, B.S. XXX, 1960).

Kundalini proceeds in this process through seven ascending and descending chakras (*chakra* is Sanskrit for "circle") which are imagined to be hierarchically located in different body segments. These localizations exhibit amazing analogies with those we described above, although we arrived at them independently on the basis of clinical observation and comparative religious and ethnological reflections.

That this Western approach should find such a widespread analogy in the East is not only sufficient confirmation, but should also lead us to see that the psychobiological basis of the human being is to a large extent the same everywhere. That is, to use Jung's language, we see how much the realities of the collective unconscious are ubiquitous and identical, i.e., archetypal, and to what degree they are identified, for example, in the East with physical structures. At the same time we do not want to forget that these representations have become much more differentiated by cultures in the East than they are by us, owing to thousands of years of tradition, observation, and experience, so that there is a good deal we can learn from them.

Nevertheless, we are not interested in making propaganda for yoga with the following presentation, because the difference between the essence of our spiritual makeup and that of Eastern man is too great for us to be able to adopt Indian philosophy. If the Shakta (member of the Bengali Tantra sects) says "whoever makes *chakra-puja* (puja = "veneration") without having fought the powers of the world and tradition will not succeed but come to harm," it is clear from the text that this attitude is identical with that which Jung always required for analysis. But yoga is also the specifically Indian road to master experience by means of introspection.

Now I shall attempt to make a table of the seven centers, using Avalon's version, although I shall have to leave out many details. Not until I finish will I be able to elaborate on several of those which are suitable for making a number of things clear to us in the West. I shall give only the basic details of the chakra description in the following sequence: (1) Sanskrit name of the center; (2) English translation; (3) location in the body; and (4) where this is probable, the corresponding localization, known to us as well, of the ganglia of the vegetative nervous system because it would be easier to assign them psychic representations should such a co-ordination be possible—at least to a certain degree; (5) the assignment to the "elements"; (6) the number of petals of the corresponding lotus—that is chakras— without reference to the very differentiated number and letter symbolism which are connected with them in India;[8] and (7) the corresponding animal symbol.

	1	2	3	4	5	6	7
1.	Muladhara	root-support	perineum	plexus pelvicus	earth	4	elephant
2.	Svadhisthana	own place	bladder	plexus hypogastricus	water	6	*makara*
3.	Manipura	jewel-abundance	navel	plexus coeliacus seu solaris	fire	10	ram
4.	Anahata	unassailable	heart	plexus cardiacus	air	12	gazelle
5.	Vishuddha	purification	larynx	plexus pharyngeus	ether	16	white elephant
6.	Ajna	episteme	between the eyes	pineal gland		2	0
7.	Sahasrara	pure con-sciousness?	on the scalp = *extra corpus*	0	empty space	1000	

The Yogi should now meditate, and from bottom to top, on one center after another; that is, not only imagine in all detail, but construct them from the elements and physically call them forth, and in *dhyana* (submersion), in a manner not readily understandable to us, realize them. That which I think becomes here that which thinks me. I am thought. The energy-libido necessary for this process is supplied by Kundalini, which has been slumbering in the lowest center and now awakens and is gradually sent upwards through the other centers, where at any given time it leads to the realization, that is, to the almost physical sensation of the chakra in question. Each of the previous steps is maintained, and then the next highest one is

[8]Whoever is especially interested (and it is of considerable interest) could consult another publication by Avalon, *The Garland of Letters* (Madras, 3rd edn., 1955), where consequent information can also be found about the mystic aspect of the sound.

attempted. Having reached the top, the order is reversed and the way is retraced, step by step, until the Kundalini in the *muladhara* is again in a position of rest. Then the yogi returns to his daily routine.

Given this hierarchy, there is no getting around being reminded of the "progressive cerebration" of Hughlings Jackson, which, although the points of departure are very different, nonetheless bears a similarity to these conceptions.

In the hope of better understanding the Tantric-like drawings of the patient referred to at the beginning, Jung invited the Indologist and Sanskrit scholar J. W. Hauer (Tübingen) to a private seminar in 1932. At its conclusion, Jung gave an appropriate psychological commentary, so that I am in the fortunate position of often being able to draw on those very talks.

1. In *Muladhara*, on the lowest rung, the level of consciousness is that of our daily existence, psychologically speaking, that is, of our family, profession, etc. The four petals of the lotus are symbolic of the material reality in its entirety, which is why the element of earth has been assigned to it. Because we are to a large degree bound up with this reality, this is a quasi-latent state where everything divine is still asleep, just like the Kundalini, and where it only softly hums to itself "like a swarm of love-struck bees" entwined as it is three and one-half times around the lingam (phallus), represented here at the base, and covering the mouth with its head. The major animal symbol for the whole is the elephant, which represents the domesticated libido in India. Beginning with this state, it is now time to ascend to higher consciousness, that is, to awaken and mobilize Kundalini —to ascend.

2. *Svadhisthana*. We are somewhat surprised to find two symbols here which, like the element water, unmistakably point to the unconscious: the half moon and a water monster, the *makara*. In the latter we can recognize a type of leviathan, the reverse side of the elephant of Muladhara. Here we are reminded of the shadow as the first step towards confrontation with the unconscious on the way to consciousness. That which is applicable for us in the West is expressed in the East as a necessity, namely to realize rather negative tendencies—as a prerequisite for more consciousness.

3. *Manipura.* The picture is of a crucible on the fire and the symbolic animal is the ram, which corresponds to Agni, the fire god. (In our astrology the ram is also the house of Mars, and Mars is a close relative of Agni.) The chakra is relegated to the element of fire. And also in the *bindu*, in the point which is on top of the inscribed Sanskrit letter, is Rudra, the destroyer of creation, because the animation of passion threatens to destroy everything again. Here we are reminded of Heraclitus, who said, "it is difficult to fight with lust and what it wants it buys with the soul." Here we are concerned with the *thymos*, with the affects, with a purely emotional psychology where I become aware only of that which makes me uncomfortable or affects my stomach (hunger) or the gall bladder; that is, with an unfree state of being and nevertheless with the beginning of a real psychology. But here we are still below the diaphragm; the conscious psychology begins above the aforementioned.

4. *Anahata* means "the unassailable" and refers to the symbol of the "self," of the Indian Atman which appears here for the first time. The term "self" as it was coined by Jung represents a more highly ordered center of the personality which is exhaustively described in the phenomenology of the Atman in Indian philosophy. The element associated with it is the air because from earth (1) comes water (2), and from this through fire (3), air (4) is derived. The element of air is represented by the lungs, in which the heart is embedded. Further, the fleeting animal symbol of the gazelle indicates air. Neurophysiologically we are also at the level of the already partly conscious control of the functions, to which, as is known, the breath is subordinate. It is at this point that the human being begins to contemplate, to judge, to differentiate. He becomes capable of setting himself apart from pure emotion. At the same time he here becomes aware for the first time of his impersonal side (self equals atman). This is the actual beginning of our conscious psychology. At this level the Christian "mystique of the heart" could be understood. The self is something extraordinarily impersonal, and to the extent to which one regards it as something objective he himself becomes impersonal. The unpleasant phenomenon we know in English as "personality" is thus eliminated. For those of us in the West, however, there is a danger in this connection—namely, identification with the self which is

tantamount to inflation, to a type of delusion of grandeur. We cannot warn often enough against this danger. I remember an impressive experience which Jung had with the Pueblo Indians in Taos, New Mexico. His Pueblo friend there complained about the Americans, saying they were all crazy because they maintained that they thought here (referring to his forehead) when everybody knows that we think here (referring to his heart).

5. *Vishuddha.* It becomes increasingly difficult for us with our Western way of thinking to imagine clearly which psychic characteristics are being referred to in the higher centers. Thus, Vishuddha is associated with the element of ether. We would say that ether is matter and at the same time no longer so; it is a purely abstract concept, whereupon this chakra becomes one of the pure concepts, that is, something purely psychic. Thus it is also the chakra of the *reality of the psychic* in general where unfortunately for us it assumes an insubstantial position about which little can be said. Western man seems to be at approximately this level of Anahata. Against this background, the world and its game here become an image of our psyche, that is our own *drame intérieur.* For the Indian, sound, language, and singing belong here. In *bindu* Ardhanarishvara is in the form of a half male half female, that is, an androgynous god which units in one the sun and moon, gold and silver—that is, the elementary opposites.

6. *Ajna* is the place of union, of the *unio mystica.* There are no more animal symbols because here the psychic experience requires no support in outer reality. Not even a god is found here because the yogi himself has become the psychic content of god through the *unio mystica*, which means he himself is the content of the psychic. The lingam once again appears, this time however, as *itara shiva*, as another lingam, which has only the form in common with the one at the first level. All of this is hardly imaginable for us in the West.

7. *Sahasrara.* For this center the qualities of Ajna apply to an even greater degree. But here we find an interesting paradox: in it is the emptiness, *shunyata*, of which is said: "That is the place where all being is no longer being. Not until now has the real been reached. Whoever has gone completely into this emptiness has achieved complete fullness. Not until this empti-

ness has been achieved does the knowledge which has been gathered during the course of this process become real." Here there is only *brahman*. And the *brahman* cannot itself experience, as it is *advaita*, that is, "not two." It is being-not being, which is the same as the idea of the *nirvana*, which is *nir-dvandva*, that is, free of contradictions. As a result of the completed union of the Kundalini (shakti) with Shiva *(hierosgamos)* in Sahasrara, a nectar *(amrita)* flows from here which means complete release (solution = *mucti*), so that the yogi comes to enjoy *advaya* (no second), that is, is identical with Kundalini.

Our difficulties with the beloved Indian metaphysical speculation on the pure subject of cognition, which is not opposed by any object, make it impossible for us to judge here any longer. We must, as W. Pauli aptly said, reject it as an indefensible extrapolation inasmuch as our consciousness presupposes the duality of subject and object or the division of the two. Pauli correctly goes on to reason that our Western idea of the unconscious begins at just this point, that is, instead of at the idea of an all-encompassing consciousness without an object. We don't want to overlook the fact that with Sahasrara we again find ourselves outside the body, whereby an unusual similarity with the primitive's bush soul (located *extra corpus*) originates. If we audaciously wish to describe this curve as the Tantrists do, we go from the bush soul of the primitive, which is completely outside the body, to the caudal end through different always higher levels to the top on the cranial end—so to say, again outside the body.

Only the libido and its circulation remain as the connection which makes itself felt, in this case by affecting the body or the different organs. Not to be forgotten is the fact that the expression "affect" originates from this experience. But is is also known here in the West that this is not the whole activity of the psyche. In this connection, I should like to repeat an important passage from an alchemist:[9]

Corpus enim nihil scit, quicquid in corpore fortidudinis sive motus est, mens facit ista; corpus tantum est menti sicut instrumenta alcujus artificis. Anima autem, qua homo a caeteris animalibus differt, illa operatur in corpore, sed majorem operationem habet extra corpus; quoniam absolute extra corpus dominatur, et his differt ab animalibus quae tantum mentem et non animam deitatis habent. (The body knows nothing of

[9]Sendivogius, "De sulphure," *Musaeum Hermeticum* (Frankfurt am M., 1678), 617.

what is in it as power or movement; this the spirit knows; the body is to the spirit only what the instrument is to an artist. Nevertheless, the soul, which differentiates the human being from other organisms, has those functions in the body. But its more significant effect is outside the body, because outside the body it governs in itself.)

Gerardus Dorneus[10] also says: "*mentis a corpore distractio necessaria est.* (The spirit must be separated from the body.) Recently, we learned from a Gnostic-early Christian source of the same spirit: "Jesus said: woe betide the flesh ($\sigma\acute{\alpha}\rho\xi$, Sarx) that is dependent on the soul ($\psi\upsilon\chi\acute{\eta}$, psyche); woe betide the soul that is dependent on the flesh."[11]

Of late the West appears to be greatly impressed by Tantrism, which accounts for the fact that Tantric texts are also now available in English. We believe that everything which is said and written in the West about levels of consciousness is afforded interesting illustrations and empirical foundations as a result of these experiences and our Jungian approach.

[10]G. Dorneus, "Philosophia meditativa," *Theatrum Chemicum*, vol. I (Ursel, 1602).
[11]*Evangelium nach Thomas*, ed. A. Guillaumont (Leiden, 1959), p. 55 (Logion 112). Now available in: *The Nag Hammadi Library*, ed. James M. Robinson (San Francisco, 1977).

Gaston Bachelard and the Poetics of Reverie

LOUIS H. STEWART

THE UNUSUAL CAREER OF GASTON BACHELARD (1884-1962), French philosopher of science and of literary creativity, began in science and ended in poetry. Having established himself as a distinguished philosopher of science at the Sorbonne, he astonished his colleagues by turning to poetry and the metaphysics of imagination. In his late career he gained world-wide recognition for his unique application of the techniques of psychoanalysis to a study of the poetic images of the age-old elements of earth, air, fire, and water. He arrived at his method through the study of alchemy. He undertook this study in order to exorcise the errors of thought which arise from fantasies projected onto matter and which distort and retard scientific conceptions. However, like the sorcerer's apprentice, he fell victim to his techniques and found himself in the power of the very images he had been seeking to eliminate. This new development was heralded by the publication of *The Psychoanalysis of Fire*, and was followed by other studies on the elements of water, air, and earth. In the titles of these later publications, he dropped the term psychoanalysis when he realized that the theory of literary creativity he was evolving could not be encompassed by psychoanalytic thought. From this point forward, he was drawn to the works of C. G. Jung. Here he found expressed a psychological theory of the imagination which matched his own experience.

It was the convergence of Bachelard's mature thought with Analytical Psychology which suggested this brief study of his life and work. Of particular interest is the focus of Bachelard's studies at a psychological level which he describes as a botanical graft. As explained by Colette Gaudin, one of his translators, "he seeks man above the graft, where *a culture has left its traces on nature.*' "[1] We take this level to be the cultural unconscious, that intermediate realm of the psyche, neither personal nor collective, which, as Joseph Henderson has postulated, accounts for the development of culture and cultural attitudes.[2] This focus of Bachelard's becomes more evident as we follow his explanations of his phenomenological method of poetic reverie.

For Bachelard, as for Jung, consciousness is active.

. . . any awareness is an increment to consciousness, an added light, a rein- forcement of psychic coherence. Its swiftness or instantaneity can hide this growth from us. But there is a growth of being in every instance of awareness. Consciousness is itself an act, the human act. It is a lively, full act.[3]

The precise point at which Bachelard intends to study this act of consciousness is in the realm of language and "more pre- cisely yet in poetic language when the imagining consciousness creates and lives the poetic image."[4] Yet he asks himself if the use of reverie as a method is adequate to the task since "a con- sciousness which diminishes, which goes to sleep, a conscious- ness which *daydreams (rêvasse)*, is no longer a consciousness."[5] But it is not simple reverie that Bachelard has in mind, it is *poetic* reverie.

This is a reverie which poetry puts on the right track, the track an ex- panding consciousness follows. This reverie is written, or, at least, promises to be written. It is already facing the great universe of the blank page. Then images begin to compose and fall into place. The dreamer is already hearing the sounds of written words . . . All the senses awaken and fall into harmony in poetic reverie. Poetic reverie listens to this polyphony of the senses, and the poetic consciousness must record it.[6]

In a similar vein Bachelard distinguishes reverie from the nocturnal dream.

. . . it is precisely by phenomenology that the distinction between dream and reverie can be clarified, since the possible intervention of consciousness in the reverie bears decisive significance. One might wonder whether there really is a consciousness of dreams. A dream can be so strange that it seems that another subject has come to dream within us.[7]

[1] Colette Gaudin, *On Poetic Imagination and Reverie* (Indianapolis and New York, 1971), p. xvii.
[2] Joseph Henderson, "The Archetype of Culture," in *Der Archetyp/The Archetype* (Pro- ceedings of the 2nd International Congress for Analytical Psychology, 1962; Basel and New York, 1964), pp. 3-14.
[3] Gaston Bachelard, *The Poetics of Reverie*, tr. Daniel Russell (Boston, 1969), p. 5.
[4] Ibid., p. 5.   [5] Ibid., p. 6.   [6] Ibid., p. 6.   [7] Ibid., p. 11.

In this distinction, as in all others, Bachelard is focusing on the poetic powers of human imagination as the touchstone. The radical difference for him lies in the relative loss of a dialectic between ego consciousness and the unconscious which occurs in nocturnal dreams.

... the dreamer of the nocturnal dream is a shadow who has lost his self *(moi)*, the dreamer of reverie, if he is a bit philosophical, can formulate a *cogito* at the center of his dreaming self *(son moi rêveur)*. Put another way, reverie is an oneiric activity in which a glimmer of consciousness subsists. The dreamer of reverie is present in his reverie. Even when the reverie gives the impression of a flight out of the real, out of time and place, the dreamer of reverie knows that it is he who is absenting himself—he, in flesh and blood, who is becoming a "spirit", a phantom of the past or of voyage.[8]

Developing this notion of the dreamer's *cogito*, Bachelard seeks to establish its validity as a philosophical counter-pole to the thinker's *cogito* of Descartes.

Reverie is a manifest psychic activity. It contributes documentation on differences in the *tonality of being*. At the level of the tonality of being a differential ontology can then be proposed. . . . The dreamer's *cogito* is less sure than the philosopher's *cogito*. The dreamer's being is a diffuse being. But on the other hand, this diffuse being is the being of a diffusion. It escapes punctualization of the *hic* and of the *nunc*. The dreamer's being invades what it touches, diffuses into the world . . .[9]

In the foregoing statement, we encounter Bachelard in his philosopher's robes defining and elaborating his concepts. But it was not in this guise that he came to discover his method of poetic reverie. On the contrary, he wrested it from his own being in the throes of a mid-life crisis that found him, in spite of having attained his long-sought goal of a chair in philosophy, unhappy and dispirited without apparent cause. It was in a confrontation with a student that the full impact of his desolate state of mind was brought home to him.

Un jour, à Dijon, un étudiant évoqua "mon univers pasteurisé."[10] Thunderstruck, he asked himself, "How is it possible for a man to be happy in a sterile world?" It is imperative that one stir up the microbes and revivify one's life. Imagination must be rejuvenated and poetry discovered.[11]

Just exactly how this insight was translated into reality is difficult to ascertain. However, it was about this time that

[8]Ibid., p. 150.   [9]Ibid., p. 167.
[10]Paul Ginestier, *La Pensée Bachelard* (Bordas, 1968), p. 10.
[11]Ibid., p. 11 (my translation).

Bachelard undertook his studies of alchemy which resulted, within a few years, in the publication of two major works, one entitled *La formation de l'esprit scientifique. Contribution à une psychanalyse de la connaissance objective*, and the other, which we have already noted, translated as *The Psychoanalysis of Fire*. It is obvious from these titles that Bachelard had also undertaken the study of psychoanalysis—as much for himself as for his research, we may surmise. In this fortuitous conjunction of alchemy and psychoanalysis, the elements of his method of poetic reverie were crystalized. The numinous impact of the transformation taking place in Bachelard himself is evident in the eloquent depiction of his discovery that alchemy was more reverie than chemistry.

Alchemy was penetrated by an immense sexual reverie, by a reverie of wealth and rejuventation, by a reverie of power. . . . Far from being a *description* of the objective phenomena, it is an attempt to *inscribe* human love at the heart of things . . .[12]

The white lady who haunts the valley comes to visit the alchemist at night, beautiful as the imprecise image, changeable as a dream, fugitive as love itself. For a brief moment she enfolds the sleeping man in her caress: a too sudden breath and she evaporates.[13]

. . . alchemy is uniquely a science engaged in by men, by bachelors, by men without women, by initiates cut off from normal human relationships in favor of a strictly masculine society. Alchemy does not receive the influence of the feminine reverie directly. Its doctrine of fire is thus strongly polarized by unsatisfied desires. This inner, masculine fire, the object of the meditation of the lonely man, is naturally considered to be the most powerful fire.[14]

It would appear that he had found his spiritual brotherhood. Bachelard was, in fact, one of those lonely men who meditate on the inner masculine fire and evoke the anima. What is perhaps pertinent in this regard is that at the age of thirty he married, at the onset of World War I, and was called into the army almost immediately. He served for five years, receiving his discharge in 1919. Scarcely a year later he was widowed and left with a young daughter. The long shadow of melancholy cast over his life by this tragedy may be inferred from numerous allusions in his writings. The initial reveries of *The Psychoanalysis of Fire*, for example, are prefaced by these suggestive images:

[12]Bachelard, *The Psychoanalysis of Fire*, tr. Alan C. M. Ross (Boston, 1964), p. 51.
[13]Ibid., p. 52.   [14]Ibid., p. 53.

It is the pensive man whom we wish to study here, the man pensively seated by his fireplace in complete solitude at a time when the fire is burning brightly as if it were the very voice of this solitude.[15]

A winter's evening with the wind howling around the house and a bright fire within is all that is required to make the grieving soul give voice to its memories and sorrows.[16]

More than twenty years later, in his *Poetics of Reverie*, he refers to the "light melancholy from which all reverie is born,"[17] and, in the same context, speaks of the profound harmony of such reveries with "the distant melancholy of a child who has dreamed a lot."[18] Pursuing this image, he declares that "within us, among all our childhoods, there is the melancholy childhood, a childhood which already possessed human nobility and seriousness."[19] And finally a poignant imperative:

All our child dreams have to be taken up again so that they will take on their full poetic flight. This task should be accomplished by poetico-analysis. But in order to try it out, it would be necessary to be both poet and psychologist. That is a great deal to ask of one man. And when I see the past again, I can only recall, with each image, these lines which in turn console and torment me, these lines by a poet who also wonders what an image is, "And often it is nothing but a bubble of childhood/Under the lentisci of grief."[20]

What can we know of that childhood? Two sources of information are available, one a brief biographical sketch, the other some autobiographical vignettes scattered through his writings. The bare-bones biography is of interest primarily for the picture it creates of the long, circuitous course of Bachelard's journey from his rural origins to his career as a professor at the Sorbonne. He was born June 27, 1884, in Bar-sur-Aube, which is situated in a sector of Champagne abounding in streams and rivers, not all of which (he notes with regret late in life) had he time to follow in childhood. He was the grandson of a shoemaker, and his parents operated a small news and tobacco stand. After completing high school, he turned abruptly to a career in the postal service, where he remained for ten years. Several years later, when he was transferred to Paris, he began his college studies, despite a sixty-hour-a-week work schedule.

[15]Ibid., p. 3.   [16]Ibid., pp. 3-4.
[17]*The Poetics of Reverie*, p. 127.
[18]Ibid., p. 127.   [19]Ibid., p. 130.   [20]Ibid., p. 123.

At 28 he received his *licence* in mathematics and began courses in engineering, which were interrupted by the outbreak of World War I. Called to military service, he spent five years in the army, three of them in the front lines. In 1919, he was discharged; returning to Bar-sur-Aube, he became a teacher of physics and chemistry in a secondary school, a position he held for eleven years. During that period, he resumed his college studies, this time in the field of philosophy, and rapidly acquired all of the requisite degrees for a university career—his *licence* in 1920, *aggregation* in 1922, and doctorate in 1927 at the age of 43. Three years later he became a professor at the University of Dijon and, not long after, was appointed to the chair of Philosophy of Science at the Sorbonne. Retired as professor emeritus in 1954, he continued to publish and to lecture on a part-time basis. He was elected to the *Académie des Sciences morales et politiques* in 1955, and received the *Grand Prix National des Lettres* in 1961. He died on October 16, 1962, at the age of 78.

An invaluable supplement to this limited biography are the personal vignettes Bachelard has woven into the fabric of his works. They evoke a lively sense of his country boyhood. The greater number of these autobiographical fragments are to be found, appropriately enough, in *The Psychoanalysis of Fire*, which was the first publication in his series of studies of the ancient elements. It may be read both as an introduction to his method and its results, and as a record of his spiritual metamorphosis. That Bachelard places himself under the sign of fire is evident in that the first and the last of his publications in this series are devoted to reveries of fire, and also by reason of the extravagant praise he heaps on the divinity of fire in his preamble to *The Psychoanalysis of Fire*.

Fire is the ultra-living element. It is intimate and it is universal. It lives in our heart. It lives in the sky. It rises from the depths of the substance and offers itself with the warmth of love. Or it can go back down into the substance and hide there, latent and pent-up, like hate and vengeance. Among all phenomena, it is really the only one to which there can be so definitely attributed the opposing values of good and evil. It shines in Paradise. It burns in Hell. It is gentleness and torture. It is cookery and it is apocalypse. It is a pleasure for the *good* child sitting prudently by the hearth; yet it punishes any disobedience when the child wishes to play too close to its flames. It is wellbeing and it is respect. It is a tutelary and a terrible divinity, both good and bad. It can contradict itself; this is one of the principles of universal explanation.[21]

One line of this paean catches our eye. It is the surprising image of the good and the disobedient child embedded in an otherwise quite generalized commentary. The personal significance is clarified through the following sequence. First the curtain is drawn back, and we are priviledged to enter the humble home in the presence of the "grave and kindly doctor" with his fiery medicaments who, Bachelard says,

. . . used to come to my bedside when I was a child and who would calm my worried mother with one learned word. It would be a winter's morning in our poor home. The fire would be shining in the hearth. They would give me syrup of Tolu. I can remember how I would lick the spoon. Where are they, those days filled with the warm smell of balsam and the hot aromas of the medicines?[22]

The father appears with the doctor and also ministers to the sick child by providing the warmth of the fire on the bedside hearth.

When I was sick my father would light a fire in my room. He would take great care in arranging the logs over the kindling chips and in slipping the handful of shavings between the andirons. To fail to light the fire would have been incredibly stupid. I could not imagine my father having any equal in the performance of this function, which he would never allow anyone else to carry out. Indeed, I do not think I lit a fire myself before I was eighteen years old. It was only when I lived alone that I became master of my own hearth. But I still take special pride in the *art of kindling* that I learned from my father. I think I would rather fail to teach a good philosophy lesson than fail to light my morning fire.[23]

These images of ministering acts of skillful men of knowledge and prestige suggest an oppressive atmosphere of benevolent patriarchy that must have weighed heavily on the sensitive spirit of a young boy. What then were the free choices? Surely not open rebellion in view of the evident admiration and respect. Secret rebellion then and the projection of smoldering resentment onto more distant authorities, say teachers? But we anticipate Bachelard. Drawing us first into consideration of the psychology of respect for fire, he observes,

[21]*The Psychoanalysis of Fire*, p. 7.
[22]Ibid., p. 8.   [23]Ibid., pp. 8-9.

If the child brings his hand close to the fire his father raps him over the knuckles with a ruler. Fire, then, can strike without having to burn. . . . the social interdiction is our first *general knowledge* of fire. . . . As the child grows up, the prohibitions become intellectual rather than physical; the blow of the ruler is replaced by the angry voice, the angry voice by the recital of the dangers of fire, by the legends concerning fire from heaven. Thus the natural phenomenon is rapidly mixed in with complex and confused items of social experience which leave little room for the acquiring of an unprejudiced knowledge.[24]

This is our introduction to the good and the disobedient child. To gain personal knowledge of fire, there now arises the problem of *clever disobedience*.

The child wishes to do what his father does, but far away from his father's presence, and so like a little Prometheus he steals some matches. He then heads for the fields where, in the hollow of a little valley, he and his companions build a secret fireplace that will keep them warm on the days when they decide to play truant from school. The city child has little acquaintance with the joys of the fire flaming up between three stones; he has not tasted the fried sloe nor the snail that has been placed all slimy on the fiery embers. He may very well escape the *Prometheus complex* whose action I have often experienced. Only this complex enables us to understand the interest that is always aroused by the rather trite legend of the father of Fire. Moreover, one must not hasten to confuse this Prometheus complex with the Oedipus complex of classical psychoanalysis. Doubtless the sexual components of reveries about fire are particularly intense, and we shall attempt in a later chapter to demonstrate this fact. Perhaps, however, it is better to designate all the shades of unconscious convictions by different formulas, until we can see later how the various complexes are related. . . . There is in man a veritable *will to intellectuality*. We underestimate the need to understand when we place it, as pragmatism and Bergsonism have done, under the absolute dependence of the principle of utility. We propose, then, to place together under the name of the *Prometheus complex* all those tendencies which impel us *to know* as much as our fathers, more than our fathers, as much as our teachers, more than our teachers. . . . The Prometheus complex is the Oedipus complex of the life of the intellect.[25]

We have quoted at some length this explication of the Prometheus complex not solely because it illustrates so well Bachelard's method and aims at this stage in his development, but also because of the light it sheds on the long course of his intellectual growth. Despite obviously superior intelligence and sensibilities, it took him longer than it would take the average person to know as much as his father and his teachers. To

[24]Ibid., p. 11.   [25]Ibid., pp. 11-12.

acquire *more* knowledge than his teachers had, another supreme effort was required of him. He had to free the feminine, to evoke imagination, and to discover poetry.

After this excursus into rebellion, we should not be surprised that Bachelard now finds himself preoccupied with the fire that "smolders in the soul."[26] This reverie begins with a learned-sounding discussion of the psychology of the pyromaniac, ends with the apocalyptic fire of the funeral pyre, and is presided over by the figure of the grandmother who holds sway over the cauldron.

From the notched teeth of the chimney hook there hung the black cauldron. The three-legged cooking pot projected over the hot embers. Puffing up her cheeks to blow into the steel tube, my grandmother would rekindle the sleeping flames.[27]

And now we meet another boy, the "hot-tempered and impetuous child" who one day "threw whole spoonfuls of soup into the teeth of the chimney hook saying, 'Eat, chimney hook, eat!' " But, when he behaves, he is rewarded with the delicious golden fire that can be eaten.

. . . on days when I was on my good behavior, they would bring out the waffle iron . . . and soon the *gaufre* or waffle would be pressed against my pinafore, warmer to the fingers than to the lips. Yes, then indeed I was eating fire, eating its gold, its odor and even its crackling while the burning gaufre was crunching under my teeth. And it is always like that, through a kind of extra pleasure—like dessert—that fire shows itself a friend of man. It does not confine itself to cooking; it makes things crisp and crunchy. It puts the golden crust on the griddle cake; it gives a material form to man's festivities. As far back in time as we can go, the gastronomic value has always been more highly prized than the nutritive value, and it is in joy and not in sorrow that man discovered his intellect. The conquest of the superfluous gives us a greater spiritual excitement than the conquest of the necessary. Man is a creation of desire, not a creation of need.[28]

With a rapid shift Bachelard turns to another axis of this reverie by the fireside, one which illuminates the aspect of change and development, and which draws the associations to fire. They suggest

. . . the desire to change, to speed up the passage of time, to bring all of life to its conclusion, to its hereafter. In these circumstances the reverie becomes truly fascinating and dramatic; it magnifies human destiny; it links the small to the great, the hearth to the volcano, the life of a log to the life of the world.

[26]Ibid., p. 13.   [27]Ibid., p. 15.   [28]Ibid., pp. 15-16.

The fascinated individual hears *the call of the funeral pyre*. For him destruction is more than a change, it is a renewal. This very special and yet very general kind of reverie leads to a true complex in which are united the love and the respect for fire, the instinct for living and the instinct for dying. To save time one could call it the *Empedocles complex*.[29]

With this development of the Empodocles complex, we can recognize the emerging pattern outlined by Northrop Frye in his preface to *The Psychoanalysis of Fire*. Substituting for "complex" the word myth, which is for him a structural principle in literature, Frye suggests that the " 'complexes' dealt with in this book are actually the points at which literary myth becomes focussed on its cardinal points of creation, redemption and apocalypse."[30] Not, of course, in that order for Bachelard now delineates the Novalis complex, "the fire-world as the unfallen world of pre-creation."[31] However, the Novalis complex does not contain any of Bachelard's personal reveries. It is with the succeeding Hoffmann complex that we pick up the auto-biographical record.

The Hoffmann complex is the complex of the punch bowl, of "the water that flames." The reverie is introduced by a vignette of the preparation of the *brûlot* (brandy burnt with sugar) at the time of the great winter festivals.

My father would pour into a wide dish some marc-brandy produced from our own vineyard. In the center he would place pieces of broken sugar, the biggest ones in the sugar bowl. As soon as the match touched the tip of the sugar, a blue flame would run down to the surface of the alcohol with a little hiss. My mother would extinguish the hanging lamp. It was the hour of mystery, a time when a note of seriousness was introduced into the festivity. . . . If the flames wavered and flickered, father would stir at the *brûlot* with an iron spoon. The spoon would come out sheathed in fire like an instrument of the devil. Then we would "theorize": to blow out the flames too late would make the *brûlot* too sweet; to put them out too soon would mean concentrating less fire and consequently diminishing the beneficent action of the *brûlot* against influenza. . . . Finally the *brûlot* would be in my glass: hot, sticky, truly an essence.[32]

This revealing reverie serves as introduction to the work of E. T. A. Hoffmann, from whom the complex receives its name.

. . . one of the most characteristic traits of the work of Hoffmann, the teller of fantastic tales, is the importance given to the phenomena of fire. A poetry of

[29]Ibid., p. 16.   [30]Ibid., pp. vii-viii.   [31]Ibid., p. viii.   [32]Ibid., p. 84.

the flame runs through his entire work. Moreover, the punch complex is here so much in evidence that it could be called the Hoffmann complex.[33]

The salamander, the creature of fire seen by Hoffmann in the flames of the punch bowl, is the immediate inspiration for Bachelard's theory of the four poetic temperaments.

... in my opinion,....a whole area of phantasmagorical literature is dependent upon the poetic excitation of alcohol. The precise and concrete bases must not be forgotten, if we wish to understand the psychological meaning of literary constructions.... If our present work serves any useful purpose, it should suggest a classification of objective themes which would prepare the way for a classification of poetic temperaments. We have not yet been able to perfect an over-all doctrine, but it seems quite clear to us that there is some relation between the doctrine of the four physical elements and the doctrine of the four temperaments. In any case, the four categories of souls in whose dreams [reveries] f ire, water, air or earth predominate, show themselves to be markedly different.

Indeed, the tetravalence of reverie is as clear and as productive as the chemical tetravalence of carbon. Reverie has four domains, four points from which it soars into infinite space. To surprise the secret of a true poet, of a sincere poet, of a poet who is faithful to his original language and is deaf to the discordant echoes of sensuous eclecticism, which would like to play on all the senses, one word is sufficient: "Tell me what your favorite phantom is. Is it the gnome, the salamander, the sylph or the undine?" Now—and I wonder if this has been noticed—all these chimerical beings are formed from and sustained by a unique substance: the gnome, terrestrial and condensed, lives in the fissure of the rock, guardian of the mineral and the gold, and stuffs himself with the most compact substances; the salamander, composed all of fire, is consumed in its own flame; the water nymph or undine glides noiselessly across the pond and feeds on her own reflection; the sylph for whom the least substance is a burden, who is frightened away by the tiniest drop of alcohol, who would even perhaps be angry with a smoker who might "contaminate her element" (Hoffman), rises effortlessly into the blue sky, happy in her anorexia.[34]

This is a fitting place to bring to a close this preliminary study. Over the next few years Bachelard completed his tetra-valent doctrine of poetic temperaments in publications devoted to the elements of water, air, and earth; *L'eau et les rêves, L'air et les songes, La terre et les rêveries du repos,* and *La terre et les rêveries de la volonté.* In the course of these studies, as his insight deepened and his knowledge of Jung's works increased, he gravitated toward a more general phenomenological approach which found its first expression in *The Poetics of Space.* Freed from his former attachment to the ancient elements, he could

[33]Ibid., p. 85.   [34]Ibid., pp. 89-90.

now examine anew "the quite simple images of *felicitous space*,"[35] the house, cellars, garrets, chests and wardrobes, nests, shells, and corners. Just how much at home he felt at that time in the realm of archetypal imagery is apparent in his last major work, *The Poetics of Reverie,* especially in an extraordinary chapter entitled, "Reveries Toward Childhood," in which he evokes the imagery of the child archetype, the well of being.

The theses which we wish to defend in this chapter all return to make us recognize within the human soul the permanence of a nucleus of childhood, an immobile but ever living childhood, outside history, hidden from the others, disguised in history when it is recounted, but which has real being only in its instants of illumination which is the same as saying in the moments of its poetic existence.[36]

Childhood is a human water. . . . What a lot of lost springs which have, nevertheless, flowed! Reverie toward our past then, reverie looking for childhood seems to bring back to life lives which have never taken place, lives which have been imagined. . . . In reverie we re-enter into contact with possibilities which destiny has not been able to make use of.[37]

And, in the course of this ever deepening reverie, Bachelard comes to one last depth in himself.

When, at the pinnacle of age, at the end of age, one sees such reveries, he draws back a bit, for he recognizes that *childhood is the well of being.* Dreaming this way about unfathomable childhood which is one archetype, I am well aware that I am taken by another archetype. The well is an archetype, one of the gravest images of the human soul.

That black and distant water can mark a childhood. It has reflected an astonished face. Its mirror is not that of the fountain. A narcissus can take no pleasure there. Already in his image living beneath the earth, the child does not recognize himself. A mist is on the water; Plants which are too green frame the mirror. A cold blast breathes in the depths. The face which comes back in this night of the earth is a face from another world. Now, if a memory of such reflections comes into a memory, isn't it the memory of a before-world?

A well marked my early childhood. I only approached it with my hand tightly clasped in my grandfather's hand. Who was afraid then, the grandfather or the child? And yet the curb was high. It was in a garden which was soon to be lost. . . . But a dull evil has remained with me. I know what a well of being is. And since one must tell everything when he is evoking his childhood, I must admit that the well of my greatest terrors was always the well of my goose game. In the middle of the softest evenings, I was more afraid of it than of the skull and crossed tibias.[38]

[35]Bachelard, *The Poetics of Space,* tr. Maria Jolas (Boston, 1969), p. xxxi.
[36]*The Poetics of Reverie,* p. 100.
[37]Ibid., p. 112.   [38]Ibid., p. 114.

The Goddess Mysteries

ALICE KENT

THIS PAPER ON THE ELEUSINIAN MYSTERIES and the two goddesses, mother and maiden, Demeter and Persephone, shows how the Archive for Research in Archetypal Symbolism (ARAS) can be used to develop and expand a dream. It illustrates one way in which this "archive . . . can serve those who are creatively concerned with the meaning of symbols in human life,"[1] to quote its director, Jessie Fraser. In April, 1971, I had this dream:

After having fainted in the middle of an analytical session, I waken on the floor, on my stomach, staring at the pattern on an Indian or Persian rug—an intricate, psychedelic pattern. As I come to, I am trying to follow the labyrinthine abstraction. Joe places beside me a piece of sculpture, a low plaque. It is of two porpoises turning in graceful design. I pick it up; it has been lying flat at my eye level. When I tilt it up, it becomes the figures of two women in Greek dress, archaically, stiffly carved—two Greek goddesses. The whole is like a wind-bell or ornament. I tap it, wondering what material it is made of. It rings. "Is this stone, or stoneware pottery, Joe?" "It is called seraph." I don't know whether he misunderstood me or was answering my question. I just say, "Oh."

Did the pattern on the rug represent abstractions seen under LSD? Had I been trying to apply vague hallucinations to real life on earth today? Was this why my wise man had handed me an earthy problem to solve, for it was my very own? Why porpoises? And unknown Greek goddesses?

I found some Bolinas clay, smelly with rotting organic material, yellow-brown as feces, the raw matter of earth. I wanted to work the clay only out of curiosity to see how two porpoises could turn into Greek goddesses. It would simply be a rough sketch that would make this dream a concrete reality. I had

[1]Jessie E. Fraser, "ARAS: Archive for Research in Archetypal Symbolism," *Spring*, 1964, 60-7. (The original archive is in New York; duplicates are in San Francisco and Los Angeles.)

never been able to paint or sculpture to my satisfaction. My aesthetic attitude was overdeveloped on the critical side, and I tried to please others. Nothing had ever turned out the way *I* wanted it—*my* way. But now I worked with the clay for a new reason, not for an outer display, but with an eagerness to put into material form this vision—for myself alone to study. The figures developed through hours of building and shaping the clay. At the same time I could dream my myth—Alice.

My two porpoises represented the basics of life—the black and white poles of creative energy—the infinity symbol—the Yin and the Yang. I had read of teaching porpoises to communicate, not in parrot talk, but by disclosing their own ideas. Mine seemed to say, "We are the primordial energy from the vast ocean of the past. We *are*, since the beginning of time."

While I modelled the "two archaic Greek goddesses," I found them growing with an inner strength of their own. I felt I must let the sculpture follow its own pattern. Indeed, if I had not been consciously playing an unaesthetic game within myself, I would never have dared tackle the modelling of Greek goddesses, nor submitted to their archaic quality before they emerged as themselves. For the two women grew to living entities who now shone through the clay figures, making them strong and vital.

What secret were they telling to each other with their eyes? As the goddesses developed, it became apparent that one was young and the other older. I wanted to make them holding hands, but instead they wished to share a four-petaled flower. Since it was unknown to me, I had to "invent it." Suddenly I realized the goddesses were mother and daughter, Demeter and Persephone! I immediately added wheat to Demeter and a field of flowers for Persephone. It was then that I realized that the four-petaled flower I had already modelled between them was a poppy being given by the daughter.

I thought about the delicate resonance when, in my dream, I struck the plaque. My Bolinas clay would make no sound, but maybe if I listened to its inner ringing I could hear a further ripple of waves. After all, it was called "seraph," the wise man said, and a seraph is a messenger angel from heaven.

Since I couldn't remember much more about Persephone than the pomegranate seed, I searched the bookshelves for assistance and came upon Kerényi's inspired *Eleusis*. The Eleusinian Mysteries, of which I had never heard, were the ancient Greek mystery rites of Demeter and Persephone, celebrated in the Temple of Eleusis. Was that book, by any chance, to be a "seraph" of my dreams to which I must listen?

Mystery derives from the Greek word *myesis*. Commenting on Socrates' quote from *Phaedrus*, Kerényi wrote: "*Myesis* can be rendered by the Latin word *initia*, 'beginnings,' . . . signifying introduction into the secret. For *myesis* comes from the verb *myeo* which denotes the action. The simpler verb *myo* implies the element of secrecy. It means nothing other than 'to close,' as the eyes do *after seeing*. The . . . object of this verb is the subject itself [she closes herself] after the manner of a flower. . . . [The secret is] that which is shut up within itself."[2] The seed.

What was this secret? Did my dream hint that I was ready for an initiation into the mystery that my two goddesses were telling each other? It had to be more than a coincidence that in every ancient sculpture of Demeter and Persephone they are looking deeply into one another's eyes, sharing some profound secret between them. Could I find the answer in books? None has a full answer.

George Mylonas traces these mystery rites back to around 2000 B.C., and they may go back to the beginning of time. However, the story of Demeter and Persephone was first recorded around 700 B.C. as the Homeric *Hymn to Demeter*.

> Long ago when gods and heroes walked in the vales of Greece, Persephone, daughter of Demeter and Zeus, was playing and gathering flowers, roses and crocuses and beautiful violets in a soft meadow accompanied by the daughters of Okeanos. When she reached out to pick a most marvelous narcissus . . . with a delicious fragrance, the wide-pathed earth yawned and out of it sprang Plouton and his immortal horses. He caught her up, reluctant, in his golden cart and bore her away lamenting.[3]

Demeter, in her grief, demanded that a temple be built for her in Eleusis. She closed herself in and refused to come out until her daughter would be returned to her, "causing a cruel year for all mankind over the nourishing earth."[4]

[2]Karl Kerényi, *Eleusis: Archetypal Image of Mother and Daughter* (Archetypal Images in Greek Religion, 4; B.S. LXV, 1967), p. 46.
[3]*The Homeric Hymns*, ed. Thomas W. Allen, W. R. Halliday, and E. E. Sikes (2nd edn., Oxford, 1936).
[4]Ibid.

Mylonas wrote *Eleusis and the Eleusinian Mysteries* after thirty years of archeological research on the spot. He says, Let us leave the myth and turn to the ruins of Eleusis.[5]

"The discovery, on the southern slope of the hill, of a few sherds belonging to the Early Bronze age indicate that perhaps the site was occupied in that remote age."[6] However, a regular settlement in the Mycenaean era, covering the years from 1500 B.C. to about 1110 B.C., was uncovered. "With the exception of the walls belonging to one structure, Megaron B, these remains are fragmentary. . . . Tradition points to [this time] as the eras in which the cult of Demeter was introduced and established in Eleusis. . . . The Hymn not only mentions that temple (Megaron B) but also indicates the [same] general locality [as today]."[7] Mylonas adds, "That slope was chosen because its area was already sanctified by previous religious use, by a cult that was celebrated there long before [a temple was needed]."[8] The temple was constructed so that the goddess could close herself up in the room behind the portico and dwell there until the return of her daughter.

By chance I had just made over a room for myself in which to meditate and write. I now called it my "Megaron B," and I holed myself up like Demeter, "refusing to come out until Persephone was returned to me from the underworld."[9] Like Demeter I had to search for Persephone, the lost dark half of myself whom I could only find in the unconscious. I spent months reading everything I could find; Harrison, Mylonas, Eliade, Otto, Jung, puzzling out my personal myth and dream along with hints about the Mysteries of Eleusis.

What was the deep inner meaning of the two goddesses, and, psychologically, what could have gone on in these well-hidden mysteries? What could have been so vital to the people that the secret of these initiation rites was sacredly guarded in the hearts of the initiated women and men of Greece and later of Rome? These are the most sacred mysteries which, according to Praetextatus "hold the entire human race together."[10]

There are some statements about the ceremonies in contem-

[5]George E. Mylonas, *Eleusis and the Eleusinian Mysteries* (Princeton, 1961), p. 29.
[6]Ibid., pp. 29-30.   [7]Ibid., pp. 32-3.   [8]Ibid., p. 44.
[9]*The Homeric Hymns.*
[10]Kerényi, p. 12.

porary sources and eyewitness reports, and the Greek drama-
tists tell as much as they dare. But nowhere has the real secret
been disclosed. By searching, reading, and playing fantasies, I
gradually built up my own vision of the rites.

Sir James Frazer, in *The Golden Bough,* wrote that in remote
times "no special class of persons is set apart for the performance of the rites.... There are no priests (at the beginning).
The rites may be performed by any one, as occasion demands."[11]

And Linda Fierz-David, in her essay on the villa of the
mysteries in Pompeii, says that man of antiquity learned to
know real life "by submitting himself to the sacred happening
of a cult drama, as it was handed down by tradition, in order to
repeat the experience of divine fate and divine transformation.[12]

Could I submit myself to the cult drama of the Eleusinian
Mysteries? For myself alone? Maybe with submission an answer
would come.

I recorded a piece of active imagination:

Earliest woman wandered the equatorial fields and woods gathering roots
and nuts, berries and fruit. She contented herself with grabbing a handful of
food when she was hungry, pulling the grains off the stalks of grasses into her
fist, and stuffing them into her mouth. Her entire life was foraging for food,
moving with the seasons, providing for her children or teaching them how to
search for edibles as her mother had taught her. She roved about with her
family, traveling in spring from the protected valley to open fields and to the
forest. Then, with winter coming on, she would pilot her family down to the
seashore, where seafood was plentiful. Here she would stretch out on the
sand under the warm sun or question the heavens at night. She was at peace
with both mother earth and mother ocean. She became aware of the moon
waxing and waning in the sky, and gradually she connected herself to its phases
with her own monthly blood-letting cycle.

She began to count the moons as the seasons changed around her. She
sensed the spring with its new growth and flowers, their gradual metamor-
phoses into pod and seed, which one moon later dropped dry and hard to the
ground. Here the final rotting took place, as did a bird's carcass, dropped on
the earth, or her dead grandmother's body, thrown into its megaron cleft in
the rock. What was behind all this? Did her all-knowing grandmother in the
cave-tomb disintegrate? And did her ghost return to earth each year to repeat
the food cycle, the lore of which she had taught her children? When the
woman had gone back to visit her grandmother's corpse, there had been the

[11]James C. Frazer, *The Golden Bough,* abridged edn. (New York, 1922), p. 411.
[12]Linda Fierz-David, *Psychological Reflections on the Fresco Series of the Villa of Mysteries in Pompeii,* tr. Gladys Phelan (unpub. ms., 1937).

evil smell of the midden, and a writhing snake had hissed at her. But later, the dead body had dropped the rotting flesh and left behind a skeletal, snakelike spine with its connecting bones lying so quietly, in contrast to the grandmother's very much alive ghost-snake twisting and expanding down there in the burial cave, protecting the remains of the old woman.

When a pig was killed and split apart for eating, it too contained the snake which came slithering out of its home in the belly. Who knew when it would arise, alive again, to strike and kill a man in revenge unless appeased? A snake was magical; it did not tear at the flesh like other beasts, but the least prick of its fang killed a man.

Woman could feel within her own body the serpent of life, either coiled calm or writhing, and angry with hunger, twisting and complaining there behind her navel. Man's snake of life, which he wore outside his body, slept quietly too, or awakened into its stiff demanding force and power of thrust. It was no wonder she reverenced and paid homage to the snake of life and death. Its coil and recoil were as changeable and unpredictable as the moon, and as important in her life.

Time passed and woman's consciousness waxed fuller. She learned to hoard grain to feed her family, but there came a time when, as she returned to collect it, she found the seeds had taken root and were sprouting with new green life. In an illumination animated by woman's irrational intuitive vision, she comprehended what she saw—the possibilities of consciously utilizing earth and seed and water for her own advantage.

Ages passed. Now woman accepted with gratitude the Earth Mother, who in ancient days taught her the full year's mystery of digging and sowing. Now she celebrated each of the four seasons with festivals of propitiation to that ancestor grandmother at her sanctuary in the megaron cave where she was first buried and now lived on in the great serpent coiled and hissing down there. And now even the festivals had gone on for so long that woman could no longer remember their beginnings.

Jane Harrison quotes Plutarch in her *Prolegomena*, "The women fasted seated on the ground because the earth was desolate; they rose and revelled, they stirred the *megara* to mimic the impulse of spring. Then when they knew no longer why they did these things they made a goddess their proto-type."[13] They created their own festivals for her.

The Greek year contained four equinoctial festivals. The spring festival was for placation of the dead of winter's ghosts and for the promotion of new life. The climax of the Anthesteria, in spring, was the sacred marriage of the chief magistrate's wife to Dionysos, the Prince of Death. Could this later be taken as the rape of Persephone by Hades-Dionysos?

[13]Jane Harrison, *Prolegomena to the Study of Greek Religion* (3rd edn., Cambridge, 1922), p. 129.

The summer festival was celebrated for fruits gathered to assure continuing fertility and in gratitude for a good harvest. Seeds of each fruit were put into *kernos* pots and shared and eaten with the goddesses.

Thesmophoria came at the fall sowing of the fields in late September, as propitiation toward fertile soil and a good crop. Swine were thrown to the snakes in the megaron chasms by maidens called Kathados (Descending Maidens), and pieces were brought back up by the Anados (Uprising Maidens).

The winter festival, the Haloa, was held at the end of the year, the dormant waiting period of winter. This festival, rich in hilarity and obscenity, celebrated the breaking loose from rigid disciplines and struggles. Also, this was the time for new beginnings, when the New Year baby was born, the spark of new fire for the future.

From these festival rites the two early aspects of the irrational mother-earth goddess gradually developed—the two branchings from the one: Kathados and Anados, *kata,* down and *ana,* up; the closing down and the bringing up, inspiration and expression, tightening and loosening.

Our goddesses, Demeter and Persephone, personified these abstract qualities. Demeter's title, Thesmophoros, meant the law-giver. "With Demeter, it is said, came in agriculture, settled life, marriage and the beginnings of civilized law."[14] The mother was the corn goddess, fostering production on earth symbolized by her grain. Her daughter, the Kore, personified inspiration and intuition, the dream, symbolized by the opium poppy she carried; she was the loosener, the up-bringer.

Man first personified his deities with natural objects—animals, trees, stones. A figure god grew out of a sanctification of serpent or tree. Herakles was a tree first, then a pillar of wood with a head and a branch, the cudgel, which still is his symbol. Hermes was a *herme,* a sign post or boundary stone, or a phallic object, before Homer gave him winged feet to fly off to Olympus. And in my sculpture the archaic goddesses are shown developing out of their fish beginnings.

An archaic Kore suggests another early harvest rite, as told by Frazer in *The Golden Bough.* He gives numerous variations from all over the agricultural world

[14]Ibid., p. 136.

In France, the last sheaf goes by the name of "Mother of the Wheat." They leave it standing in the field until the last wagon is about to turn homeward. Then they make a figure out of it, dress it with clothes belonging to the farmer's wife and adorn it with a crown. At the dance in the evening this Ceres is set in the middle of the floor, and, after the dance, a fire is made. The girls place Ceres on the fire along with the flowers with which she is adorned. The girl who has first finished reaping sets fire to the pile, and all pray that Ceres may give a fruitful year.[15]

Theocritus tells us that in Greece, "in the sweet-scented summer time, the farmer brought the first-fruits of the harvest to Demeter"[16] . . . The Maiden makes the fields fertile, and her rustic effigy of straw stands smiling there, with corn and poppies in her hands.

When and why did the agricultural Pelasgian people give up their outdoor rites and build walls around the megaron at Eleusis? For, as Mylonas says, the temple to Demeter (still called her megaron) was built on the same already sacred ground. We know that, as time went on and men migrated north and south, a new race of men, the Achaeans, came down from the North with their male attributes of the hunt, the chase, the kill, and their male gods hungry for burnt sacrifice of meat. Rostovtzeff dates the beginning of this invasion at 2000 B.C. and says that the first walled cities were built during this period.[17]

Was it at that time that our matriarchal Pelasgians, the original inhabitants of Eleusis, felt the need to enclose their sanctuary with walls to ensure privacy against the invading heathen? Here within their new megaron temple, I believe, they consolidated their rituals into two festivals—the two Mysteries. The spring festival with its marriage in the underworld and its objects of fertility, became the Lesser Mysteries while the autumnal equinoctial rites marked both the fall sowing and the winter festival of the birth of the new spark of fire, and they became the Greater Mysteries, the Epopteia.

By the time the Homeric Hymn to Demeter was composed, in 700 B.C., the place and rituals of the Eleusinian Mysteries had already been fixed by the Greeks. The myth of Demeter and

[15]Frazer, p. 401.   [16]Ibid., p. 396.
[17]M. Rostovtzeff, A History of the Ancient World, tr. J. D. Duff, vol. 1 (Oxford, 1926), p. 177.

Persephone proved to all people that the rites had come from the goddesses *with* the help of the Olympian gods.

At the time of Perikles, about 300 B.C., the Eleusinian Mysteries, which had been sacred since time immemorial, had not only reached the zenith of aesthetic and architectural development in outer manifestation but were also the most complete interpretation of the symbolic expression for spiritual understanding. The active imagination of my initiation into the Mysteries employs this period for the backdrop.

The rites of the Lesser Mysteries were held in the spring to celebrate Persephone's return from the underworld. Undoubtedly it was a continuation of the early Anthesteria, when ancestors were fed the fertility sacra in the megaron, and the maiden was married to Dionysos.

In the reliefs on the Lovatelli urn we have hints of what occurred, for they depict the purification and initiation of Herakles. This is a hint in itself, for Herakles had to be purified and initiated before he descended into the underworld in order not only to face the Queen of the Dead, Persephone, but also to dies and yet return to the world of men—to go down and bring back.

A picture from the ARAS slide collection (3Pa.049) shows Herakles bringing his pig to be sacrificed. Herakles will be purified through sacrificing his animal nature to the gods. At the same time the hierophant hands him a plate containing Persephone's gift, the visionary poppy capsules. These he must chew as he drinks the kykeon from the hierophant's right hand. A heavy veil is thrown over him to simulate his death into darkness. As many have experienced with LSD or peyote, the first stage of the trip is often a descent into the awesome abyss of death and nothingness. The blackness and silence are terrifying. Herakles must go through the ordeal to reach a better state. A priestess is holding a liknon over his head. This scoop-shaped basket, used in ancient Greece for winnowing the grain, was also used for gathering fruit, or as a cradle for a new-born babe. (In the Homeric *Hymn* to Hermes, the infant Hermes is put into a *liknon* at birth.) The liknon over the head of Herakles, therefore, signifies new birth; Herakles is born again out of the darkness. In the next episode Herakles is standing before Demeter, goddess of earth's bounty. But, rather than looking at him, she is facing her daughter as if to say, "This is your ceremony, not mine." Demeter sits on the great *cista mystica,* the covered mystery basket. Around the basket twines a huge snake whose head is in Demeter's lap. Herakles, with his right hand, strokes the head raised to greet him. The serpent is also a symbol of regeneration, for it was believed he died, shed his skin, and was reborn each year. In the mystery basket are stored the secret sacred objects symbolic of life. The basket, of course, is the container, symbol of the female receptacle, while here the twining serpent represents the driving male phallus.

What happened beyond this moment which must never be told? All we know is that those who completed the initiation had to call out these passwords in order to enter the Greater Mystery: "I have fasted, drunk the *kykeon,* taken things out of the big basket and, after performing a rite, put them in the little basket, whence I put them back in the big basket."[18]

What was the meaning of these mysterious words? I followed the steps alone, trying to sense deeply the secret of what Persephone's eyes exchanged with the penetrating gaze of her mother. What did they know together which was beyond words? Who am I to tell in words a secret that is far deeper than words? I followed Herakles and the ceremony depicted on the Lovatelli urn. When I came to Demeter and the snake, I recognized that the serpent symbolized creative generation. I must hold the serpent's head in my hand and accept his vitalizing energy. Until I dared to stroke the terrifying snake, I could not reach into the basket.

I put my hand into the basket and withdrew some raw material of creativity. My "raw material" was my porpoise dream, which had come up from my unconscious mystery basket. I put this into my little basket, my *liknon,* my consciousness, to winnow as I could, separating the wheat from the chaff, keeping the small collection of fertile seeds as I tossed the material into the air for the breeze of controlled thinking to choose what to blow away. Then I returned the seeds to the *cista mystica.* What did this mean? To me, this last gesture of the return of my individual creative effort into the big basket was the real message to be learned in the Eleusinian initiation. Persephone's immortality comes with the understanding that nothing is cre-

[18]Kerényi, p. 66.

ated by one's ego alone, nor belongs to one's ego self. Everything is part of a greater eternal whole, symbolized by both the snake and basket combined in one completeness. Anything I will produce as an individual is not for me, nor by me, nor to enhance my ego, but comes from a combining of the elements, water, fire, earth, and air, as they balance themselves within me. I am only a unique centering instrument for the elements. Whether this creation is my personal physical body and cell structure, as it makes and remakes itself, or my creative sculpture, which I might believe I make, or even children born to me, I am only an individual instrument to be used. In life I am given the opportunity to remove and winnow the product, but must return it to the source basket. My immortality lies in realizing this and in thinking of my life not as a product of myself, for then it dies, as I do, as my ego dies. If I separate myself from the whole and am not part of it, I am nothing. "When that which is perfect is come, then that which is in part shall be done away.... For now I know in part; but then shall I know even as also I am known." (I Corinthians 13:10-12, AV).

This then was the first of the two great Eleusinian Mysteries of immortality. It was Persephone's mystery, and it was on the material level, a physical manifestation, whether it was of seeds, clay, or generative organs. It had to be deeply fathomed before it could lead to the sacred, Great Mystery, the Epopteia. This was a purely spiritual mystery, more difficult to comprehend or explain for there are no words for it. Indeed, the initiate could not go through the Greater Mystery the same year, but had to wait a year and a half in order to grasp fully the significance of the Lesser rite.

The Greater Mysteries were held once a year in late September and October, the time of the autumnal equinox—the sacred month for the Greek world.

In Athens, after five days of feasting and purifying themselves, the people assembled for the brilliant procession to Eleusis. The initiates wore festive clothes and were crowned with myrtle wreaths; in their hands they bore the mystic bacchos (*fascis* made up of branches of myrtle tied together with strands of' yellow wool).

A wooden statue of Iaccos, bearing a torch and crowned with myrtle, was placed on a carriage to lead the procession, followed by the priests of Eleusis. Then came the holy priestesses with Demeter's round mystery baskets on their heads, later memorialized in marble by the karyatids at the entrance gates into the Telesterion temple. The baskets contained the secret sacred objects of fertility used in the initiation rites.

Following the priestesses came women, men, children, and initiates, a vast throng of people. The road from Athens to Eleusis is about fourteen miles long. "The procession went slowly but with enthusiasm and animation, and the road and the hills surrounding it echoed and reechoed the festive cry of the participants."[19] "Iacchos, Iacchos!" is their equivalent of our "Allelulia"[20] and they personalized it with the figure of the youth with the fiery torch in his hand—the morning star ahead of and heralding the sun.

In the late afternoon, the procession had to cross the Kephisos River. There on the bridge, old women and jesters in masks were waiting. They hurled insults against important persons to the laughter of those around. They also did obscene dances to ribald songs. The tension of the weary throng was broken up with laughter and joking. "In a joyous mood, with torches lit, the pompe would finally reach . . . the outer court of the sanctuary."[21]

By now they were inebriated by both the excitement and the fermented *kykeon* drink, made of barley water and mint, that they all carried. The courtyard blazed with torches, and the great dance platform was crowded with figures bending and turning. The women carried lighted *kernos* pots on their heads (the same earthenware vessels with small cups as were used in the summer festival). But the little cups of these pots were shallow and could not hold seeds; instead there was space for candles or even small hearths for charcoal fire. The women danced with these on their heads, as can be seen in the Niinnion tablet.

What a spectacle this fire dance must have been, with all the torches lit and the hundreds of flickering *kernos* on the dancing women's heads, in addition to a moon and the reflections of it all onto the surface of the sea below!

The Kernophoria was a fitting climax to an inspiring day, leaving the initiates filled with anticipation for the morrow.

[19]Mylonas, p. 254.   [20]Harrison, p. 413.   [21]Mylonas, p. 256.

The sixth day, the Telete (which means "initiation"), was spent in resting, purification and fasting, so that the initiates would be ready for the full initiation ceremony. Very few definite facts remain of what occurred. After those to be admitted entered the gates, all we know is that the initiates went through "certain experiences which left them . . . overflowing with bliss and joy."[22] Nothing can be proved, but the following is how I came to fantasize the mystery, using art of the time and vague hints from books written by men who had been initiated but who had sworn never to divulge what they had experienced.

Flashes of the puzzle were suddenly joined together while I was sitting in my Megaron B staring at a copy of the ground plan of the sanctuary. I could visualize myself taking part in the events. Here is the dance platform, and here are the outer and inner gates, the Propylaia with the great priestess karyatids holding the mystery baskets on their heads. What happened beyond these gates? Further along the Sacred Way we see narrow steps built for people to stand on. Why? To view a pageant? No one knows what needed to be seen. The steps are in front of the cave dedicated to Plouton. Behind the cave Mylonas uncovered small steps cut in the rock with an entrance hole in the rear big enough to allow a young girl to enter from its steps.[23] Could the maiden have been Persephone returning from the underworld? Here is the Mirthless Rock where the myth says Demeter sat and mourned her daughter. Here is the long marble paved Sacred Way into the Telesterion itself. In this temple there was room for many people, and again there were narrow steps around the back to stand upon for a view over the heads of the crowd. Here, in the center of the Telesetrion, is the little room, the Anaktoron-Megaron, the holy of holies since time immemorial, the same spot sacred even before the building of the first small Megaron B. The Telesterion had a roof, and there was no light from outside, but there was no roof over the Anaktoron room, and the chimney-like opening to the sky could have served to allow fire and smoke to escape. One quote from Plutarch says: "At the very moment when the cries [of Iacchos] were heard, a light [which could be seen from Athens] flashed across the bay from Eleusis: the light from the sanctuary."[24] Hippolytos writes that "the Hierophant officiated

[22]Ibid., p. 261.   [23]Ibid., p. 148.   [24]Kerényi, p. 10.

at night 'under the great fire.' "[25] Remember that Frazer's *Golden Bough* tells of a world-wide harvest ritual in which the last sheaf of grain was made into the figure of a goddess and later burned in a bonfire with prayers of supplication for a good harvest. Maybe at Eleusis, in order to keep women's rituals secret and sacred, the straw maiden, which had been burned with the chaff on the sacred ground in the open, was now hidden each year in Demeter's Anaktoron-Megaron on the same sacred spot. And maybe, having filled the little holy of holies with chaff from the thrashing, one could, at a given signal set fire to it, with the straw maiden standing in the center of the pile. No one will ever know, but my own initiation came together in one illuminating fantasy.

Night is coming on. It is dusk. The procession of the men and women ready for the second initiation moves slowly forward. There is genuine sadness, as we, too, depict the great goddess who worries and longs for her abducted daughter. We are imitating her in dark dress, with one shoulder bare, heavily veiled as we take on her sorrow, leaning on our pilgrim staves.

Along the Sacred Way we come to the cave of Plouton. Here, resting on a stone called the "Mirthless Rock," a personification of Demeter mourns, awaiting the return of her daughter from the depths of the cave where Hermes has gone to fetch her back to earth. The procession stops, awed at seeing the goddess herself. The initiates can stand on steps to watch and wait, too, in the dying daylight. There is much speculating, which is hushed as the viewer senses, with Demeter, her anticipation. A light appears at the yawning mouth of the cave. It is Persephone, carrying two torches, one held high, one lowered, signifying light from above and light from below. She sets them on either side of the cave's entrance. The mother rises, radiant and loving, and runs to her child.

Persephone clasps her mother in the long-awaited embrace. They look into each other's eyes with complete understanding and oneness. The daughter has brought back to the mother the fresh spark of inspiration from the dark fiery deeps. She reveals this to the mother through the warm, new-kindled look in her eyes. The crowd is overjoyed. They understand the gratitude of a mother for the return of her daughter, and they

[25] Ibid., p. 92.

know that the gift of a plentiful harvest will now come from
Demeter. To receive their worshippers, Demeter, goddess of the
productive earth, sits upon her covered mystery basket, while
behind her sits the dark Persephone, queen of the shadow world
upon her throne. Between their thrones rises the Om-
phalos, the navel of the world, the center between the underworld and heaven. The two goddesses receive their worshippers
in this place which symbolizes the balance of the two Great
Mysteries, the first the Mystery of material, physical love and
creativity, and the other the creative ecstasy of immortal love.
At the navel, the two are brought together as one creative and
psychic energy.

By now it is night. Iacchos steps up to the cave's entrance to
take the torches brought by Persephone from the underworld,
and following the blaze, the adoring *mystai,* dancing and singing
behind their leader, light their torches and bring their gifts and
sacrifices to the feet of the goddesses.

Then once more the procession starts up the Sacred Way
toward the Telesterion, toward the most awesome of initiations,
the Epopteia (the state of "Having Seen"). Now, all but the
torch of Iacchos are extinguished. The crowd is again subdued
by the darkness of the night around them and the fearful
expectation. The *kykeon's* fermented potency and perhaps some
opium seeds to chew upon have taken hold of the fears of the
crowd, no longer boisterous. Ominous silence intensifies the
muffled shuffling of feet as they feel their way along the dark,
stony path lit only by the flickering torch of Iacchos at the lead.
Behind this "torchbearer" priest walks the sacred boy,
Demophoön, the boy of the hearth, a youth who has been
chosen to take a major role in the coming ceremony. He carries
an unlit torch.

The throng enters the Telesterion, passing through the entrance doors into the cold tomblike sanctuary. Here, in the
hushed blackness, they fan out to the right and left of the
Anaktoron, in the center of that solemn enclosure. The door of
the Anaktoron is closed. No words are spoken; this highest of
initiations is beyond words. The Hierophant, "he who makes
holy things appear,"[26] takes his place under a canopy to the
left, which is attached to the small sanctuary. Except for the one

[26]Ibid., p. 90.

fitful torch in the hand of Iacchos, the blackness of the Telesterion closes in oppressively, and an empty quiet hangs
shroud-like over the awestruck audience. The feat and apprehension are appalling.

At the very moment when the intense black silence becomes
unbearable for these drugged and frightened mortals, the crash
from an enormous gong deafens the throng. The *echeion*, the
bronze instrument of Hades, beaten by the Hierophant, calls
upon Persephone to rise up with the same thunderous voice
with which it summons the dead down to the underworld.

Simultaneously, the door to the Anaktoron is flung open.
Iacchos also invokes the maiden to appear, throwing his fragile
torch into the holy of holies. The entire room is instantly
ablaze. The spectators are so blinded they must turn away,
unable to face the heat and glare, but not before they have
glimpsed in the holocaust the vision of Persephone, arms out-
stretched, rising immortal in the flame, her ineffably beautiful
form ablaze with joy and welcome. The Hierophant, under
cover of his canopy, for the heat is intense, pushes forward the
young Demophoön. This year-baby thrusts his unlit torch into
the immortal flame. As the torch catches the fire, the door to
the Anaktoron closes with a clang. The Hierophant calls out his
song, "Brimo has given birth to Brimos! that is, the Strong One
to the Strong One."[27] In the ensuing, expanding echoes, the
High Priest, by the light of the new fire held by the child,
silently produces an ear of wheat, holding it high for all to
share. Its form, too, is torchlike.

The hall rustles with sighs of participation in this second
mysterious source of energy, the single ear of wheat. The
tension is eased; the deafening gong is still; the blinding blaze is
shut away. The multitude, which had been struck mute by the
overwhelming drama, can once again exchange whispers and
embraces, wondering at the power and the glory they have
experienced in shared vision but will never be able to speak of,
for there are no words to fit this inner revelation. It only *is* and
forever. From now on, the initiated will be as joined as the bundles
of myrtle branches they carry. For they have witnessed together
both the macrocosm—love, the unindividualized blinding fire
of life's force, the driving force of the psyche, as personified in

[27]Ibid., p. 92.

the fire by the immortal maiden—and the microcosm of the ear of wheat, representing the unending, growing power of food energy on earth. Both are forever producing and delivering sustenance for man's twin driving forces, sex and hunger. Forever and ever, around and around, never static, no death, only return and return and return.

There is no death. Demophoön, the new year-baby is also immortal. He rekindles his torch each year from Persephone's flame before she returns to the underworld of the unconscious to be fired anew in the embrace of Dionysos, the Lover, the Loosener. In the grains of wheat, she too will now return to the soil, where, in death, she will be born again on earth, to renew life's energy. "Blessed is he who, after beholding this, enters upon the way beneath the earth: he knows the end of life and its beginning."[28] Those poetic words are from Pindar.

"The source of life lies deeper than the beginning of life."[29]

Dawn is coming. The crowd moves slowly out of the great Telesterion, back down the Sacred Way. They halt for one more important ceremony at the cave of Plouton. On either side of the cave stands a tall jar, shaped like a top, full of fresh water, the *plemochoai*, placed to the west and to the east of the chthonian chasm. There the Hierophant waits. When all are gathered to watch and partake, he steps up to the vessel on the east. He lifts it up; and, as he empties the liquid into the cleft, the entire crowd looks up to the clouds hiding the dawn and calls out "Hye!" perhaps meaning "rain" or "flow." Then he turns to the western *plemochoè*; and, as he pours, while all look this time toward the earth, he and the group call out "Kye!" These words, too, are untranslatable, except perhaps as "be fruitful" or "grow."

According to Hesychius, the Hierophant then faces toward the crowd and calls out over the newly initiated the words: "Sound the conch—enough."[30]

---

[28]Ibid., p. 15.   [29]Ibid., p. xxxiii.   [30]Harrison, p. 161.

A Study of Authors with Reflections on Language and Jung's Typology

WAYNE K. DETLOFF

HUMAN LIFE WITHOUT LANGUAGE would be difficult for us to imagine. Language is intimately related to thought and consciousness and is absolutely vital to our educational system and day-to-day functioning. Regardless of one's general level of native ability or one's natural aptitude for language, there is evident need for everyone to develop a certain minimal competence with it.

In recent years various aspects of language have captured my attention. One has to do with the basic sounds which make up words. A system that deals very effectively with this originated in Japan and is known as the Kototama principle. The translation of Kototama is "word soul."

In the period immediately following World War II, when Japan's emperor relinquished the divine aspects of his traditional role, a number of secret traditions carried by the emperor's family became available. The main recipient of this body of material on the Kototama was Sensei Koji Ogasawara. In the United States, it was introduced by Sensei M. Nakazona, who is also one of the most eminent experts in Aikido. The amount of material in English is still quite limited. The Kototama principle is closely linked with the *I Ching* and especially with Shintoism and the *Kojiki*. It is said to date back some 4,000 years, which would be considerably before the introduction of written language to Japan (around A.D. 700). I understand the Kototama is not well known in Japan at the present time and does not appear to be gaining any significant popularity.

According to the Kototama, the sounds are the most central essences, to which trigrams of the *I Ching*, numbers, elements, color, etc., are related. The sounds contain all the essential possibilities and thus together form a complete matrix or "mirror" for reflecting almost any content. These sounds are the basis for building words regardless of the specific language. To draw an analogy with chemistry, sounds make up words as the elements make up molecules. Thus, in our framework, the sounds are related in a deep, essential, elemental way to the archetypes.

Apparently language followed the Kototama principle more closely 2,000 years ago than it has in recent times. The principle was "hidden" in order to make possible the next stage of civilization. There is an implication that a kind of consciousness existed which needed to be sacrificed to allow for the development of science and the space age. Now that the scientific era is well established, the Kototama principle can be revealed again. Thus, there is an attempt also to understand this principle in relation to history.

One can grasp some of the concepts of the Kototama intellectually, but the real essence requires deep concentration through time. It is truly one of the most introverted approaches I have encountered. It can be fully appreciated only when viewed much more broadly than merely as a basis of language. When one develops the right deep connection with the Kototama, it becomes a "mirror" against which one reflects his concerns in order to have a better sense of their nature, place, and relationship to a totality.

Working with very disturbed patients with whom relationship and communication are tenuous and extremely difficult often leaves me reflecting about what makes possible those beautiful moments which so deeply move both the patient and me, and which seem to affect the process and endure in the patient's later consciousness. Most often, tuning in to the affect and the archetypal aspects of gesture, posture, and the fragmented verbal expressions is clearly central. I also feel there are aspects of language to be studied so that we can more consciously facilitate the process and perhaps help sensitive therapists improve their work. Psychological type is another consideration in this area but obviously not the only one. I have contemplated the problem a great deal. Usually I have had to settle for some general statement about intuition, Eros, or relationship with the unconscious. The subtle aspects elude me, and truly satisfactory formulations are not forthcoming. We are dealing more with an art than a science, but I've never abandoned the urge to include science also.

Working with children also demands attention to language. Non-verbal approaches, such as sandplay, are valuable, but often they are not, in themselves, sufficient. I have been interested in aspects of learning problems and in the sub-group of children presently called "minimally brain-damaged." Some of these children could be better understood and helped by Jung's contributions. From clinical experience over the years, I have developed a conviction that Jung's typology is very important in studying and understanding this group. An example may help to clarify how this might work. Of all the types, introverted feeling-sensation or sensation-feeling appears to occur with least frequency. It may be that, by natural inclination, people so typed have less need to communicate. But it is also possible that early attempts to communicate have gone badly when others failed to hear or appreciate what for them was the intrinsic message. When this happens, the sense of frustration and disappointment that follows readily reinforces any natural disposition to be silent. In my experience, one often has to be extraordinarily patient in encouraging persons of this type to give full expression to their thoughts. There are some generalizations about teaching and learning which seem especially important for these people. In giving them oral instruction or assistance, one has to be especially careful to pace it at just the rate that can be taken in and related to in a completely individual way. Especially to persons whose typology is different, these people may appear slow and negativistic. Often trying to relate to their way and trying to be available for only minimal, concise direction or demonstration can be far more effective than elaborate, thought-out formulations which may overwhelm them.

Jung's typology has been of enduring interest to me. My clinical and research experience has convinced me that there are much deeper implications in it than have generally been appreciated or explored. In my view, it is more accessible than some other aspects of Jung's contribution to the kind of experimental approach acceptable to research methodologists. It can be taught well enough to have utility for educators who have not been deeply analyzed and trained as analysts. I see some urgency to studying this problem in relation not only to reading, writing, and spoken language but also to mathematics, which can be viewed partially as involving a special kind of language.

The functions give a sense of the patterns of the development of consciousness, that is, "normal" ego organization, with definite implications for the relationship of the conscious to the unconscious. The functions are considered qualitatively different and are much more than mere clusters of attitudes, preferences, and behavior patterns. It is believed that this typology cuts across cultures, though any one culture may favor the development of certain types, and the superficial manifestations will differ from group to group.

I have often wondered about the degree to which one could perceive changing consciousness on a collective level within his own lifetime. Jung's first paper on typology, in 1913, dealt almost exclusively with introversion-extraversion,[1] and, within a decade later, his complete description of typology appeared.[2] It seems reasonable to suppose from this sequence that, at that time, even for a person of his calibre, it was easier to become conscious of the attitude than of the functions. A few years later, there was a flurry of interest in questionnaires for introversion-extraversion, but none of the reports in the literature dealt with the functions. It was another two decades before the articles of Gray and Wheelwright appeared, and neither their work nor that of Myers and Briggs attracted much attention until the 1960's. During this time, introversion and extraversion became household terms which loosely approximated Jung's concepts. The functions did not become known outside the small Jungian circle. Brief mention of the typology was occasionally made in textbooks, but these short passages showed little understanding, especially of the functions. Professionals and laymen now seem to have a greater interest in the subject and are able to grasp it more readily than seemed possible a decade or two ago. I do not believe this is due merely to clearer

[1]"A Contribution to the Study of Psychological Types," CW 6, Appendix 1.
[2]*Psychological Types* (orig. 1921), CW 6.

and more dynamic presentations of the material, though this may be a factor also. I am inclined to see it as evidence that, even among professional psychologists and psychiatrists, nearly half a century was necessary before the concept of the functions and their dynamic clinical implications could be assimilated. Among recognized Jungian analysts, there is a considerable range of appreciation and interest in the concept of typology. Along with that are significant variations in the understanding of the depth and dynamic aspects of the theory. This is consistent with Plaut's survey.[3] It would seem that changes in the levels of collective consciousness are clearly related to the problem of understanding Jung's typology.

*   *   *

For quite a long time, I have speculated about language and whether patterns in writing style might be related to typology. The area which seems to offer the best avenue for research is that of stylometry. In this field, intriguing work has been done by A. Q. Morton and his colleagues at the University of Edinburgh. They have recently developed a quantitatively based method for studying disputed authorship.[4] Morton is a student of history and first developed his techniques with the Greek language. More recently he has worked with English texts and documents, for example, the plays of Shakespeare and the writings of Alexander Hamilton and James Madison in the *Federalist* papers. He is now involved in forensic work. This includes studying the authenticity of documents, e.g., written police statements or pages of a will. His work has been accepted in the courts of Great Britain and Canada.

Morton's method involved selecting simple words which occurred with such frequency that a statistical approach could be used to study their use in a sample of two thousand words or less. According to a count of the text of American magazine articles in the 1930's, the ten most frequent words make up about 22 per cent of the total words used. The same count shows that the fifty most frequent words account for about 42

[3]A. Plaut, "Analytical Psychologists and Psychological Types: Comment on Replies to a Survey," *Journal of Analytical Psychology* 17 (1972), 137-52.
[4]S. Michaelson, A. Q. Morton, and N. Hamilton-Smith, *To Couple Is the Custom: A General Stylometric Theory of Writers in English*, unpublished; A. Q. Morton, S. Michaelson, and N. Hamilton-Smith, *To Couple Is the Custom: A General Solution to Problems of Authorship in English Texts and Documents*, unpublished (read in ms.).

per cent of the writing.[5] Morton's way of increasing efficiency over previous attempts to study uniqueness of style was to note the preferred position of the word in the sentence; for example, whether the word was first or last. More often he has studied collocations—i.e., instances in which the word is preceded by, or followed by, another commonly occurring word or class of words such as an adjective. These combinations and proportions are more important than the mere frequency of the single word.

Morton apparently was challenged by a statement made by William Allan Neilson and Charles Jarvis Hill, editors of the *New Cambridge Shakespeare*, who wrote in the introduction to *Pericles*, "Shakespeare's hand is present and predominant in Acts 3-5, but scarcely if at all detectable in Acts 1-2."[6] Morton presents a statistical analysis and comments, "It is difficult to see such grounds for his confidence; there is no statistically significant difference in any preferred position or collocation."[7]

In order to determine whether the literacy style of one writer could be imitated by another, Morton examined a novel Jane Austen had begun to write during her lifetime but that had been completed many years after her death by an admirer and student of her work. The novel was *Sanditon*, first published in London in 1975. The title page reads, "Sanditon; a Novel by Jane Austen and Another Lady." Morton compared a sample from the section Austen had written with samples from two of her other novels, *Emma* and *Sense and Sensibility*, and with a sample from the section written by The Other Lady. The differences he found were significant, and he concluded, "The probability that the work of The Other Lady could be accepted as a genuine sample of Miss Austen is less than one in one thousand million."[8]

Morton made a similar study of Sherlock Holmes stories published after Sir Arthur Conan Doyle's death at the instigation of the owner of the copyright, who sought to capitalize on Holmes's popularity. These books, patterned after Doyle's suc-

[5]Edward L. Thorndike and Irving Lorge, *The Teacher's Word Book of 30,000 Words* (New York, 1944).
[6]William Shakespeare, *Complete Plays and Poems*, ed. William Allan Neilson and Charles Jarvis Hill (Boston, 1942).
[7]Michaelson, Morton, and Hamilton-Smith.
[8]Ibid.

cesses, were the work of two professional writers, Nicholas Utechin and Austin Mitchelson. Utechin had written several books about Holmes and was admired as a successful imitator of the "Holmes style." Morton found marked differences in style between the works of Doyle and the Holmes stories written by his imitators. The study also revealed pronounced characteristics in the styles of both Mitchelson and Utechin that readily identified the portions each had written.

Another interesting observation of Morton's was that the literary characteristics of an author are stable over the years even though crucial events occur in his life. For example, he studied Sir Walter Scott's *The Antiquary*, written in 1816, and *Castle Dangerous*, written fifteen years later. The events in Scott's life during the intervening years included a period of great prosperity, which ended with sudden bankruptcy in 1826, and the loss of his wife in the same year. He suffered attacks of gallstones from 1817 to 1819 and a series of strokes, first in 1823, then two in 1830, and a fourth in 1831, before the fatal one in 1832. Morton also examined the works of Henry James to determine whether his move from America to England in 1875 had affected his writing style. The books he studied were *The American*, published in 1877, and *The Ambassadors*, published in 1903. He found that the writing styles of both Scott and James did not change in spite of marked alterations in their life patterns.

When Morton developed his technique for studying uniqueness of style, it seemed he had also provided a method which could be used to investigate whether there are generalized patterns related to psychological type. Morton had gathered data on ten authors with considerable care, tedious work, and expense. The authors, their birth dates, and the writings which were sampled are shown in Table 1.

From each author's writing, Morton and his colleagues amassed 70 counts. In most instances, he made a count of key words, and, in addition, he counted a particular usage of that key word, such as the preferred position. For example, he counted the number of times such words as "for," "in," or "that" occurred and the times each was used as the first word of the sentence, also the times it occurred as the last word. Other counts of the special usage were collocations, an example of

TABLE 1

Author	Dates	Book Sampled	Words in Sample
Greene, Graham	1904-	Brighton Rock, 1938	4,245
Huxley, Aldous	1894-1963	Point Counter Point, 1928	4,463
Lewis, C. S.	1898-1963	That Hideous Strength, 1945	6,108
Maugham, Somerset	1874-1965	The Moon and Sixpence, 1919	4,757
Murdoch, Iris	1919-	The Severed Head, 1961	5,022
Snow, C. P.	1905-	The Masters, 1951	4,462
Waugh, Evelyn	1903-1966	The Loved One, 1948	4,538
Wells, H. G.	1866-1946	Tono-Bungay, 1909	7,257
Woolf, Virginia	1882-1941	Night and Day, 1920	8,292
Wyndham, John	1903-1969	The Seeds of Time, 1956	4,800

Note: The sample of writing for each author ranged from 4,245 words to 8,292 words, with a mean of 5,394 and a standard deviation of 1,397. For statistical analysis, the data were adjusted by proportion to make each author's sample size comparable to 5,000 words per subject.

At publication date of the book sampled, the mean age of the authors was forty-three years with a standard deviation of six years and a range from thirty-four to fifty-three years.

which would be the times the word "for" is followed by "a" or the number of times it is followed by "the." In most of his analysis, it was possible for him to deal simultaneously with two figures: the key word and the special usage. Thus, his 70 counts were reduced to 49 comparisons when studying the similarity or difference of the two samples of writing.

Morton's study is interesting in itself, but he has also made a specific contribution to a new area of research by designing a method of quantifying very specific, subtle aspects of style. This allows for a quantitative method of relating generalized patterns in writing style to psychological type. He has chosen a particular set of comparisons, but the list could be expanded for other uses. The number of comparisons is limited only by the frequency of occurrence. That is, there must be reasonable expectation that the sample of writing chosen will include an adequate number of the words to be compared. The words chosen are mostly function words (articles, prepositions, conjunctions) and are relatively free of content, probably differing very little regardless of whether the subject matter is social science, natural science, or the arts.

With Morton's generosity in permitting his data on these authors to be used to study another aspect of writing style, an interesting pilot study was formulated. The purpose of this pilot study was twofold.

First, from the point of view of theory, the data amassed by Morton on these ten authors were studied for generalized patterns of writing style. The discovery of patterns which occur in as yet unconscious ways would suggest that something transcends, or operates independently of, the educational system. The confirmation of a relationship between writing style and Jung's typology would be further evidence that there is a deeply inherent propensity for individuals to develop according to the patterns sketched by Jung in his scheme of psychological types.

Second, the data were studied to determine whether the variables with which Morton worked might be the basis for developing a new technique for establishing psychological type. This would be important because it would be on the basis of a stable performance rather than of transparent, stated preferences, as in multiple-choice questionnaires, where the marked items have high face validity. (Face validity here means that an item would appear to measure what it is intended to measure.) On these questionnaires social desirability or wishful thinking can influence the response of individuals who have a little knowledge of Jungian concepts. Unless one made a concerted effort to contrive a different style based on specific research findings, misleading results would be minimized or probably eliminated in this new approach. By being able to evaluate type at different levels, one could better take into consideration the innate disposition of the subject in contrast to environmental influence. This would be especially important in cases where—for example—the subject is oversensitive to expectations of his family or others and attempts to live up to their image of him.

Special skills and adaptation that have been achieved through discipline and training may differ in quality from an innate function that becomes fully developed in a natural way. This emphasizes the fact that possessing a well-developed function may be different from being able to do a specific task for which a particular function would ordinarily make a special contribution. In other words, a good level of general intelligence and persistent attempts may compensate for an otherwise poorly developed function. Also, there may be instances of special access to a function in a circumscribed situation, e.g., that of an artist who uses a generally less accessible function in certain creative work. We would like to have tools to study these problems.

In short, this method might allow a more subtle evaluation and perhaps penetrate to a deeper level than is possible except in deep and successful analysis.

The first task in this study was to establish the psychological type of the ten authors. Previous research experience had confirmed the clinical observation that one's own typology tends to bias his view of the problem of psychological type.[9] Further, the authors and their work were not well enough known to me to be typed by myself.

It was decided to obtain from informed friends and colleagues a consensus of ratings of the author's type in Jungian terms. Raters were asked to give their impression of a writer's type in each instance where they felt they had a valid impression, realizing that the amount of biographical information or familiarity with the author's writing would vary from rater to rater. This kind of "loose structure" would surely tend to reduce inter-rater reliability, but the compromise was necessary in order to make the task of getting the ratings a reasonable one. Raters were sought who were familiar with literature. None was aware of the aspects of style with which this pilot study is concerned. All the raters had considerable personal Jungian analysis and had a working understanding of the theory. Ratings were made by placing a check along a 12-cm. line with the mid-point indicated. This made possible a scale value which would include the rater's confidence in the rating and/or the degree to which the author was differentiated on that axis. At the same time, the rating could be dichotomized according to Jung's theory. The format is as follows shown below (reduced in size):

[9]Katherine Bradway, "Jung's Psychological Types: Classification by Test versus Classification by Self," *Journal of Analytical Psychology* 9 (1964), 129-35.

		Cannot evaluate
Author	_____	
Extrav.	_____	Introv.
Sensation	_____	Intuition
Thinking	_____	Feeling

For ease of exposition, I have previously introduced two additional terms, which Jung did not use.[10] These terms, "axis" and "dimension," will be used interchangeably in this paper to refer to any of the three pairs usually experienced as polar opposites: attitude (introversion-extroversion); perception or irrational (sensation-intuition); and judgment or rational (thinking-feeling). This follows the concept of the three-dimensional model of a sphere representing the whole, with the three axes being uncorrelated and 90° to each other, thus also fitting the simplest factor analytic model.

Consensus was not clearly decisive for some authors on one or more dimensions, partly because they were less well known and partly because the raters' responses were so divided as to differ minimally from chance. From an overall statistical point of view, the reliability was quite satisfactory. Consensus was based on the median of the raters and is shown in Table 2.

Using the consensus ratings shown in Table 2, an item analysis of the available data was made. The original 70 variables were used, and, in addition, 49 ratios were created from the original 70 variables. Where Morton had used two figures simultaneously, a ratio was created so that a single value could be used. Each of the total of 119 variables was studied for each axis. At eight levels of significance from $p < .0001$ to $p < .1$, there were consistently more items on each of the three dimensions than would be expected by chance. This immediately suggests that the group of variables studied are indeed related to the psychological types.

The items were also studied by using cluster analysis[11] and orienting the axis according to Jungian typology. For practical reasons, only the 87 most promising of the 119 were retained. Approximately two-thirds of the variance could be accounted

[10]Wayne K. Detloff, "Psychological Types: Fifty Years After," *Psychological Perspectives* 3 (1972), 62-73.
[11]Robert C. Tryon and Daniel E. Bailey, *Cluster Analysis* (New York, 1970).

TABLE 2

Author	Attitude	Judgment	Perception
Greene, Graham	Introverted*	Feeling*	Sensation*
Huxley, Aldous	Introverted*	Thinking	Intuition
Lewis, C. S.	Introverted	Thinking	Intuition
Maugham, Somerset	Extraverted	Thinking*	Sensation
Murdoch, Iris	Introverted	Thinking	Intuition
Snow, C. P.	Extraverted	Thinking	Sensation*
Waugh, Evelyn	Extraverted*	Thinking	Sensation
Wells, H. G.	Extraverted	Thinking	Intuition
Woolf, Virginia	Introverted	Feeling*	Intuition
Wyndham, John	Introverted	Feeling*	Intuition*

*Rating not clearly decisive.

Note: Since Wyndham was not sufficiently well known for statistical analysis, he was omitted from the reliability figures below, and consensus was determined by a discussion with a small group of raters.

The average correlation among the 28 raters, who rated ten or more of the 27 ratings utilized in this study, was .41. When this is adjusted by the Spearman-Brown formula, as suggested by Guilford,[12] the overall reliability is .95.

An overall split-half reliability for all dimensions is .81; with a Spearman-Brown correction, it is .89. For introversion-extraversion only, the split-half reliability is .86; corrected it is .92. For sensation-intuition, it is .84; corrected, it is .91. For thinking-feeling, however, it is only .40; corrected, it is .57.

Individual ratings for each author on each dimension were dichotomized and compared to 50-50 chance. The overall variation from chance was considered very highly significant, in the range of one in a hundred thousand.

The means of the ratings for each author on each dimension were compared (single sample t-test) with the midpoint of the scale (theoretical population mean). Seventeen (63%) of the 27 reached the .05 level of significance. The number of authors rated at the .05 level of significance was evenly distributed among the three axes (attitude, 6; perception, 6; judgment, 5).

After inspecting these two approaches, the asterisks were added to the above table to indicate the most doubtful classifications.

[12]J. Guilford, Fundamental Statistics in Psychology and Education, 4th ed. (New York, 1965).

for by three clusters approximating the three Jungian dimensions. When three additional oblique clusters, which appeared
to be mixtures (extroverted-thinking, introverted-feeling;
intuitive-thinking, sensation-feeling; and sensation-thinking,
intuitive-feeling) were included, 95 per cent of the variance was
accounted for. A large number of items had very high factor
loadings, and 74 items were actually scored. Each cluster had
uncommonly high reliability, each above .97. Some of the very
high reliability could be understood as a known overlap in
items. Much of the overlap is due to the fact that ratios were
created from variables which were retained. However, the
cluster analysis suggests considerable internal consistency in
the variables. This seems less likely if the items that appeared to
be significant were merely chance happenings which occurred
because the sample was small.

Utilizing the discriminant function and the best individual
variables or cluster scores, the authors' classifications on each of
the three dimensions were reconstructed with 100 per cent
accuracy. This, in itself, is not surprising, but the extent of the
separation had a $p < .0001$ for attitude and $p < .00001$ for
the functions when the best individual variables were used. If
one included selected cluster scores with individual variables,
the probability figure was way beyond the one in a hundred
thousand. Further, for the functions, there were enough variables remaining after the first run to again classify correctly all
of the authors on both axes with a $p < .0001$.

It is important to note that the discriminant function is a very
powerful statistical method, the number of authors was small,
and the scores were being applied to the same population as
that utilized to select the variables. Also, there are problems in
utilizing levels of significance in reasoning about strength of
relationship and importance. It would be unlikely that future
applications will do as well without considerably more research,
but, in spite of these qualifying considerations, these findings
would suggest that this line of research seems worthy of further
investigation.

It is interesting to note that the number of variables identified in this study as being related to judgment or perception is
greater than those related to attitude. In addition, when the
very best variables were used to reconstruct the type of the

authors, the separation into the polar opposites was significant to a greater degree for the functions than for the attitude. This is in contrast to previous work where attitude is associated with greater statistical significance. For example, in studying congruence between self-type for a group of Jungian analysts and questionnaire indices,[13] there was good agreement on attitude (range of 87 to 96 percent) while on the other two axes the agreement was less (range of 76 to 83 per cent). The Gray Wheelwright was used in both of these studies; the Myers-Briggs was also used in the first study. What is suggested by these findings is that this new approach might help fill in just where the greatest problem in studying typology has been encountered.

The findings of' this pilot study are consistent with the hypothesis that subtle aspects of' language style are related to psychological type. Further, there are converging findings to suggest that a method may be developed for evaluating attitude and function by studying writing style.

[13]Bradway, *op. cit.*; Katherine Bradway and Wayne K. Detloff, "Incidence to Psychological Types among Jungian Analysts Classified by Self and by Test," *Journal of Analytical Psychology* 21 (1976), 134-46.

A Psychological Interpretation of Meyrink's *The Golem*

NEIL W. RUSSACK

THE GOLEM, a novel by Gustav Meyrink first published in Germany in 1915, is narrated in the first person. We do not know much about the narrator. He does not even have a name. he is a stonecutter working in the ghetto of Prague; he is also able to restore old manuscripts. He is suffering from amnesia, and that means loss of personal identity. We do not know till the end of the story that this loss of identity is due to his having taken Athanasius Pernath's hat by mistake. We only know he is under some strange influence. It is a sort of psychosis. His memory of his personal unconscious has been eclipsed, and therefore he has a direct connection with the unconscious images in their pure form. In this sense his strange experiences are similar to those of a patient in a mental hospital.

The main characters include Hillel, a Kabbalist, who helps the narrator put the experiences he has into a natural order. There is also Hillel's daughter, Miriam, with whom he falls in love and who helps him to appreciate the mystery of the spiritual aspect of life. And there is Athanasius Pernath, whose name Jung says means the "immortal one", clearly one of the images of the self. There are too many other figures and all too many experiences to relate here. But I thought I would relate four important scenes that will give a sense of the story. The central figure is the golem. It is known that somewhere in the ghetto there exists an autonomous figure known as the Golem, and there is a window to an unknown room in one of the houses where he is supposed to live. The narrator, in a strange state of mind, encounters the Golem without knowing it and only later realizes that it is causing evil things to happen whenever it appears.

Gershom Scholem, in *On the Kabbalah and Its Symbolism*, presents the legend of the Golem as it was described by Jakob Grimm in 1808.

After saying certain prayers and observing certain fast days, the Polish Jews make the figure of a man from clay or mud, and when they pronounce the miraculous Shemhamphoras (the name of God) over him, he must come to life. He cannot speak, but he understands fairly well what is said or commanded. They call him golem and use him as a servant to do all sorts of housework. But he must never leave the house. On his forehead is written *emeth* (truth); every day he gains weight and becomes somewhat larger and stronger than all the others in the house, regardless of how little he was to begin with. For fear of him, they therefore erase the first letter, so that nothing remains but *meth* (he is dead), whereupon he collapses and turns to clay again.[1]

Meyrink portrays the Golem as one who has escaped, a form the Polish Jews recognized. Instead of being a servant, he has become an autonomous being similar to Frankenstein's monster. This is a figure not in itself evil but having an evil effect because it is an unrecognized bearer of self-realization.

Scholem compares the Golem to Adam, the first man:

At a certain stage in his creation Adam is designated as "golem." "Golem" is a Hebrew word that occurs only once in the Bible, in Psalm 139:16, which Psalm the Jewish tradition put into the mouth of Adam himself. Here probably, and certainly in the later sources, "golem" means the unformed, amorphous. There is no evidence to the effect that it meant "embryo," as has sometimes been claimed. In the philosophical literature of the Middle Ages it is used as a Hebrew term for matter, formless *hyle*. . . . In this sense, Adam was said to be "golem" before the breath of God had touched him.[2]

In Scholem's description of the first creation of Adam as Golem, which indicates the long history of the legend, we see that the Golem represents medieval man—in contrast to psychic or spiritual man, in the Kabbalistic tradition.

In Meyrink's novel, the first indication that the problem to be solved is redemption of the archetypal shadow comes in the chapter called "Awake." The narrator has been in a psychotic condition, with catatonic symptoms, in the previous chapter.

Hillel speaks to the narrator:

"Hear and understand. The man who sought you out, and whom you call the Golem, signifies the awakening of the soul through the innermost life of

[1]Gershom Scholem, *On the Kabbalah and Its Symbolism*, tr. Ralph Manheim (New York, 1965), p. 159.
[2]Ibid., p. 161.

the spirit. Each thing that earth contains is nothing more than an everlasting symbol clothed in dust. . . . Nothing that takes shape unto itself but was once a spirit.

"Two paths there are, running parallel courses—the way of life and the way of death. You took unto yourself the book of *Ibbur* and read therein. Your soul is fecund now with the Spirit of Life.

"Men tread not a path at all, neither that of life nor death. They drive like chaff before the wind. In the Talmud it is written: 'Before God made the world, he held a mirror to his creatures, that in it they might behold the sufferings of the spirit and the raptures that ensue therefrom. Some of them took up the burden of suffering. But others refused, and those God struck out of the Book of Life.' But you tread a path you have chosen of your own free will, even though as yet you know it not. You are self-elected. Do not torture yourself. As knowledge comes, so comes also recollection. *Knowledge and recollection are one and the same thing.*"[3]

Hillel explains to the narrator that the Golem has sought him out in order to awaken him, and the healing experience is described as a death and rebirth, which means an awakening to consciousness. Hillel is his guru here, and, although Hillel is not old (only forty-five), he has the wisdom of the Wise Old Man archetype, when he says "knowledge and recollection are one and the same thing."

The narrator then has the following vision.

I looked up, and suddenly became aware that the room was full of forms that stood round us in a circle. Some were in white robes like grave-clothes, as worn by rabbis of olden days; others wore three-cornered hats, and shoes with silver buckles.[4]

This is the vision of former rabbis who seem to be emerging from the past in a revival of life from death. In other words, the spirit of resurrection is evoked, along with the memory of previous ancestors from the eighteenth century (thus the three-cornered hats). At the end of the chapter he has another vision.

The book of *Ibbur* rose before me, with two letters flaming in it: one signifying the Archetype Woman with the pulse that beat like an earthquake, the other, at an infinite distance, the hermaphrodite on the pearly throne, with the crown of red wood upon its head.[5]

The reconciling symbol appears first as the "Archetype Woman with the pulse that beats like an earthquake," presum-

[3]Gustav Meyrink, *The Golem*, tr. Madge Pemberton (London and New York, 1928; repr. 1972, Prague and San Francisco), pp. 71-2.
[4]Ibid., p. 73.   [5]Ibid., p. 77.

ably to counteract the negative power of the shadow, but then it gives way to the "hermaphrodite on the pearly throne" as reconciling the opposites. The word "Ibbur," according to Meyrink, means "The Soul's Conception."

But all this is anticipatory, like initial dreams in analysis. The hero still has to encounter the full force of the archetypal shadow.

Then he meets the Golem in his human form in prison. His name is Laponder.

A little, slender, still youngish man, carefully clad, though without his hat, like all newly introduced prisoners, stood bowing politely before me.

He was clean shaven, like an actor, and his large, almond-shaped eyes, with a bright green gleam in them had the strange peculiarity of not seeming to see me, for all they gazed at me so directly. Almost as though his spirit were absent from the body.[6]

Laponder admits to the crimes of murder and rape. Meyrink makes us realize that the narrator is now somewhat identified with Athanasius Pernath, whose hat he took by mistake. Athanasius tells Laponder of his earlier vision in which he encounters a headless man. The headless man is the Golem in the general archetypal image of the shadow, while Laponder is its human form. In place of a head, there is a nebulous globe-shaped mist. Athanasius tries to put many sorts of heads on the torso, but the only one that fits is that of the Egyptian Ibis. Ibis is the emblem of the Egyptian god Thoth, who resembles, in classical mythology, Hermes or Mercurius, the bringer of change. The headless man offers Athanasius a handful of little red and black seed pods. Instead of accepting them, however, Athanasius knocks them out of his hand. Laponder, the murderer-rapist, tells Athanasius that he too had experienced the same vision but says that he took the pods.

"So you struck them out of his hand?" he murmured thoughtfully to himself. "Never would I have believed that a third way could have been found."[7]

Had Athanasius accepted the pods, he would have chosen the path of death as did the murderer. Meyrink labels the colors red and black, both colors of death, which he calls bad. If Athanasius had simply refused them, he would have chosen the

[6]Ibid., p. 242.   [7]Ibid., p. 253.

path of life. But he neither accepts nor rejects them; instead he knocks them out of his hand, thereby choosing a third way. He does not accept the offer as it is presented. By refusing to accept an either/or situation, he denies the validity of the offer. He will not even allow himself to enter into a dialogue with the Golem. He refuses the situation that the Golem puts before him.

By denying the Golem, he seems to redeem the whole history of man. At this point in the story, the images of all the faces of his ancestors pass by him, century after century. It is not only himself that he is saving but all mankind. The conscious work the individual does has an impact upon the world. By denying the shadow, the hero finds a new religious attitude. Laponder says,

"If you had refused them, then would you most certainly have chosen the path of life, but the pods, that signify the powers of magic, would not in that case have remained behind. You tell me they rolled on the ground. That is to say, they stayed behind here, and will be in the custody of your forefathers until the time of their ripening. Then will the faculties still latent within you spring into being."

I could not understand. "My forefathers . . . you say, those pods will be in their custody?"

"All those things you have experienced," explained Laponder, "you must partly interpret in the way of symbol. That circle of blue luminous entities that closed you around was the chain of the diverse inherited personalities each mother's son is born into the world with. The soul is not 'one and indivisible'; it will ultimately become so, and thereby attain what man calls immortality; your soul consists of infinite component parts—egos innumerable, like an ant-heap is composed of multitudinous ants. You bear within yourself the *spiritual vestiges* of thousands of your forebears, the original progenitors of the face from which you sprang. It is the same with all creation. How otherwise could a chicken hatched from an incubator instantly seek forth its own peculiar nourishment, did it not contain, innate within itself, the accumulated experience of hundreds of centuries? The presence of 'instinct' reveals in both one's body and one's soul the undeniable fact of our own ancestors."[8]

If Athanasius had accepted the pods, he would be identifying with the shadow. He would then have become the shadow. Psychologically, that would mean that, if one had bad thoughts, he would identify with them. He says, "Those thoughts are who I am." If he takes them literally, he would fall into a depression.

[8]Ibid., pp. 253-4.

If I think I am what I feel, then I am accepting the seed pods. Identification with the shadow causes depression. The shadow takes over the ego.

By not accepting them, he chooses the path of life. He says, I am not the shadow. I do not have to be that thing. But it is the opposite and is too one-sided. It does not include death. He is not even conscious of the shadow.

It is a paradox. He has to accept it and reject it at the same time. That is the third way. It is the path of immortality, or individuation. It is neither death nor life. The third way is not accepting one or the other. To accept a thing means to become identified with it. One must keep one's own ego. He must accept neither death nor life and thereby become identified with neither. By knocking the seeds out of his hand down onto the earth, new life can come. Something new comes out of the destructiveness of the past. It is the path of redemption. That is the point of the book, to redeem the Golem. To bring spiritual life into man, to put the spirit into matter; that is the task of us all.

God created Adam like clay. The old Adam is unchanging and sinful. It is Adam before he has a soul. The Golem is Adam in his first creation. The Golem is the archetypal shadow. He is mechanical man. The new Adam is regenerated man. He has been redeemed.

Jung says,

The Golem is an entirely negative figure, the complete shadow of the immortal one. He began as a lump of clay and was brought to life by black magic, by writing the holy name on his brow. So he is a living being that has no soul,—a mechanism which can only be killed by wiping out the holy name. The figure occurs in many ancient Jewish legends, and Meyrink used it in free form, a personification of the horrible troubles that befall the hero through those visions.[9]

There is a third shadow figure in addition to the image of the headless man and Laponder. This person is Aaron Wassertrum, the old Jewish pawnbroker. He embodies the Golem-like materialistic man in whom no soul is apparent. He might represent that aspect of the cultural Jewish shadow.

In Meyrink's novel, the beginning of the healing process

[9]Jung, *Notes on the Seminar in Analytical Psychology; Dream Analysis*, Part 5: Winter 1929/30 (Zurich; privately circulated), pp. 93-4.

occurs with the emergence of the rabbi, a Kabbalist named Hillel, who embodies the archetypal image of the Wise Old Man, and his daughter, Miriam, who embodies the spiritual aspect of the anima. This is in contrast to the worldly aspect represented by Angelina, the other woman Athanasius cared about. It is through his relationships to these two women that he learns to love. It is the wisdom embodied in the archetypal image of the Wise Old Man and the life and love of the anima which is compensating to the ego and shadow. But real healing and redemption can only come through the ego's relation to the self. Athanasius is, of course, the self-image.

At the end of the story, the narrator comes to the simple house where Hillel and Miriam are supposed to be living. But in the morning he sees the house has been transformed.

The night before it had been the same place. Now in the morning I see that it is by no means a simple place but a very beautiful gilt gate, quite an elaborate thing, and there are two yew trees that rise up from low bushes or flowering shrubs, flanking the entrance. I see now that the wall around the garden is covered with a beautiful mosaic, made out of lapis lazuli. The God himself, an hermaphrodite, forms the two wings of the gate, the left side male, the right side female. The God is seated on a precious throne of mother-of-pearl, and his golden head is the head of a hare. The ears are erect and close together, looking like the two pages of an open book. The air is full of the smell of dew and hyacinths and I stand there a long time, astonished. It is as if a foreign world were opening before my eyes. Suddenly an old gardener or servant in the costume of the 18th century opens the gate and asks me what I want. I give him the hat of Athanasius Pernath, which I had wrapped up in paper. The servant disappears with it, but in that moment before he shuts the gate behind him, I look inside and see not a house, but a sort of marble temple, and on the steps leading up to it, I see Athanasius with Miriam leaning on his arm. Both are looking down upon the town. Miriam catches sight of me, smiles and whispers something to Athanasius. I am fascinated by her beauty. She is so young, just as young as I saw her in the dream. Athanasius then turns his head towards me and my heart almost ceases to beat. It is as if I should see myself in a mirror, such is the similarity of his face to mine. Then the gate shuts and I only see the resplendent figure of the hermaphroditic God. After a while the servant brings my hat which was in the possession of Athanasius and I hear his voice, deep, as if from the depths of the earth. He says, "Mr. Pernath is much obliged and asks you not to hold him inhospitable that he does not invite you in, since it is a strict law of the house since old that guests are not invited. He also says he has not used your hat as he noticed at once that it was not his, and he hopes that his has not caused you headache."[10]

[10]Ibid., pp. 94-5.

Meyrink ends the story with a humorous touch. This lets the reader know that these archetypal images originate in the collective unconscious and belong there. We could say the hat belonged to that principle of renewal connected with immortality. Under the influence of the hat, the hero is able to experience the death-and-rebirth archetype. Like many people, he has a close relationship with his unconscious in which he is able to identify with these archetypal images and learn from them. The danger lies in becoming inflated from a permanent identification with them. This does not happen to the hero in *The Golem*. The gate in the form of the hermaphrodite indicates a way of entering into a certain kind of knowledge, which means that, in a relative sense, the opposites are joined.

Notes on the New Culture

THOMAS E. PARKER

WE ARE LIVING IN AN AGE where our consciousness is out of tune with society. Our social system is not in keeping with our new state of consciousness, and there must be a sacrifice of the old social system. As the population's consciousness changes, it comes more and more into conflict with our social institutions. Therein lies the great source of danger, the source of violent confrontation. In a period of such change there is a need to remove the restrictions and binding influences of the past.

For example, as people stop wanting to acquire material goods, our economic system is thrown out of balance because it is based primarily on consumption. Likewise, our social system is thrown out of balance because its status is largely based on the acquisition of material goods (the good life). Until these systems are changed to function on some other basis, we have chaos. When we have a society that is functioning partly on one basis and partly on another, we have not only chaos but conflict and confusion. Our culture seems to be in this stage at the moment, and the conflict between these opposing systems and states of consciousness is rapidly reaching a climax.

The fact is that Western culture is unbalanced. It values its own products too highly. It feels in control of itself and that it has solved many of the important problems of the world. It often feels it has imposed stabilization on the world, as though it had gained control of the cycles of creation and destruction.

There is a positive side to destruction. It, as well as creation, is a cosmic principle, yet we have a natural fear and aversion to it. Destruction is associated with pain, discomfort, fear of the unknown, a sense of loss. Destruction means giving up attachments to things we consider dear to us—human relationships, relationships to experiences and ideas, to the natural world, and to our social structure.

In 1918 Jung pointed out that our civilization is standing at a great transition point.[1] Sixty years later this is still true. We are approaching the climax between man's conscious state and his social structure. Most likely this climax will come before the end of this century. Certainly the signs of social disintegration are around us everywhere. Jung noticed in 1918 that what was being interpreted as a materialistic problem was really a psychological one. Problems of World War I could not be solved economically but only with a change in man's consciousness. Now we are facing the next phase, which is to change the outer social view to coincide more accurately with the new consciousness that has already arisen but is not yet fully developed.

No society, country, culture, or group has yet successfully provided the structure necessary for this new manifestation of consciousness. A change is required of everyone and of all groups. To build the new, one must first remove the old, especially when one can see that its foundation is faulty. The new spirit can manifest itself only when the old attachments and impediments are swept away. If we allow our attachment to our own ideas and the way we think things should be to stand in the way, we will be destroyed. If we give them up, help comes, pushes our old ideas aside, and clears the way for the new manifestations.

The flaws in our previous way of thinking are only now beginning to be generally known, even though some have seen them for a long time. We have felt we knew how to make things right, at least for ourselves if not for others, and that a continuation of our development in technology would soon make things right for others as well. We have tried to create an ever-expanding society with more material possessions and without the need for limitation and sacrifice. We have expected to take all we wanted from the world without having to pay back anything.

This is only beginning to become apparent to most people, especially through our lack of resources, many of which cannot be replaced. We have had the attitude that the world should be an all-giving mother, or at least one that we could control through our science, so that, if we made a mistake, we could always develop something new to keep from suffering the

[1]"The Role of the Unconscious," CW 10, pp. 3-28.

results of that mistake. We do not like to sacrifice anything, but we are going to be called on to sacrifice a lot. Almost all of our social forms must be destroyed and will be.

Jung himself said that the world hangs by a thread, and that thread is man's psyche.[2] It is primarily the consciousness of man that is undergoing such a dramatic change, and it foreshadows the new culture. The new age will be a spiritual socialism—spiritual values, but socialist in that everyone will be seen as equal. Equality of spirit, however, is not to be confused with equality of development. Not everyone is the same.

In this period of rapid change, the new culture, primarily a change of consciousness, has to come into being in a short time. The real revolutionaries today are those people who are truly changing their own consciousness and giving up their attachment to their own ideas and ways of seeing things. This change began several hundred years ago and is reaching its climax during this century. We are leaving behind an age of darkness and materialistic consciousness.

The new consciousness is not completely established. Many changes are occurring and will continue to occur, but nevertheless the new consciousness has outstripped the changes made in our cultural institutions. The conflict is that the social institutions were formed and developed during many ages of strict materialistic consciousness. The foundations of that consciousness have begun to crumble because the concept of energy has been discovered. Science has penetrated the veil of matter and discovered energy. The delusion that matter is solid has been broken. Man's consciousness has accordingly expanded to include new realms of previously unknown knowledge. In passing the veil of the seemingly solid material universe, science found something else behind it.

Many, including Jung, have said that behind the materialistic universe is something more. For Jung it was the *unus mundus*. Others have said the world is like a great thought rather than a great machine, but our social institutions do not reflect that state of consciousness. This has produced a very unstable situation, because, when the outer forms for expressing consciousness are not in keeping with consciousness itself, conflict occurs.

[2]*C. G. Jung Speaking*, ed. William McGuire and R. F. C. Hull (B.S. XCVII, Princeton, 1977), p. 303.

Consciousness has changed everywhere throughout the world. It will continue to change until a new point of view is established in man's consciousness and his social systems.

A point of view very different from that of Western culture may provide us with a more balanced attitude toward life on this planet. India's conception of Kali, the divine goddess of nature, can be of help to us, for she contains the regenerative and destructive cycle all within herself. The passage through the world seems to be important to Kali, for she gives birth, we live, and then she consumes us at death, having nourished us in between. But there are lessons to learn during the passage through this earth. For example, we wonder why we have to die. Wouldn't it be nicer to live on forever? But what would be the result if we had to stay in this human body without dying?

First of all, there would be a tremendous limitation of experience and consciousness. We would be limited to whatever experiences could come into this particular body with its spatial problems and defects, its particular structure, as well as the collective defects that exist in our human bodies. We would be limited to knowing only about this little section of the universe. Even our limited senses give us an idea of how vast the universe is. We are like ants stuck on one tiny sand hole and only guessing what goes on somewhere else.

We are limited by the thoughts we are able to have. Just as physical tissue makes a certain commitment to development, so does the psyche. Our mind, because of the experiences we have had in this particular body, has made certain developments. Certain other developments are automatically prohibited because the structure of the mind and thoughts has gone in a certain direction. All of these are limitations. They are limitations of the infinitude of development available to each soul.

During Jung's severe heart attack, he found himself a thousand miles above India and became acutely conscious of the humiliating limitation of his body on his return to his physical form. It is India's goddess Kali, through her cruel destructiveness, who saves us from this limitation. To us her destructiveness seems cruel because it removes things we have come to consider dear. But the dearness of these attachments is a delusion and merely covers the joy that comes from the experience of consciousness which these attachments greatly inhibit.

Kali wears the skulls of many decapitated heads garlanded around her neck and carries a knife in one hand. She also has one hand upraised in a gesture that means "This is not what it seems." The decapitated heads stand for thoughts we have about ourselves in this world. These thoughts become integrated into a personality and world view. Our attachment to these things keeps us in delusion. Actually, it is only the delusion that Kali is removing, but, because we are attached to these things, we are filled with fear. If man can understand that there is nothing to fear and can let go of the old ways, he may save himself from the chaos and destruction that will otherwise overtake him.

All the universe is Kali's body. It includes suns, moons, stars, planets, animals, and human beings. She seems to object to our wanting to spend our entire existence in one little closet of that vastness. She throws us out of our non-adventurous state. Isn't this what Jung discovered when he said there is a force in life that constantly pushes one toward greater consciousness?

The earth has all sorts of aspects that range from containment to harsh devouring. There is nothing that has not been there all the time. It depends on our ability to perceive the changes. Essentially each person makes his own discoveries and perceptions. Nobody can do it for him. He cannot do it until he is ready. Our perceptions three thousand years ago depended on who was there to perceive, what state his consciousness was in, and the collective consciousness that was available. To people with deep insights, their perceptions were not limited to the collective consciousness.

For example, the attraction of the force we call gravity always existed and was noticed and understood by some even if not by the general population. There always have been people of superior perceptivity because of their higher state of development. They have understanding of the world even if the mass of people live in a particular ignorance. Not infrequently they have lived shielded from the world in seclusion. Sometimes they have been exposed to the world view but were not understood. What they talked about was not common knowledge and was often considered to be nonsense because the mass of people were not able to perceive what was there.

All knowledge and wisdom have always been there. In the

East they have always been aware of it. They have a cyclic view of knowledge. Ours is a linear one. What we are discovering now has been there all along. It's just that we haven't been aware of it. We think we are discovering something new.

There's an entirely new culture coming into being. United States, as compared with Europe, has been founded during the last 200 years. During that period, there has been a slow building-up of the new culture. We have more seeds of the new culture than Europe has.

The East has what the West needs, and vice versa. Bringing together these two cultures will show the way for the new culture to develop, but, if we try to explain India from the point of view of the West's successful materialism, it is not understood at all. It is easy to try to explain India without having any idea of what India is about. India is about the spirit. For those who still feel that all of creation is only what one can see with the naked eye, that all of creation is only that part which we can perceive with our ego consciousness, India's goddess Kali is certainly a fearsome figure.

In India she is a powerful figure. Many come to her to develop or borrow that power. Others come for enlightenment and development of the divinity within themselves. People from all castes, classes, stages of intellectual development, stages of consciousness, worship her. Some take her image literally and often perform animal sacrifices at her feet. Even human sacrifices were made at one time. But the meaning and instruction of the aspect of the Divine are nonetheless there to be received by one's own consciousness, depending on one's state of development.

Kali is considered to be dark, but we have to learn to see the dark and light as equally necessary. In the West we have not accepted enough of the darkness as a necessary part of the universe. We tend to see the darkness as negative rather than just as darkness. However, on a printed page we do not think of the print as dark or negative. Without both we could see nothing. Darkness is not meant to injure us; it is necessary to see the light.

Even the active pull of evil is necessary so that we can fight against it and become strong. Kali is the front line fighter of evil. She fights it so strongly that many people identify her with evil. They see her as the instrument of evil and death. Kali sees it as being attached to misery and limitation. Mother Kali is direct and open, even harsh. Evil, on the other hand, is cunning, indirect, manipulative, covert, hidden. For example, the sacrifice of animals for Kali is upsetting to us, but it is not upsetting to us that we have slaughterhouses where animals are killed. There is repression involved here. We must keep in mind that there is spirit in an animal, rather than killing an animal as though it were an object.

The Divine Mother, the feminine, is dark but luminescent also. She is closer than the father. One goes to the father to meet the law, but if one goes to the Divine Mother with an open heart, she forgives. If we misunderstand Kali, we misunderstand the whole process of moving on to greater consciousness. We must pay attention to the lessons she teaches. If we do not, we are "spanked" until we begin to understand. Divine Mother nourishes us after birth and cares for us but takes life away when we become used to the toys in her universe. We are forced to go through this process over and over until at last we learn to hold on to the joys of our own divinity, to the joys of our own expanded consciousness. It is only when we become the "naughty child" of the Divine Mother, and refuse to play with the toys she gives us, and cry only for her that we become free. It is like the game of hide-and-seek that children play in India. When a child tires of the game, he goes to the grandmother, who sits and watches the children, and puts his hand in hers. Then he can no longer be tagged. So with Divine Mother, or Kali: when we are tired of the game we can return to her. By accepting her wisdom rather than seeking out only ours, we can find that she represents our freedom from limiting attachments. She is the center of our own divinity.

Jung points out that what is within is also without. The first path to be trod has to be within. However, individuation is not enough. Something more has to be accomplished. Jung stated that knowing more demands a corresponding development of morality. That is occurring now, but it develops unevenly in society as well as in ourselves. Some members of our society want to continue in the old ways while others want to forge ahead. In each of us, part of us wants to hold on to the old while another part wants to move to the new.

We are forced to become more and more aware of how the world really operates. The entire universe is Divine Mother. We are part of her body. This produces a different psychic dimension from the one where we live on the earth not knowing where God is, not knowing that He acts on the inert material of the universe. We have been in a state of transition for several hundred years. The transition has progressed to the point where the incompatibility of the new consciousness with the old is becoming increasingly apparent and pressing. It is fast becoming impossible to tolerate the conflict. Soon something must change. The outer form will always follow the inner consciousness. The important leaders now are the ones who are changing themselves. Others may be more visible, but they are less important. It is important to select the right leaders to help us make this transition.

Until now our leaders have all talked in terms of the past, of modifying or altering the social system, rather than of the need to shake out the excessive materialistic concepts of the system. Of course the leaders are going to be chosen through our collective consciousness. We have to get that straight to get the proper leaders. Along with the rest of the world we have the leaders we deserve, but the crisis approaches rapidly and our time is limited. We need the right consciousness in order to get the right leaders who can pull us through a very dangerous period.

In other words, we are on the brink of the destructive aspect of the Divine Mother. A change of consciousness always precedes a change of social structure. In the present period, the inside is developing and coming out. The spiritual, as opposed to the religious side, pops up everywhere. For example, in San Francisco there is rock music on the spiritual side—how to talk to God. A new consciousness about spirit and spiritual things is coming about.

Transition is always a point of danger. As one struggles to arrive at a new point of view, one is exposed to dangerous forces during the crossing. Our world stands on the brink of such a crossing. The real hope lies in the underlying spirituality of the people of the United States, founded on the tradition of religious freedom. In this respect the United States will be one of the leaders. Our country occupies a special place in this transition because its historical beginnings lie mostly within the last two hundred years, and it contains within itself the seeds of the new structure. The United States was founded after the beginning of this change, which is now reaching its climax.

The United States is not as rigidly rooted in the past as are the institutions of Europe, whose long and still visible history extends back into the dark ages. Even though we are fettered by many differences, they are not as severe as those of Western Europe. But even for us the tie with the past is strong and will have to be broken to allow a manifestation of a growing and changing consciousness.

As Jung said, "All old truths want a new interpretation, so that they can live on in a new form."[3] For every psychological development there is a cost. The cost for our age is to give up the old ways of our being and doing and make way for the new culture.

[3] *Jung Letters*, ed. Adler, vol. 2, p. 169.

Part Three

A Hidden Life

MARY JO SPENCER

Nature loves to hide.
Heraclitus

*We are a psychic process which we do
not control, or only partly direct.*
C. G. Jung

A PATIENT WHOM I SHALL CALL JANET told me this experience from her childhood. When she was between the ages of seven and nine, she was walking along a woodland path in the backwoods hill country near the mining town in Kentucky where she lived. It was a warm summer day, and she was aware of buzzing insects in the foliage. But behind the drone she became aware of music, faint and distant at first, but gradually getting louder and closer. Finally she could distinguish a chorus of voices very light and high, but not children's voices. She stopped to listen, entranced, became aware that someplace on the path ahead there was an aura of light—not bright, but soft and luminous; it blotted out the landscape beyond. It seemed to pull her onward, and, as the singing grew louder, she began to move in its direction. Although she walked towards it, she could get no closer. It was always the same distance from her. It did not fade for some time. She was enchanted and then grieved by her experience.

Many people have had such experiences. They seem to hint at something real, but just beyond our grasp; almost within reach, but never quite attained; almost remembered, but never becoming quite focused; tangible as a fragrance, but elusive at every turn.

Their presence suggests another life hidden within us, which may touch us with an odd momentary sense of being someplace else, or of knowing something wordlessly and without conscious images. Haunting, provocative and irritating, such borderline intuitions draw us on we know not where. There is often an uneasy sense that one has forgotten something vital.

Since often there are neither words nor images, such experiences fall away easily into forgetfulness, only to surface again unexpectedly, nudged into remembrance by some seemingly trivial occurrence. Some do linger on as Janet's vision did. There was enough imagery in such a vision to give the memory capacity of the ego something to hold. Or we can be quickened into a remembering awareness by some evocative and overwhelming feeling in a dream. A memory may also surface as a by-product of the pursuit of a meditative state. And it is obvious, of course, that drugs also produce altered states of consciousness.

In presenting the clinical material in this paper, it is my hypothesis that such intangible and evocative experiences of "otherness" relate to those moments when one stands on the borderline between ordinary daily ego consciousness and altered states of being.

It is a known fact that there are "state memories" which exist only when one is in that state. In daily consciousness they are obliterated. The fact that there is a memory at all—even if it is not always available—implies a continuity. And this, too, is part of my hypothesis for the material I present. The foundation and the theme of the paper are the belief that there are such hidden lives within us all, that they are continuous, and that they do run parallel to our daily waking lives. The secret that human beings are to themselves is as mysterious as the far-flung universe.

The pivotal point of this presentation is one culminating event which surfaced, apparently quite suddenly, in Janet's therapy. It was a crucial experience for her, and one can say that it transformed her life, though little changed outwardly. The enormous change was in her attitude towards herself and towards her daily outer life—the life of the limitations of time and space, of five senses and a human body.

Her therapy was never an analysis in the formal sense; and yet I could not have wished more for her. I think of the lines of Elizabeth Barrett Browning:

> *God's gifts put man's best dreams to shame.*[1]

Janet was sixty-eight years old, widowed and childless. Her

[1]Elizabeth Barrett Browning, *Complete Poetical Works* (New York, 1919), p. 624.

jobs, her relationships, and her manner of life were cramped and limited, falling far below her intellectual abilities and her capacity to relate to people. Because of severely inhibiting factors beginning in early childhood and continuing through much of her adult life, she had never developed the ego strength necessary for a better adjustment.

There was in her an underlying current of intense sadness, at times approaching a tragic grief. She felt that life had passed her by, or, to put it more actively, that she had not lived her life. Indeed little did, or could, change in her outer life. She had neither the resources of physical energy nor those of psychological strength necessary for a radical shift in her pattern of living. Nevertheless, at the end of nine years of work, a major shift took place in her attitude towards herself and her life in a relatively short period of time. It began with the culminating event mentioned above, which follows almost exactly as she wrote it.

I use the word "event" because I do not know what else to use. She insisted that, although it occurred at night, it was neither a dream nor a vision. And I think her greatest fear in talking about it was that I might not believe her utter sense of its reality, that I might try to interpret it or understand it as a symbol or as a psychological metaphor. If I had, she would have thought that I was seeing it as a "nothing but" sort of experience, when what she was feeling was that nothing in her whole life had ever been so real.

There are three things to note about this event. One, it was not induced by drugs nor by a technique of meditation. It came naturally, as if born after a long period of incubation into our world of time and space. Two, for the most part it describes an ordinary daily life, as opposed to an ecstatic or other-worldly experience. Three, it was as real as, if not more real than, her waking consciousness.

The Beginning: I am with a crowd of young people on a ship nudging itself into a New York pier. As the ship settles to its berth, the inner lining of the ship (like an inner core) slides out into the street, lowering wheels and taking all of us riding with it. We go down a street (complete with its old red brick, as it used to be) and we are all young and gay, in bright costumes and waving banners. It is like a float in a parade, and we are a merry juggernaut, taking up the whole street.

(The foregoing is like a fantasy prelude in a dream; the rest is real.)

The Self That Lived with Piedr: I have just come to New York, and am living in an apartment with my sister and my cousin. This is the same apartment I *did* come to in 1927. And, in this other life, my age and the time and the street seem about the same; that is, the situation *feels* parallel.

But it is different because I meet a young Norseman and, after the first laughing date, we are in love. A flash shows him as I first remember him—a tall young man who wears a knitted cap and the kind of dungarees that men who spend their lives around boats wear as a regular costume. He is posed against the ship's rigging. His name appears like a subtitle: Piedr. (I no longer know how to pronounce it.) He is not a sailor, exactly, but works on a ship from his homeland, which I now think is Norway. . .

Piedr does not think that it is a good life for me, with my sister and cousin. I agree with him that it is not "right," and I move to a very tiny apartment on the other side of the street. There I can have my life with this Norseman whenever he comes back to New York. I cannot tell you what the warmth and rightness of this time with Piedr were like. It is not just like clinging to something, or someone, to keep out the cold—but a joy in the completeness that we know for each other.

Piedr is concerned that I am alone when a voyage takes him away from New York. I do not really mind the waiting, though, because the warmth is always there.

Piedr and I marry very soon and I go with him to live in his land. I know that my parents are clamoring somewhere in the background, but I enter this life with great serenity, as though their objections were a small matter. I do not let my sister interfere, either, and she fades most quickly from my mind.

The rest of it is my life in Norway. ("Norway" because I have to give this land a name; it is now my land.) The pines are like the pines of my childhood but they are darker, and the sky in my new land is a different blue. It stands high, and the blue seems washed with white.

The house we live in is white, built taut and snug the way that ships are fashioned. It is somewhere near an inlet, but not right on the coast. I would not like the strong winds that blow forever on the outer coast. Leading up to the narrow porch steps is a dirt path; yellow flowers (daffodils, crocus?) are clustered on either side.

I remember that for a long time my people do not communicate with me. When I do get a letter, my mother is complaining in some way about my sister. But I am needed in my new life. My mother has lost me, and I have none of that anguished fretting that hurts because I have lived "against her orders."

My kitchen shines with a curious pale-yellow light. As I move around in it, I notice an embroidered strip that hangs as a decoration, and there are many things that suggest I keep house as do the others in this land. I am one of them. Things are now so familiar to me that nothing stands out, though I am aware of touches of red in the shelf strips and the pottery ware.

Once I am sitting by the table, waiting for Piedr to come home, up the hard earth walk. I rest my hands lightly on my big belly and feel a surge of wonder and warm content. This is a stray memory from my first pregnancy, because, later on, I know that I have two girls. There are scenes in which I go into their room late at night to see if they are well covered.

Sometimes, at night when the girls are in bed, Piedr and I sit by the stove (such a funny-looking stove!) and we try to talk a bit in English. But I have forgotten my first language and we laugh. It is not bitter at all, but warm and amusing, because I am needed here and do not have to "hang by a word," any word in any language.

One night I tell Piedr about a man with strange eyes who had come to the door. Piedr listens and suggests that I be careful about admitting strangers. I reply, rather comfortably, that "he was hungry." It seemed understandable for me to answer this way because my life is the taking care—the feeding, really—of the ones I trust.

Then there is a memory of seeing the girls off for school on that last morning. I check to see if their clothes are in order (their skirts swinging straight) as they go down the path, their satchels of books hanging from their shoulders. This must be a spring morning because my girls are not wearing any kind of headgear; their hair shines as it falls free.

This is the end of this self's life with Piedr. My body is lying in a corner of the room; the strange man has come back and I have been killed. Up above the shapeless husk is a misty twining; the other selves are gathering. It is known that one of them must coalesce because the need for that self is over. (There are more than two selves; in fact I do not know how many.) But before this happens we are together, hoping that Piedr will come up the path first. We do not want—we cannot have—the girls coming home to this. It would shock and, in some way, distort them. They are young enough to still be hurt by a broken doll, and to see this scene by themselves would be cruel. As these misty, moving selves all hope together, Piedr's step is on the path outside. We know that he will come in first. He is a man and will bear it in a man's way; he will know what to do.

This is our last thought together.

The After-Word: I can't explain it—I was too busy living it. And it wasn't sad at all but rich and lovely and complete. May all my other selves be as needed!

For reasons which will I hope become evident, I should not like to categorize this extremely important and crucial experience of my patient as merely a manifestation of the animus or of the ghostly lover. There is a qualitative difference between the ghostly lover who seduces a woman away from life and Janet's experience, which seemed to be for her a link which connected her to herself and to her life as she had never been before. The figure of the man with the strange eyes, however, who comes to the door, is clearly an animus, and a deadly one. We will have more to say about him later.

I think of what Jung wrote in the prologue to *Memories, Dreams, Reflections*:

My life is a story of the self-realization of the unconscious. Everything in the unconscious seeks outward manifestation, and the personality too desires to evolve out of its unconscious conditions and to experience itself as a whole. . . . Thus it is that I have now undertaken, in my eighty-third year, to tell my personal myth. I can only make direct statements, only "tell stories." Whether or not the stories are "true" is not the problem. The only question is whether what I tell is *my* fable, *my* truth.[2]

The Life with Piedr is clearly Janet's truth.

Let us turn to two thirteenth-century legends of the Virgin Mary. Each one tells a story of a hidden life running parallel to the daily conscious existence. What is implied is a double life lived simultaneously. The difference between these and Janet's experience is that the ordinary time sequence is uninterrupted in them. In Janet's case she lived simultaneously in two discrepant time spans. All the while that her life with Piedr was taking place, she knew perfectly well who she was and that she was lying in bed in her own house.

The likeness between the legends and Janet's experience is that the simultaneous other life surfaces into ego consciousness at a given point in time. Before that, the states of being are mutually exclusive. Quite suddenly they meet on the plane of ego awareness, and the ego becomes fully conscious of both lives and continues to remember both. The theme of the sudden emergence of one life into the daily waking ego consciousness also implies that there has been a period of incubation, in which the alternate life went on, so to speak, in darkness and underground.

The first legend is called "The Knight of Kirkby:"

A knight on his way to a tournament stopped to hear a mass in honor of Our Lady and lingered so long that he missed his tournament. As he rode out from the church, his friends congratulated him for deeds of honor that had been miraculously performed in his absence.[3]

The second is the story of Beatrice, a devout nun who was made sacristan of her convent. And, although her devotion increased with her new responsibility and freedom,

[2]Jung, *Memories*, p. 3.
[3]Beverly Boyd, *The Middle English Miracles of the Virgin* (San Marino, California, 1964), p. 135.

A certain cleric, seeing and desiring her, began to use enticements. When she scorned his wanton talk, he became so much the more eager, and the old serpent hotly tempted her, so that her heart could no longer endure the fires of passion, but going to the altar of the Blessed Virgin Mary . . . she said, "Lady, I have served thee as faithfully as I could; behold I resign to thee thy keys. I can no longer withstand the temptations of the flesh." Placing the keys on the altar she went in secret after the cleric, and he, after dishonouring her, within a few days deserted her. And she having no means of living and being ashamed to return to the cloister, became a harlot.

Having lived publicly for many years in this wickedness, one day she came in her secular dress to the gate of the convent, and said to the gatekeeper: "Do you know one Beatrice, formerly the custodian of this convent?" And he replied, "Yes, she is a very worthy lady, holy and without reproach from her childhood, who has lived in this convent to this day."

She, hearing these words, but not weighing their meaning, was about to go away, when the Mother of Mercy appeared to her in the form of a woman and said: "For fifteen years I have filled your office in your absence. Return now to your home and do penance, for no one knows of your departure." The Mother of God had actually in her shape and dress taken her place as guardian. At once she returned, and as long as she lived gave thanks to the Virgin Mary, and in confession made known to her confessor all that had happened to her.[4]

Psychologically, the story of the knight can be seen as a tale of a man's devotion to one of the higher forms of the anima. When this relationship is honored, the story seems to suggest, the outer world with its obligations of status and responsibility will function on its own.

The tale of Beatrice hints more at the image of the self. There is also another strand in this story, not so clearly evident, but one worth mentioning at least: the implied theme of the mother and the daughter.

Eileen Power says:

As to the origins of the cult of the Virgin and the various strands out of which this characteristic and quite original creation was woven, it is difficult to give a simple answer. Something it certainly owed to influences older than Christianity. The remnants of that devotion which had once been lavished upon the Great Mother in all her various forms, lingered on and were inevitably now lavished on the Mother of Christ. Isis, Diana, Ceres and Rhea all left something to her. Their statues sometimes did duty as the Virgin in Christian churches in the South of Europe and the fact that Isis and Ceres are often represented with a child in their arms accounts for the ease of the transference. Briffault notes that "at Castrogiovanni on the site of ancient

---

[4]Johannes Herolt, *Miracles of the Blessed Virgin Mary*, tr. C. C. Swinton Bland with an intro. by Eileen Power (London, 1928), pp. 44-5.

Enna, the great shrine of [Ceres'] . . . worship, there is still a statue of the Virgin whose divine child is not a boy but a girl, the figure having served as Ceres and Proserpine in a previous sanctuary of the goddess."[5]

It is also possible that there is, in this story of a Divine Mother and her human daughter, a faint echo of the rape of Persephone. For the myth of Persephone too is the story of a hidden life, whether it is taken as a myth, from agricultural times, of the dormant cycle in nature, or whether it is seen as the loss of a woman to a community of women when she leaves to marry and to encounter the strange, and sometimes fearful, Other—a man. In the eyes of the medieval church, it was the serpent (with the hint of sexuality connected to that symbol), the devil, the lord of the underworld of Hell, who tempted Beatrice away.

But Mary was as strong as Demeter when it came to claiming her own. So great was her power of snatching sinners worthy of Hell away from the devil, even at the very gate to his own kingdom, that he and his cohorts used to call her *illa mulier*, "that woman." Eileen Power says, "The evil ones never minded an appeal to the God of justice in case of a difference of opinion," for he was as rational as they in his standards of morality, "but they could not bear an appeal to Mary, for they knew that whatever a soul might get of her it was not justice."[6]

There is a hint of the psychological concept of the self in this. For the Self does not ask for righteousness and rationality but moves towards wholeness. The departure of Beatrice and her return to the convent can be seen in contemporary psychological terms as a hint of the price of that wholeness, even though told in medieval terms strange to our current modes of thought.

There is another theme, in addition to that of Mary and Demeter as aspects of the self in the psyche of women. This is the theme of the descent—the descent of the Virgin to earth, Beatrice's descent into a life of sin, the descent of Persephone into Hades. We shall be picking up the theme of descent when we come to discuss the dream which Janet named "The Dream of the Black Psyche."

Among Sufi tales there is one called, "The Sultan Who Became an Exile." The Sultan and some learned men were dis-

[5]Ibid., pp. xi-xii.   [6]Ibid., pp. xxx-xxxi.

cussing the subject of the Night Journey of the Prophet Mohammed:

> It is said that on that occasion the Prophet was taken from his bed up into the celestial spheres. During this period he saw heaven and hell, conferred with God ninety thousand times, had many other experiences—and was returned to his room while his bed was yet warm. A pot of water which had been overturned by the flight and spilled was still not empty when the Prophet returned.[7]

An argument arose; some said it was possible, some disagreed. The Sultan said it was not possible. Some of the sages said that all things were possible to divine power. But this did not satisfy the Sultan. A Sufi sheikh, hearing of this dispute, presented himself at court saying that both interpretations were wrong. And, after some demonstrations of his power over unnatural events, he asked the Sultan to put his head in a vessel of water brought into the audience chamber for that purpose.

The Sultan did so and, enraged, found himself stranded on a remote and lonely seashore with absolutely nothing. He found his way to a city, however, married a wealthy woman, sired a son, and squandered all the wealth of his wife. Poverty-striken, he was forced to seek work as a porter, but he could not make enough in one day to cover one tenth of his needs. He went again to the seashore. Seven years passed. He washed his hands before prayer and was suddenly transported back to his court and lifted his head from the vessel of water. He roared at the sheikh,

> "Seven years of exile, evil man! . . . Seven years, a family and having to be a porter! Have you no fear of God, the Almighty, for this deed?"
>
> "But it is only a moment," said the Sufi master, "since you put your head into this water."
>
> His courtiers bore out this statement. The Sultan could not possibly bring himself to believe a word of this. The sheikh, apparently a prudent man, perceiving himself about to be beheaded, exercised his capacity called the Science of Absence, which caused him to be instantly and corporeally transported to Damascus, many days' distance away.
>
> From here he wrote to the king: "Seven years passed for you, as you will now have discovered, during an instant of your head in the water. This happens through the exercise of certain faculties, and carries no special significance except that it is illustrative of what can happen. Was not the bed warm, was not the water-jar empty in the tradition?

[7] Idries Shah, *Tales of the Dervishes* (New York, 1969), p. 35.

It is not whether a thing has happened or not which is the important element. It is possible for anything to happen. What is, however, important, is the significance of the happening. In your case, there was no significance. In the case of the Prophet, there was significance in the happening."[8]

In this Sufi story we see an illustration of collapsed time, as in Janet's case. The Sultan lived for seven years as an exile in a moment of his daily life. Janet lived years of adult experience in one evening of her ordinary life. The difference is that Janet maintained a double consciousness, while the Sultan completely lost contact with one of the states of his being.

The most important point of the story—indeed, the most important point in all of the amplifying material—is the Sufi's statement to the Sultan. "It is not whether a thing has happened or not which is the important element. *It is possible for anything to happen.* What is, however, important, is the significance of the happening."

Janet's rational mind struggled with the odd and unusual happening in her life, but it had a significance which she was powerless to deny. It may have been the inescapable sense of significance so powerfully and directly experienced which gave her life with Piedr its quality of simple, undeniable daily reality.

The final illustration of the theme of a hidden life is from a novel by George Du Maurier, *Peter Ibbetson*. Although I can include only a few details that relate to my paper, the novel as a whole is a fascinating document, published as it was in 1891, of the mood and climate which were to produce Freud and Adler and Jung and which heralded the explosion of interest in depth psychologies and alternate modes of viewing the human experience, rather than those of the purely rational or traditional points of view.

The novel is written as if it were the autobiography of Peter Ibbetson, and its main theme is the story of a long and shared life between him and the Duchess of Towers, a lovely and eminent lady. They had been playmates as children, were separated by tragic events in the lives of their families before adulthood, and later meet three times in external reality as adults. Their life together is lived out in an out-of-the-body state, though Du Maurier does not use that term. It begins after

[8]Ibid., pp. 37-8.

Ibbetson is confined in a prison for the criminally insane for a crime he committed. Since this is a romantic novel, however, it is a suitable noble crime.

Peter and the Duchess of Towers do meet, to their mutual astonishment, in one out-of-the-body experience, before he commits the crime for which he is finally imprisoned. A few excerpts from this meeting illustrate a process Peter Ibbetson later learns to call "dreaming true."

It begins with a nightmare, during which he finally perceives the Duchess of Towers at a distance and desperately makes his way to her. The nightmare vanishes, and he says,

I felt that this was no longer a dream, but something else—some strange thing that had happened to me, some new life that I had woke up to.

For at the touch of her hand my consciousness, my sense of being I, myself, which hitherto in my dream (as in all previous dreams up to then) had been only partial, intermittent, and vague, suddenly blazed into full, consistent, practical activity—just as it is in life, when one is well awake and much interested in going on—only with perceptions far keener and more alert.

I knew perfectly well who I was and what I was, and remembered all the events of the previous day. I was conscious that my real body, undressed and in bed, now lay fast asleep in a small room on the fourth floor [of a hotel in Paris]. I knew this perfectly; and yet here was my body, too, just as substantial, with all my clothes on; my boots rather dusty, my shirt-collar damp with the heat, for it was hot. . . . I felt in my trousers-pocket; there were my London latch-key, my purse, my penknife. . . . I looked at my watch; it was going, and marked eleven. I pinched myself, I coughed, I did all the things one usually does under the pressure of some immense surprise, to assure myself that I was awake; and I *was*, and yet here I stood, actually hand in hand with "the Duchess of Towers" who seemed much tickled at my confusion.[9]

He wonders if he has died, but "some instinct told me that this was not death, but transcendent earthly life—and also, alas! that it would not endure forever!"[10]

The Duchess then gives him some very specific instructions on how to "dream true." She tells him that he will soon learn to do it, that it is very easy; and she tells him in just what position he must lie as he goes to sleep. Then she says, "you must never for a moment cease thinking of where you want to be in your dream till you are asleep and get there; and you must never forget in your dream where and what you were when awake. You must join the dream on to reality."[11]

[9]George Du Maurier, *Peter Ibbetson* (New York and London, 1891), pp. 202-3.
[10]Ibid., p. 206.   [11]Ibid., p. 208.

After a sequence of events, he wakes in his room. He feels that he is not a bit more awake than he had been a few minutes ago in his strange vision, not as much! He wonders if he has gone mad. He thinks about the five senses as known organs of apprehension, and then wonders, "Is there, perchance, some sixth sense embedded somewhere in the thickness of the flesh —some survival of the past, of the race, of our own childhood even, etiolated by disuse? or some rudiment, some effort to begin, some priceless hidden faculty to be developed . . . ? some nerve that now can only be made to thrill and vibrate in a dream, too delicate as yet to ply its function in the light of common day?"[12]

Du Maurier's novel describes the same sense of the utter reality of a life lived in a non-ordinary dimension as Janet had. The description of the actual sense of physically being in two places simultaneously also fits with what happened to Janet. She knew perfectly well who she was and that she was lying in her own bed during the entire period when the self that lived with Piedr went on with its life too.

The instruction of the Duchess of Towers to Peter Ibbetson that he must "join the dream on to reality" is interesting. Though Du Maurier says it from a different perspective, it could be a description of the process of analysis, for analysis too "joins the dream on to reality," widens reality, deepens it, and sometimes focuses it from a perspective entirely beyond the capacity of the ego alone.

In going back over Janet's dreams (not really very many considering the number of years we worked together) it was interesting to see that every theme of the self that lived with Piedr, had been worked over carefully by the dreams; that when the dreams were finished with one of the themes, it gradually faded out and another became energized, so to speak, and moved into the focus of the dreams.

None of this had ever quite come to the surface in our work together. When she was dreaming of young women, she did begin a correspondence with a young niece. When she was dreaming of infants and small children, she did find herself deeply drawn to children she saw and knew. And these were important experiences for her. But some final connection be-

[12]Ibid., p. 218.

tween herself and these feelings never seemed to happen. She remained in some sense split or detached from a part of herself until the meeting with Piedr. However, the dreams showed that the work on these aspects had been well and thoroughly done, even though it had not surfaced into waking consciousness.

I began to be aware of the long internalized time of incubation in Janet's psychological process—that process which was also illustrated in the story of the Knight of Kirkby and especially in the story of Beatrice the Sacristan. The recognition and the integration of the incubated content are necessary for the human wholeness of the Knight, of Beatrice, and of Janet. "The Sultan Who Became an Exile" is, on the other hand, an example of an "initiation manqué." He does not grasp the meaning of his experience; he does not admit it—odd as it is—as an aspect of his being. Therefore it remains without meaning, without significance, simply a psychic accretion, like a barnacle, on the surface of his ordinary life.

Some of the biographical data from Janet's background are implicit in what has been said up to now. But the specific difficulties of her life will throw light on why so much of it went on underground for so many years.

We began working together in 1968. At that time she was 58. She terminated her work with my agreement in 1977 when she was 68. She had married twice. The first marriage soon ended in divorce; the second was a late marriage, not terribly successful, ending with her husband's death. The positive thing they shared in common was an intense and joyful interest in language and literature. The negative things which bound them were negative mother complexes, which, although seeming opposite on the surface, were equally destructive and inhibiting in effect. Her husband had been crippled emotionally by a mother who doted, and leaned on, and controlled him through love of her "good boy." She also treated him as her servant. I came to feel, as we worked together, that Janet's mother had either become psychotic or, if not, nearly psychotic with rage over impossible living conditions in the small backwoods mining community where they had their home. There were no comforts, no amenities, and sometimes not enough food. Janet had one sister three years older. The rivalry between them was intense and bitter, fanned often, it seemed, by the mother. My patient was the loser except in matters pertaining to school or where a trickster-like imp in her played practical jokes which looked accidental on the surface.

School was her refuge and her stronghold, though even in that area her mother threatened and stormed and punished her with slaps for being "uppity" when she talked about it or referred to things she had learned. On the other hand, sometimes she was punished when, out of sheer terror, she became unable to talk. By the time she was in seventh grade she could not speak at all in class, but, in spite of this, she maintained her scholastic standing and was graduated with the best grade average in the history of the school.

After high school, her mother sent her to New York to join her sister. They were expected to earn money and send it home. She was so ill adapted to the world of external reality, however, that she could not tell time, did not know how to take a bus or a subway, nor how to use a public telephone. Needless to say, her life at this point was one long nightmare.

It was also the middle of the depression. Nevertheless she found work and has always managed to do so. The positions were usually clerical. In the beginning she was often promoted but would soon ask to be relieved of the better job because she could not take responsibility for other people nor give any kind of order or direction to others.

Inevitably in every office she met her mother—whether she recognized her or not. But she never left the job just as she had never been able to leave home of her own free will, for her feelings of helplessness crippled her.

She came to see me originally because her mother-in-law, whom she hated, had died. Her own mother had died ten years earlier. She did not experience the sense of relief at the death of her mother-in-law which she expected; on the contrary, she began to feel that she was falling apart. It was clear that her only sense of being was as the fearful and polarized satellite of a powerful and destructive feminine figure. Without that presence she ceased to exist; with it she was in a constant state of panic and suppressed rage.

As we continued, she brought dreams and reported psychic or near-psychic experiences which seemed clearly to illustrate her situation in metaphor. Although she was very close to her unconscious material, much closer than many other people, she was unable to make any useful or meaningful connection with it. It always hovered "out there," someplace just beyond her grasp, out of reach, much as it did in the early childhood vision reported at the beginning of the paper. She brought these dreams and experiences because I asked her to, simply because she did anything any authority figure asked her to do. But it was difficult because she was ashamed of them. She had a gift for writing, and her literary side regarded them as crude and fragmentary. It was very hard to persuade her not to tidy them up—to recognize that they had a value in themselves just as they were.

It was a frustration for me, at times mounting to despair, that nothing in our work together seemed to help her make a meaningful connection to her dreams. She was like an empty chamber through which events and images, inner and outer, passed without pause—no one thing more meaningful than another. Nothing had significance. Her only affect was anxiety; her only mode of action, flight. Flight in our sessions took the form of a barrage of words which effectively distanced us from each other and made any but the most minimal communication impossible. But it did allow her to stay in a one-to-one situation with a woman. I was often reminded of a bird poised fearfully for flight at the faintest move from another being.

She said she had often wished to be invisible, so that she could wander in and out of people's houses—in order "to see what people do and how they do it." She felt that people knew a secret that she didn't know, that she was forever shut out. There was also a tag of thought which frequently floated to the surface of her mind, and she wondered if this ever happened to other people too. This was the phrase "The child is dead," and it came and went at its own will as if carried on some invisible current unconnected with her mood or the events in her external life.

She *had* very nearly died of typhoid fever when she was between two and three. The convalescence may have taken close to two years, and she had some vivid memories from that time. One was of her hunger, and one was her fear that she would die before she was old enough to go to school. It is my impression that her mother cared for her and nursed her with

great devotion throughout this period in her life. She read to
Janet a great deal, and this is interesting in terms of her later
success in school and her writing. It seems possible that the
nurturing she had from her mother at this time was the basis
for an ego which was able to endure the later onslaughts of her
mother's irrational and devastating rages.

There was another kind of early death experience, it was a
memory that her eighth year was the last year she "fought
back." Something in her "gave up trying," she said. From other
associations and other comments about that year, it seems that
something in her *did* disappear, go underground as it were. A
part of her became hidden from herself. Something in her fell
away into darkness, apparently lost forever. Some aspect of her
being slumbered in unconsciousness from that time on.

During the second year of our work, she had a dream which
she entitled, "The Black Psyche Dream." It intrigued her,
piqued her curiosity, and brought back painful memories. For
me it was a relief, because I finally felt I had a glimpse of what
might be going on beneath the surface and a clue as to how our
work together might proceed. I became less concerned about
making interpretations, less concerned about what seemed like
a fatal lack of capacity for insight, and much more willing to
endure the flow of words, a flight of ideas, which at times
seemed to be pathological in proportion. It filled the room and
inundated us both in every hour. For it seemed as if something
very real and very important were going on—indeed, had been
going on all along.

The Black Psyche Dream: The landscape at the beginning of the dream . . . was up
at the rim of the world. Everything was softly colored—not unlike a moon-
scape—and the lakes of water had easily sloping earth rims. The whole thing
curved a little and went gently toward the horizon. There was a feeling that I
had been in the water but was reassuring someone (or myself) that there was
no "hurt" and apparently I did not get wet.

I came to the steep cliff down which I must go to get to the picnic (or the
gathering of dim figures) at the bottom. At the side of the moving figures,
where I must go, was the ruined house (our old ranch house of which there
were left just a few weathered dark timbers). The cliff was our old meadow—
from the ranch—but tip-tilted to a cliff. I knew that there had been an old
path down it and tried to descent it within those bounds. The earth was dark
red and spongy, and there were apertures, like shallow caves, in which there
were statues. The statues were white, not a glistening white but a pale mush-
room white, and I feel that they were not of as hard a substance as marble. . . .

I reached a shallow cave in which I saw the white figure of Psyche. (I have forgotten now whether I thought they were all Psyches or not.) The descent here was perilous; it all was, unless I caught hold of the figure and lowered myself. I knew that, if I did, it would damage the Psyche. But she told me to go ahead, that it was all right! She wanted me to go on, and not to mind. I caught hold of her, and part of her statue-body slid away, but I was successful in getting down farther, and the rest of the climb down was now feasible. But near the end of my climb, on this treacherous, spongy red earth, down almost to where I "must" go..."they" began to question me about the Black Psyche. "You know," they kept insisting. I tried to evade them and to deny that I knew the Black Psyche or where she was. But during the questioning, I felt guilty and alarmed, because I felt that somewhere, somehow I did know the Black Psyche, and where she was, and what she meant.... I have remembered. It is on the next page.

...I noticed at our last meeting that, whenever the Black Psyche is mentioned, my heart beats faster. And that night, sleep seemed far off, and a curious exhilaration came when I thought...I knew!

It was a place of dirt. Nothing but gritty dirt, and a little tent house in which only one room had a "floor"—the kitchen. So you really lived on the earth! It was way out somewhere in the Kentucky hills; my folks spoke of it as "when we lived out to the mine." When we went there, I was crawling, not walking. In reality my mother, in later years, spoke bitterly of my crawling to a dump of some sort and chewing burnt wood. The charcoal would run down my chin and all over my clothes. "The drinking water was packed twenty miles by muleteam." "I used the clear part of the dishwater to scrub the floor." "Your sister saw her reflection in a barrel of water and spit at it, but we couldn't throw the water out." These things in quotation marks are probably said by *them,* my parents in later years...but also, it is no doubt true that they were saying these things at the time.

I must have nursed for a long, long time. *Because they never shut up about it.* "You got ashamed of it yourself." "If we had company, you used to go up and whisper in your mother's ear to get her out of the room so that you could nurse." "We tried to shame you"—and now, these are only scraps, but true scraps, I'm sure:

"We put black"—charcoal? coal dust? the smoke from lamp chimneys?— I don't know—"on your mother's breast, so you wouldn't nurse, and you cried and cried. We would ask you if you still wanted Num-num, and you would cry and cry."

Also, the doll. I do not truly remember this doll. It is shut out of my actual memory, *except for the long skirt* which hid, again, some of the Black Psyche. I asked my mother once, years and years later (I was still ashamed) who gave me the doll? But she, too, had forgotten. They would hand me this doll—it had a long skirt—and say "love the baby," and I was eager and would hold it to me. Then *they* would grab the doll and turn it over (tip-tilting), and the doll had a black face, and the skirt would cover the regular baby face. "How you would cry," they said in after years. "You cried and cried, and would try to push it away." "You would cry and we would laugh."

Several themes in this dream are important: first, a traumatic separation from the nourishing breast, blackened and darkened and denigrated in feeling, one can predict that henceforth trust would become difficult; second, a split between the dark and the light infant, represented by the doll, a split remaining in herself as an adult. Third, and most important of all in the dream, is the implied fact that she knows both where she must go and what she is seeking. She knows on some level of her being who the Black Psyche is and where she must journey to find her.

It is by going down past the dimly lit figures closer to the surface of the earth. Can we say those which were closer to ego consciousness? Can we say that she will find her way? Even Psyche herself, in her light aspect, is to be sacrificed. Janet must destroy that image in order to go still deeper. But the light Psyche herself told her "to go ahead, that it was all right! She wanted me to go on and not to mind."

We can discern a final theme and I think it is particularly important to note it in this life situation: the solution, the journey is down into the earth. I remind you of the theme of descent mentioned earlier, the Virgin's descent to earth, the descent of Beatrice into a life of sin, Proserpine's descent into the kingdom of Hades. Marie-Louise von Franz says that women with a negative mother complex walk by the first half of life.[13] But whoever finds and knows the Black Psyche could surely no longer remain a restless little ghost hovering outside of other people's windows, or hiding invisibly in corners to see "what they do" or what it is like to be ordinary and alive and human! She will know it from the depths of her psychic being. And this manifestation of Psyche, though black and clearly of the underworld, is not associated with death. It is the human child who died in spirit, although the body went on living.

Naturally we were both very much intrigued with the Black Psyche, neither one of us ever having heard the term before. She went on living with the Black Psyche. This was her privilege and her pain, while I found the theme often in my mind as I listened to other patients, or read clinical or symbolic material.

The alchemical treatise called *Aurora Consurgens*, "the rising

[13]*Aurora Consurgens*, ed., with a commentary, by Marie-Louise von Franz (B.S. LXXVII; 1966), p. 88.

dawn," with Marie-Louise von Franz's commentary, was in the end the document I turned to most often. In it there were metaphors and concepts which seemed to underline and illuminate the archetype of the Black Psyche.

The treatise describes the encounter of a man with a divine feminine figure. Though in essence she is black and unknown, the author of *Aurora Consurgens* bathes her in a luminous half light. She becomes suffused by the soft peripheral glow of an experience barely on the border of consciousness, which remains dark at its core like the dark moon, not pearled by reflection from the sun, but existing in and of itself unillumined by daylight consciousness.

She is variously equated with the Queen of the South, that is with the dark Queen of Sheba who made a journey to see Solomon because she regarded him as a man equal to, and worthy of, herself. She is also equated with the mysterious Woman of the Apocalypse, she who was crowned with twelve stars. And she is known as Sapientia Dei or Scientia Dei. In alchemical literature the parallel to this is the Mater Naturae, the mother of Nature. As Sapentia Dei in patristic literature she was interpreted "as the sum of the *rationes aeternae* (eternal forms), of the 'self-knowing primordial causes,' exemplars, ideas, and prototypes in the mind of God. She was also considered the *archetypus mundus*, 'that archetypal world after whose likeness this sensible world was made,' and through which God becomes conscious of himself. Sapientia Dei is thus the sum of archetypal images in the mind of God. Other patristic interpretations equate her . . . with Mary. In modern psychology she would be interpreted as a feminine personification of the collective unconscious."[14]

Von Franz goes on to comment that the author of *Aurora Consurgens* equates "his feminine figure with the 'soul in matter' and with the 'filius philosophorum' or *lapis*, thus lifting her out of her purely ecclesiastical framework into the empirical sphere of scientifically based alchemy and bringing her closer to individual human experience."

Further she says, "It is important to remember that the thirteenth century, to which *Aurora* presumably belongs, was a time when the worship of Mary was on the increase. Psychologically,

[14]Ibid., pp. 155-6.

this would point to a need, rising from the collective unconscious, for a feminine figure to be given a place in the purely
masculine, patriarchal Trinity, as the representative of the
anima of a man and the self of a woman."[15]

Reading *Aurora Consurgens* in this light, as material which
could be related to the self in women, was useful as background
for the clinical work. The stories of the Virgin referred to
earlier also fall in the thirteenth century and belong to this
development of the collective unconscious. But they reflect as
well the underlying continuity of the older, more remote
mother religions, hinted at too in *Aurora Consurgens* in the
figures of the Queen of Sheba, the Woman of the Apocalypse,
and as the archetype for the creation of the world.

Von Franz says, "In *Aurora* the anima appears as she does in
the Gnostic texts, on the one hand as the Biblical Wisdom, on
the other hand as the *anima mundi* sunk in matter and calling
for help."[16]

Janet's experience of descent differs from the Gnostic interpretations here, and from the experience of Beatrice the Sacristan. The theme of being sunk in matter and calling for help
is nowhere indicated in the Dream of the Black Psyche. On the
contrary, this is the descent into the darkness of matter in its
most positive sense. It is the exact opposite of the point of view,
historically prevalent in our Western culture, which strove to
free the psyche from the life of nature, from the life of the
body and the ego, so that it might find the life of the spirit. In
this dream the descent into the earth to find the Black Psyche
represents neither a death nor an annihilation. Though it does
not say so specifically, it may be hinting at the search for the
child who is dead, or who has disappeared into darkness or the
underworld. The archetype of Demeter, the mother who has
lost her child, may be behind this descent as well.

Although the theme of the descent is positive, there is nowhere any suggestion that it was easy. The descent was perilous,
especially at that point, the dream says, where she had to break
the figure of the white Psyche in order to continue her journey
—and the footing all the way down was on "treacherous, spongy
red earth."

Von Franz quotes from the *Turba*, another alchemical trea-

---

[15]Ibid., p. 157.   [16]Ibid., p. 191.

tise, that "the substances must be tormented with an 'ancient black spirit' until they change."[17] And in the beginning of *Aurora*, itself, is a passage about the Wisdom of the South, the Black Queen of Sheba, "She . . . that Solomon chose to have instead of light, and above all beauty and health . . . ," which says, "Her ways are beautiful operations and praiseworthy, not unsightly nor ill-favoured, and her paths are measured and not hasty, but are bound up with stubborn and day-long toil."[18] Certainly the paths of the Black Psyche were "measured and not hasty."

That in my patient's case the descent is positive may be related not only to her core problem—that essentially she had not been able to get down into her own life, her own being— but perhaps also to the fact that the Black Psyche is for her an aspect of the self and therefore is an experience of whole-ness rather than one of fragmentation or dismemberment or separation.

The next significant dream in this sequence occurred almost six years later, in December 1975, and Janet entitled it "Take Me to My Twin." She later saw this dream as a forerunner of the experience with Piedr, as if it were the twin, the other half of herself which lived that life.

Take Me to My Twin: I am stranded somewhere along a highway; there is some kind of noisy bar in the background. The people whom I approach to give me a lift back to "where I belong" are rather threatening. I feel weak—rather second-rate, like a "B" picture—but I know that it is vital that I get back to the Other Person, who also seems to be me. This Other Person, a kind of twin, is in my mind like the original, and this stranded-me is like a throwaway copy.

I am not successful in identifying myself to the group that surrounds me; they say that they "know" the other person. Whatever I say is crushed . . . I cannot prove anything.

The more I try, the more threatening they grow. I feel as if I were fum-bling at a locked door in the dark.

They sneer at my attempts to tell them that I am the Other Person, though they do not shake my own belief. I am forced into a car that I know "goes in the wrong direction." Other cars follow making it a kind of funeral proces-sion. Men drive the cars, but I know that none of them is "the boss"—it is a woman in the background with a loud voice.

Somewhere as I fight my way out of the car, I tear my coat; this makes me look more like a castaway in appearance. I catch hold of the back of a truck that is going along the highway. . . . I am not strong enough to pull myself up

[17]Ibid., p. 218.   [18]Ibid., p. 35.

on the truck bed but just run along in back holding on to the tailgate. The truckdriver shouts something back at me, like "Drop off now or you'll be killed," and I realize that he, too, is one of the enemy.

The truck swings into a deserted gas station, and my enemies pile out of the other cars and surround me again. Their threatening ways are more purposeful now. I realize that they are going to take me somewhere and kill me. I think the Other Person will be without me, and, though I am a rather limp person, I know that the waiting twin *has* to have me, too.

The woman enemy, who is my "most enemy," is in front now and very clear. She is dressed in a black gown; the top is black chiffon with loads of glass beads. I think of the lot of them, whom this woman seems to be the heart of, as being vulgar, oafish, and in "bad taste."

Though away from the Other Person, I am only half alive. I protest and try to throw their hands off. I keep saying that if I am released to find "the other person," they will *see* who I am—that I am not to be killed and discarded.

The woman in the black dress says something loud and coarse, and suddenly I am very angry and not afraid at all. I turn on her and pull at the dress top of chiffon and glass beads. It rips, and the beads bounce all over, even out to the highway. It is like the beginning of a hailstorm.

She is surprised, but she yells at the rest to grab me. I am overpowered; there are too many of them. I know that they are going to take me away so that I shall never find the Other Person again, but my anger keeps me from being afraid. (End of dream)

This is a note out of my memory: When I first came to New York (I was eighteen) someone took me to a dance hall. I was sort of ashamed of being there; I felt that it was tawdry though I did not dare to say anything. When the orchestra quit thumping for a while, a mature-looking woman appeared on the stage and sang. She had red hair, a bronze-red dress, and wore some dangling beads. She also had a shelf-like bosom and powerful lungs and she belted out, "Me and My Shadow."

Another tag end of memory: I do not *know*, really, what the woman in the dream said to me that made me so angry. *But* the sudden blast of rage is similar to what I used to exhibit when my sister would make fun of some of my bits of attempted poetry. . . . Anyway, I did not cry as I might have at other things, but I would actually dive for her, trying to bring my enemy to the ground. She was lots bigger, but in this kind of encounter—!! I felt no pain or fear, only rage.

Her words, although informal, might have come straight out of a Gnostic text. "This Other Person, a kind of twin, is in my mind like the original, and this stranded-me is like a throwaway copy." The Gnostic reference to the transcendental self is clearly evident in this dream.

Hans Jonas writes of a Persian word, *grev*, found in Manichean fragments, which can be translated either by "self" or by "ego."

It denotes the metaphysical person, the transcendent and true subject of salvation. . . . It is called "the luminous nature," "our original luminous nature," or "inner nature." . . . Manichaean hymns call it the "living self" or "the luminous self." The Mandaean "Mana" expresses the same idea and makes particularly clear the identity between this inner principle and the highest godhead. . . . It is between this hidden principle of the terrestrial person and its heavenly original that the ultimate recognition and reunion takes place. . . . It is no exaggeration to say that the discovery of this transcendent inner principle in man and the supreme concern about its destiny is the very center of Gnostic religion.[19]

In another sentence in the dream, which moves in a slightly different direction, Janet says, "I think that the Other Person will be without me, and though I am a rather limp person, I know the waiting twin *has* to have me too."

This seems to point to the idea that the transcendental self needs its human aspect in order to become fully what it is. It explains the significance of Janet's deep sadness and fear that life would pass her by, that she would die without ever having lived her own life. The implication is that a deeply desired aspect of being can only be completed and fulfilled within a human existence. If it is not lived fully in all its humanness, it will dangle forever at loose ends throughout eternity.

Now a dream from late January 1976, thirteen and a half months before the Self That Lived with Piedr.

I had climbed a hill almost to the top when I stopped and looked up. There was a wonderful white wall, shutting off the top of the hill—and stretching as far as the eye could see—and I could go no farther.

While I stood there, a voice said: "Everything's on the other side."

At first I thought that the wall was so wonderfully fitted together that no one could see where the stones were joined, and then I saw a tiny uneven crack down the face of it. I knew that this line meant a gate. The voice told me again: "Everything's on the other side."

Notes: This is one of my "Picture Dreams," and usually I feel that I am just *shown* a scene; no voice comes. These scenes appear very beautiful to the dreamer: in this case, the bulging hill with the dry yellow grass, and the wall of snow-white stones, so beautifully joined together that at first the jagged line of opening is not seen.

I feel bemused afterward, as if I had stumbled into a holy place.

It is clear that there is finally a passage, a connection to the other side. But it is like the strait and narrow gate, like the eye

[19]Hans Jonas, *The Gnostic Religion* (Boston, 1963), pp. 123-4.

of the needle, like the door in the Sufi story which opens only one second in every hundred years.

Then, in February 1976, two dreams on the same night.

I am hurrying across a meadow, or a kind of park. I am going to a poetry concert, and I am afraid I am late. They are going to read a poem of mine, and, since I have never heard it read, I am both excited and worried. It is not a new poem, and I have almost forgotten how it goes, except that it has long lines and a wavelike motion. I *have* to hear it read, I shall never have another chance.

The woodland is crowded with people; I can find no place to sit. After I have hunted for a place, I remember a little dip in the grassy area and hurry toward it. I walk around, and over, lots of seated people and make my way to this hollow. But there are people there, too. I crowd in by a Mrs. Turner, who has voluminous black skirts. (She was a rather belligerent elderly woman whom I knew long ago in a WPA poetry class; she used to argue with the teacher, and, with that man, it was easy to do). Now she tells me: "No, you can't sit here; there won't be room for my legs." I try to smile at her—not answering, just smiling—so that she won't belabor me with words. I brush some of her full skirt aside and sit down, because I *have* to hear my long-ago and half-forgotten poem read at last. She is still muttering as I strain to hear the far-off voice that is coming from a stand somewhere.

This dream is included because it indicates a shift in attitude. Here too is the large, formidable, powerful woman dressed in black who tells her that there is no room for her, even though the occasion is a celebration and a marking of her own creation and achievement—a poem she has written. But for the first time she does not retreat, nor does she fight back. She simply brushes some of the woman's full skirt aside and sits down, because she has to hear her long-ago and half-forgotten poem read at last.

"It is not a new poem," she says, "and I have almost forgotten how it goes." That is, it represents a content once familiar, but half hidden from her now. It is to be read in a public place where all may hear. This implies that it is valued, regarded as worthy of being held up in the light of day, in consciousness, and that it can not only stand by itself but it can also give something to others. It says that she too will hear it and be reminded of what she knows and what she has done. What is hidden and on the other side is now about to be seen and heard.

The second dream of the night speaks for itself.

I am standing near an open door to another room. I can see in the other room, and there is a light beginning to gather. I know that this means that someone loved is coming back to see me. I am like a knot of joy, and I, too, seem to glow as I move toward the visitor because I know that it is someone loved who is "coming back."

This was like experiencing a vision, except that it was during sleep.

The episode which she described as "The Self That Lived with Piedr" occurred a year later: her courtship, her marriage to Piedr, her happy life in the white house in Norway—not too near the coast where the strong winds blow, but sheltered among the pines with the blue sky high above. Here her two children are born, and she is busy about her house and with the care and feeding of the ones she loves and trusts. Here it is that the man with the strange eyes comes to her door—the man who, in spite of Piedr's warning to her, eventually murders her.

The brutal ending to a life so longed for and so valued was initially the most difficult aspect of Janet's experience for me to comprehend and to deal with. I thought about the murder for some time afterwards, and I finally began to understand that, yes, there had been a murdering animus in her psyche, that something had died or been killed which prevented her living out her life as a wife and a mother in external reality, and that this fact, too, was present in her human experience and was a part of her fate.

There had been a number of dreams in which she was already dead or about to be killed. But in the end her greatest terror did not befall her, the fear that she would always be like a ghost and never know nor possess her own life. She had been able, in a layered fold of time, to live all that she had longed for and missed. It does not seem to matter much, *sub specie aeternitatis*, in what state of consciousness or transformation she lived her own unique life. The fact for her was that she did live it; she did have it.

In *The Feminine in Fairy Tales*, Marie-Louise von Franz says that the ultimate stage of transformation is what one would call plain, positive humanness. I think this was the transformation for Janet—to live the experience of being plainly and positively human in whatever state of being it happened.

Although the Self that lived with Piedr dies, "up above the shapeless husk is a misty twining; the other selves are gathering.

It is known that one of them must coalesce because the need for that self is over. There are more than two selves," she says, "but I do not know how many."

It is not after all an annihilation. It is a tragedy dictated by the currents of her own fate. But, like genuine tragedy, it evokes "pity and terror." It is not without meaning. It has significance.

Although the process which culminated in "The Self That Lived with Piedr" went on in the realm and under the guidance of the Black Psyche, I do not think it would have happened without the therapeutic situation and the therapeutic relationship. It would be difficult, however, to say exactly what factor in the therapy quickened and brought to life the intrapsychic functioning within Janet which healed one of her grievous wounds. Perhaps it was as simple a thing as providing, in Dora Kalff's terms "a *free and sheltered space*"[20] within which the inner process could flow according to its own gradient and in its own fashion.

It seems that the Black Psyche allowed an organizing process to take place quietly and in darkness. It is as if an alternate ego complex found the shelter and the ground in which to grow. Some interrupted process began to move forward again, albeit in the dark, unseen on the surface and only hinted at in dreams. It went on unperceived and in secret until the day came for the hidden aspect of her life to rise to the surface of consciousness.

The word "secret" is derived from Latin *secernere*, "to set apart." It can be broken down into *se*, "apart," and *cernere*, "to sift." It was this sifting and ordering by the alternative ego in darkness which seemed to have been going on behind the scenes for all those years.

The realm of the Black Psyche was set "apart" below the earth in the dream. It could only be reached by using the light Psyche, which in turn would be damaged by this use. The implication here is of a transition which is destroyed as it serves its function. It suggests that there will be no way to turn back. She can only, if she chooses to find the Black Psyche, walk on in darkness. The evidence suggests that she did so. It is the *via negativa*. I wonder if it is the voice of the Black Psyche in the dream which then tells her, "Everything is on the other side."

[20]Dora Kalff, *Sandplay* (San Francisco, 1971), p. 18.

In *Aurora Consurgens*, the dark but luminous feminine image is also perceived as "Wisdom," the wisdom of God, or of the soul in its likeness to God. The alchemist Senior calls this wisdom the "tincture," that which can change things "from potentiality into actuality."[21] Perhaps it is this dark wisdom of the soul which changed the potentiality of a life into an actuality of experience for Janet.

Marie-Louise von Franz writes:

Jung says that women with a negative mother-complex often miss the first half of life, they walk past it in a dream. Life to them is a constant source of annoyance and irritation. But if they can overcome this negative mother-complex, they have a good chance in the second half of rediscovering life with the youthful spontaneity missed in the first half. For though, as Jung says . . . a part of life has been lost, its meaning has been saved. That is the tragedy of such women, but they can get to the turning point, and in the second half of life have their hands healed and can stretch them out for what they want—not from the animus or from the ego, but, according to nature, simply stretch out their hands towards something they love. Though it is infinitely simple, it is extremely difficult for it is the one thing the woman cannot do, it needs God's help. Even the analyst cannot help her—it must one day just happen, and this is generally when there has been sufficient suffering. One cannot escape one's fate, the whole pain of it must be accepted, and one day the infinitely simple solution comes."[22]

It is all in Janet's own After-Word. It is the principle of Eros, so lacking in her early and formative years, which is summoned from the depths, which rises into her consciousness, and which survives. "I can't explain it, I was too busy living it. And it wasn't sad at all but rich and lovely and complete. May all my other selves be as needed!"

[21] *Aurora Consurgens*, p. 173.
[22] Marie-Louise von Franz, *Problems of the Feminine in Fairy Tales* (New York, 1972), p. 88.

Introversion and/or Schizoid Personality: Clinical Thoughts

THOMAS B. KIRSCH

THIS PAPER IS IN LARGE PART an outgrowth of a previous paper on an extrovert's approach to dream interpretation. In that study I examined my work with people who did not know I was a Jungian analyst. I found that I tended to relate their dreams to outside reality rather than to the subjective contents of the unconscious. I attempted to discuss some differences in dream interpretation depending upon the psychological type of the analyst. I noted that most Jungian studies tended to emphasize the introverted subjective aspects of dream interpretation. Early in my professional life I had tended to agree with that approach; yet, through my analysis with Joe Henderson, I came to realize that my own natural extroversion needed another way of approaching dreams. Another interesting facet emerged from this previous study: I found there existed in my practice a large subgroup of introverted women. As a group these women were generally successful in their careers but felt extremely isolated in their interpersonal emotional life. It was as a result of the feeling of isolation that they would usually seek analysis, since their emotional isolation would lead to various forms of depression. That I seemed to work well with this group I attributed to two basic factors: (1) psychological type differences and (2) orientation towards the mother complex.

As an extroverted intuitive-feeling type I could do most of the work in bridging the relationship and therefore help the analysand feel more at ease. I could "sense" intuitively certain feelings which these analysands would have and present the possibilities to them. This would tend to open up various affects and emotions of which they were unaware. I had to be careful about these "hunches," because at times I would be wrong and then be at complete odds with the patient. Furthermore, analysands have an ambivalence to exposing these feelings, so defenses would rise. They would feel as if they were being invaded by something alien to their own natures. I have become quite aware that one must be extremely careful with one's intuitive-feeling hunches, because they can cause as much harm as good. Clinical examples of this phenomenon will be shown later.

All these introverted women had deep negative mother complexes which were primary factors in their emotional isolation. They were usually profoundly self-critical, full of negative judgements towards themselves, and they generally viewed the world in a pessimistic fashion. The future was bleak, and it was felt that nothing could change to make life more meaningful. My own orientation towards the mother complex was positive, and I saw life as full of possibilities and growth. At first I was extremely naïve in my overall optimism. Therefore, often a polarity was constellated between the patient and me, which had to be threshed out in each individual situation. As my life went on and my analytic experience grew, I realized that it was not correct to label all the behavior patterns of these women as introverted. There was something other than introversion at work. It was more than helping shy women overcome their shyness, introversion, or whatever. Clearly there was a pathological complex at work, and I found these people could best be described as schizoid. A conflict arose for me at this point between the psychiatrically oriented nomenclature of the schizoid personality disorder and Jung's description of psychological types based upon normal psychology. For instance, much of what psychiatrists describe as schizoid, analytical psychologists would consider normal introversion. In the *Comprehensive Textbook of Psychiatry*, Brody and Santa describe the schizoid in terms of "a tendency to avoid close or prolonged relationships with other people. A corollary of this is a tendency to think autistically. . . . The cornerstone of the adaptive-defensive system in their instance is withdrawal. . . . In his isolation, he may invest his energies in nonhuman objects, and with sufficient talent and persistence . . . [to] provide an adaptably useful structure for his life."[1] All these attributes may just as well describe the introvert.

So wherein is the difference between the two terms? Is it important to make the distinction? I think that there is a great difference between normal introversion and schizoid personality disorder. The difference lies in the fact that the introvert is able to make a meaningful interpersonal connection when he chooses, whereas the schizoid person is unable to do so.

Clinically, one may ask, what difference does it make? Analytical psychologists in general are not terribly interested in diagnostic categories, and, if the analysis works, it does not matter. But I have found that it is important for me to have some formulation in order to assess where the patient is. Some of these people have done extremely well in analysis, but others have been some of my most horrendous failures. Therefore, knowing what can be seen as introversion and what can be seen as schizoid has been most helpful in the analytical work. Furthermore, within the category, schizoid, it has been most helpful for me to assess the degree of isolation. Often these patients present a thick barrier which it has been extremely difficult to penetrate. It is the degree of isolation which ultimately determines whether analysis is possible or not. A colleague, Melvin Kettner, has described this sort of person as a "workable schizoid." I have seen a large number of such women, and I think that they are drawn to a Jungian analysis because they see in Jung a legitimization of their psychology. Jung accepts the reality of the inner experience and does not reduce it to a pathological entity. I would like to present some clinical examples of such schizoid persons.

In one case for which the analysis did not work well, the patient was a young single woman in her mid-twenties. She had become interested in Jungian analysis as a result of taking a course. She had been seeing a married man with whom she felt quite involved, although he did not appear to reciprocate her interest. In the initial phase of analysis we discussed that relationship extensively, and she expressed much affect, crying

[1]Alfred M. Freedman and Harold I. Kaplan, eds., *Comprehensive Textbook of Psychiatry* (Baltimore, 1967), p. 941.

frequently and seeming to feel vulnerable. She came to see herself as playing the little girl role vis-à-vis the man, and she was gradually able to disengage emotionally from him. Over a period of one year her outer life stabilized. Her job went well; she was involved in courses, had a few friends, and the analysis seemed to go well. She presented dreams which mainly centered around her childhood home.

Her history revealed that she came from a Jewish father and Catholic mother whose f:amilies had emigrated from Europe. She had always been competitive with her mother and favored by her father. Her background did not seem unusual through high school, but at college her life became somewhat chaotic. She changed colleges each year until graduation, whereupon she went to Europe for several months. In Europe she became unable to cope on an emotional level, and her mother had to bring her back home. After several months of recuperation she got a job and gradually found herself in one short-term relationship after another.

None had been particularly significant until the one which brought her into analysis. I felt that the therapeutic relationship was good. She expressed warm, positive feeling towards me, and I liked her. The analysis was working. Then she became genuinely involved with a young man ten years younger than herself; she was 29 and he was 19. She felt it was crazy, but they were both in love. Life was going better for her until he began to pull away from her, because he wanted more independence. She began to withdraw more into her shell, and all my extroverted feeling could not bring her out. She reported many fewer dreams and then began to leave the sessions early. She stated that she had nothing to say, and, after a few attempts on my part to get her to talk more, I would let her go early. This pattern continued for one year until the period after I returned from a summer vacation. At the first session after my return she came in extremely heavily made up, which was unusual for her. She announced that she was going to stop therapy, that it had reached the point of diminishing returns. I urged her to continue and see if we could work through the block, but her decision was final. At the last session she was on the verge of tears throughout the session, but she would not give in to them.

I have reflected on this case, because it was a type of patient with whom I have usually done quite well. Furthermore, the initial phases of the analysis had gone well. After two years of therapy with her, I had dreamt that I was married to her. I had taken this as a positive sign that I was deeply connected to her, but I did not understand the further meaning. Now I think it has to do with my own schizoid anima that I have been married to and that I've wanted to rescue from that fate. With the actual patient there has been only a partial resolution of that schizoid nature. She did make many changes in her psyche over the four years of therapy; she was not, however, able to break out of a certain schizoid isolation which remained untouched. She was more comfortable in her professional life, but she was not able to form a meaningful relationship—either to a man or woman. Perhaps it is too early to say, but I do not think that she will return for further therapy.

Another example follows where the problem of distinguishing schizoid personality from introversion became important. The patient, a woman in her mid-thirties, married, but with no children, came to me after she had been in therapy with another man for three years. Her previous therapist had a bioenergetics orientation, and a conflict between them had developed concerning his approach. She decided to leave him in favor of someone with a Jungian orientation, since she thought Jung's approach would validate her more readily. She particularly liked the theory of psychological types, and she saw herself as an introverted thinking person.

She had grown up in a small town with an intact set of parents and two older brothers. The family was extremely poor during her youth, but the parents always put on a good persona for the community. She never felt close to her mother, and the father had serious brain surgery during her adolescence.

The initial three months went quite easily until I made some comments about masculine and feminine aspects in one of her dreams. Before the next session I received a long letter, a warning of sorts, not to label things in masculine or feminine terms. I tried to explain the way Jungians use the terms, that they represent attitudes rather than belonging to only one sex or the other, that we all have both. We were able to come to some sort of resolution. I agreed that I would be careful how I used the words "masculine" and "feminine," since they were so loaded in the general culture.

The next major issue was my interpretation of a dream. She dreamt that she was going to a doctor's office in a clinic; she was going to tell him a dream. She did not tell the dream to the doctor but went to the next office where her husband was. I saw this dream as presenting a major problem. In reality she was telling dreams to her husband before she brought them in to the analytic hour. I experienced the energy as going away from the analysis rather than coming into it. I suggested that she tell the dreams to me first and then talk them over with her husband if she wished. She reacted extremely negatively to my suggestion. We began a battle which lasted for the remainder of the therapy. She felt since it was her analysis she could do whatever she wanted, whereas I tried to explain my point of view in terms of the alchemical *temenos*, where it is important to keep the material contained and not have a leak, which dilutes or drains the content. In actuality she found there was a big difference in whether she told me or her husband the dream first. If she told him the dream first, most of the energy would indeed be dissipated during the analytical session. A related issue was that she would talk only about dreams which were weeks or months old. She would not relate recent dreams, as she had not yet assimilated them herself. She required a certain distance from me, and I felt that I was working too close in for her comfort.

Another major issue was the use of tranquilizing medication. She required tranquilizers to calm her diffuse anxiety. She was taking more than the recommended dose, and I felt that she was becoming psychologically and physically addicted. My medical conscience would not allow me to prescribe such large doses for her. Again it was the issue of who was in control of the therapy. I ended up by writing the prescriptions, at the same time I was cautioning her against overuse.

A further issue was money, but not in the way it usually comes up as a problem. She and her husband were not in the best shape financially during much of the time of her analysis. As a result I did not raise her fee when I made a general overall rate increase in my practice. When I made a second rate increase, I hesitatingly asked her for the first increase. She became furious with me for not telling her about the first increase. Why did I take it out of her control and decide unilaterally not to raise her fee the first time? She ended up by paying me retroactively so that her fee was like everyone else's.

These vignettes highlight the issue around control in which we were engaged. It appeared that she had a solid wall around her, her schizoid character, which I with my extraverted feeling was unable to penetrate. I genuinely felt supportive towards her and felt that I wanted to help her. In other words, my anima was generally positive in relationship to her. She did not want to let me in because that would have been too threatening. As I saw it, she could not allow me to enter her world with her and I was always outside. Behind the defensive armor there seemed to be extremely positive feelings towards me. She always came punctually, gave much time and thought to the analysis, and she did not wish it to end. After three years of this, however, I had worked to the limit of my tolerance for being excluded from the process and felt that we were locked in an endless and destructive power struggle which was not helping either of us. I suggested termination and referral to another Jungian therapist, a woman. The patient agreed, and I understand that she is doing much better now.

If I look back and wonder what went wrong here, I think it has to do with the two factors I thought to be helpful with this type of patient. It seems that both my extraverted intuitive-feeling responses and positive mother complex threatened her. She felt attacked by my reaching out or wanting to give to her. Instead of helping her to come out of her shell, it made her retreat further within her defensive armor.

A third and less complicated example was a woman, married, in her middle thirties, with a successful career as a book editor. In addition to being quite isolated interpersonally, she had phobic symptomatology, such as not being able to bear crowds, stores, etc. In the early phases of treatment she had several dreams in which she tried to meet with me, but something would be wrong, such as the time or the place of meeting. I felt that this had to do with a resistance in the analysis. By being unable to make a connection with me in the dream, she was unable to make a connection with herself as symbolized by me. Initially her ability to express affect of any sort was quite limited. Dreams and crying were her major modes of expressing anything deeper than persona issues. For instance, during this phase of the analysis she would enter each session and cry for the first ten minutes without being able to say why. It seemed as if a dam were breaking which had been holding her emotions in check by only the greatest of efforts. The dreams centered mainly around family matters, particularly relating to childhood. In many dreams she was in her childhood home, with her five sisters and mother, and would not be able to talk because there was too much noise in the room. She sensed that she was caught in the *participation mystique* of the family and could not express her individual needs. She felt completely caught in the subliminal demands, attitudes and expectations of the family, and hence she could not find an individual mode of expression. The family values were those of a typical Midwestern family, where she was caught up in an extraverted life. We were able to trace the sense of isolation which developed in spite of being surrounded by the rest of the family. Many dreams included an interaction with her mother, wherein the analysand felt duty bound by the mother's wishes and expectations. These dreams were most helpful in the reductive aspects of the negative mother complex.

The analysis progressed more or less smoothly for several years until a crisis developed. In the marriage the pattern had been for her to take all the initiative. She planned all social events, even made her husband's appointments with his doctor, and generally took charge, although in a not too overbearing manner. The crucial time came when her husband had to decide about a job change. His local office was closing and he expected to be transferred. In a subliminal way she was being asked to make a decision for him: should he move with the company or look for another job locally? She became quite anxious and phobic, and many of her initial symptoms returned. After several months of indecision, we threw the *I Ching* on my suggestion. The result was "Waiting" with no changing lines. It seemed that she needed to wait and let events happen as they would. She should not try to influence her husband in any way. As difficult as it was for her, she did wait and let him make the decision. On the last day of his old job, he found a job in another division which was not being relocated, and they remained here. Shortly thereafter she had a dream which indicated that she was ready to finish therapy. She dreamed that I was visiting her home, and she was showing me her kitchen. Afterwards we walked through the hallway into the living room and then I walked out. After all those early dreams in which we did not connect, she had finally brought the symbolic me into her house. I suggested that it was time to finish therapy, with which, after her initial surprise, she concurred.

My extraverted intuitive-feeling approach was most helpful with this schizoid woman, who is also an introverted-sensation type. She gradually has been able to drop many of the extraverted expectations placed upon her and accept her own more natural introverted way. My intuition raised numerous possibilities where her own associations were quite sparse. She was able to pick up on those possible interpretations which seemed to be right for her, and then was able to continue with her own associations; a meaningful dialogue ensued. She also needed my feeling function and positive mother complex to help her feel comfortable. Of the three examples this one has had by far the most favorable outcome.

Analytical psychology generally does not place much emphasis on clinical diagnosis. We speak rather in terms of psychological type or the activation of a particular complex. In the beginning of the analytic work I tended to overuse the terms introvert and extravert as a way of describing certain of my analysands. It has become important for me to be more specific, especially in relation to the overuse and overevaluation of the term introversion. In each of the three cases reported, there exists a schizoid element above and beyond normal introversion. An important consideration has been whether this schizoid element could be changed or not. In each case, that element has been analyzed with varying degrees of success. I have pondered what effect my own psychological type and positive mother complex have had on the process. At first I thought that my being able to reach out would have a helpful effect. It has turned out that the results have been mixed. Some schizoid introverted women can respond to my extraverted feeling and nurturing approach, whereas for others it is pure poison. The deciding question is whether I am able to reach behind the barrier and tap the emotional isolation. If I can, then they become the "workable" schizoid. So, contrary to my original notion, my psychological type is not always as helpful as I originally thought. This clinical problem has been extremely important to me since the variations on the introversion-schizoid theme account for approximately one-quarter of my practice.

Empathy in the Analytic Process

CHARLES H. KLAIF

THERE IS, I BELIEVE, A PREVAILING STEREOTYPE, at least in the San Francisco Bay Area, that the typical psychoanalyst is cold, unresponsive, unfeeling, and lacking in empathy and that the typical Jungian analyst is warm, responsive, feeling, and empathic. As with most stereotypes there is probably more error than truth here. However, it may be fruitful to examine the attitudes of the two schools regarding the relationship aspects of our work, with particular emphasis on the parameter of the analyst's feeling responsiveness, i.e., his empathy.

In undertaking this study, I met in myself precisely those difficulties and anxieties that Fordham suggests arise when we undertake the "microscopic study of the analyst-patient inter-action." It was a concern whether "bringing analysts' activities to light might interfere with valuable spontaneity in their relation with patients."[1] While trying to arrive at a tentative formulation of the concept of empathy, I found myself attempting to determine, during hours with patients, whether I was "being empathic" and whether such an observation might be an appropriate one to include in my paper. This extraneous and distracting personal aspect, of course, totally precluded the appearance of the phenomenon in question. One cannot, obviously, make a successful effort to be spontaneous and, as I will suggest below, the empathic response is a spontaneous phenomenon.

Without doubt, an excellent case can be made for the view of a friend and colleague of mine whose response, upon hearing that I was writing on this subject, was, "Hmm, I always thought

[1] Michael Fordham, "Technique and Countertransference," in *Technique in Jungian Analysis* (Library of Analytical Psychology, 2; London, 1974), p. 260.

that empathy was one of those things that just is!" In a very real sense I believe she is right, in that the empathic response derives in part from the non-ego, non-conscious portions of the psyche. My hope, however, is that our observation of our spontaneous activities can help us differentiate the valuable, spontaneous reactions which help to move the analytic work along from those idiosyncratic intrusions which impede the process. There is reason for concern that at some point the analyst's self-observation and self-evaluation can indeed affect his spontaneity. Although Fordham attributes the wish for privacy to "infantile anxieties,"[2] the problem of observation influencing the thing observed is well known in the physical and biological sciences and is even more likely to be an obstacle where a major portion of the observed phenomena occur within the observer.

Psychoanalytic Views: Freud's attitudes and ideas regarding the transference evolved remarkably throughout his lifetime, and psychoanalysts continue this healthy evolution. Many of us Jungians began our journey (as did Jung) by studying Freud, and we may have been excessively impressed by Freud's emphatic admonition to "model themselves during psycho-analytic treatment on the surgeon, who puts aside all his feelings, even his human sympathy, and concentrates his mental forces on the single aim of performing the operation as skillfully as possible."[3] Freud's justification for this acknowledged "emotional coldness in the analyst is that it creates the most advantageous conditions for both parties," and very significantly he felt that it insured "a desirable protection for [the physician's] own emotional life."[4]

In this same paper, however, he suggests that the analyst "turn his own unconscious like a receptive organ towards the transmitting unconscious of the patient. . . . The doctor's unconscious mind is [then] able to reconstruct [the patient's] unconscious."[5] In 1923, Freud described the analyst's appropriate attitude for listening to his patients as a "surrender [of] himself

[2]Ibid., p. 261.
[3]Freud, "Recommendations to Physicians Practising Psycho-analysis" (orig. 1912), Standard Edition of the Complete Psychological Works, translated under the general editorship of James Strachey (London), XII, p. 115.
[4]Ibid.   [5]Ibid., pp. 115-6.

to his own unconscious mental activity" in order to "catch the drift of the patient's unconscious with his own unconscious."[6] This clearly suggests an attitude of inner responsiveness and of allowing oneself to resonate to one's patient. The response on the part of the analyst would then presumably enhance the understanding of the patient's unconscious. The emphasis here is on the cognitive aspect of understanding, in which the "feelings" are put aside and viewed as either distractions from the "single purpose" or as threatening to the wellbeing of the analyst.

Consistent with Freud, Olinick, in writing on empathy, sees the analyst as able to "experience his own internal and internalized processes as a way of supplementing his knowledge of the patient."[7] He refers to empathy as "a perceptual mode that is available to both analyst and patient; it has been studied by psychoanalysts as a means of perceiving aspects of the patient."[8] It is a means of "more direct seemingly nonmediated knowing."[9]

Also emphasized here is the idea that empathy must be checked to differentiate it from countertransference[10] reactions, since both give a sense of certainty, and that self-observation must be continually employed. "In any case, it is not desirable to communicated either the empathic perception nor an interpretation directly arising from it without taking into account the usual cautionary principles having to do with interpretation."[11]

Jungian Views: Jung uses the term empathy at several points in *Psychological Types*. In the chapter "The Type Problem in Aesthetics," he discusses the relationship between the individual's typology and his way of sensing art and beauty. Empathy is described as "a form of extroversion" and as a "kind of perceptive process, characterized by the fact that, through feeling, some essential psychic content is projected into the object,

[6]Freud, "Two Encyclopaedia Articles: (A) Psycho-analysis," Standard Edn., XVIII, p. 239.
[7]Stanley L. Olinick, "Empathy," in *International Encyclopedia of Psychiatry, Psychology, Psychoanalysis, and Neurology* (New York, 1977), vol. 4 p. 315.
[8]Ibid., p. 314.   [9]Ibid., p. 315.
[10]I assume the term is used with the traditional pathological implication rather than in the sense of Fordham's syntonic countertransference.
[11]Olinick, p. 316.

so that the object is assimilated to the subject and coalesces with him to such an extent that he feels himself, as it were, in the object...."[12]

By "object" Jung seems to be referring to natural objects or works of art (although this is not clearly stated and there is some ambiguity here). Empathy is thus defined as one kind of aesthetic experience in which the aesthetic appreciation of a thing depends on the unconscious contents which are projected upon it. The opposite attitude is referred to as "abstracting" and corresponds to introversion. The individual with an abstracting attitude "withdraws into himself...and builds up a protective antiworld composed of abstractions."[13]

Willeford follows Jung's definition of empathy, referring to it as a "process of extroversion and introjection, based on impulses of attraction and repulsion."[14] This is in contrast to Fordham, who equates empathy with the capacity to "relate intimately."[15] It is a product of the free flow of projections and introjections and the "raw material for interventions."[16] "The likeness of the analyst's experience with that of his patient leads, because of his familiarity with what is going on, to a capacity to project himself, i.e., put himself into his patient's place, or to introject, i.e., experience the patient's feelings inside himself: these twin processes form the basis for flexible and complex identifications, necessary if he is to relate intimately [empathize] with his patient."[17] He feels that empathy provides the raw material of interventions. In the context of this paper, interventions must be understood as interpretations. Fordham states that, since an analyst knows about his affects, he need not act on them but understands them as indicators.

Jung wrote little about the actual conduct of the analytic hour and, beyond the discussions in *Psychological Types*, did not address himself directly to the question of empathy. Questions of "technique" are not much addressed in his writings either. Perhaps the clearest exposition of technique was that presented at the Tavistock Clinic in 1935. Although not using the term

[12]"The Type Problem in Aesthetics, " CW 6. par. 486.
[13]Ibid., par. 492.
[14]William Willeford, "Towards a Dynamic Concept of Feeling," *JAP* 20 (1975), 18-40.
[16]Fordham, p. 272.   [16]Ibid.   [17]Ibid.

empathy, Jung's description of his technique seems pertinent to our discussion. In giving his reasons for using the chair instead of the couch during the analytic hour, he said he did this "in order to be able to show my patients that their reactions have arrived in my system, I have to sit opposite them so they can read the reactions in my face."[18] "It is quite good to have a reserve of sentiments which you can allow to play."[19] The same point is made in "Principles of Practical Psychotherapy," where Jung refers to the "reciprocal reaction" between the doctor and the patient. He advocates a "dialectical procedure . . . unhampered by my assumptions. In this way his [the patient's] system is geared to mine and acts upon it, my reaction is the only thing with which I as an individual can legitimately confront my patient."[20] The same point is made when he says that "the relation between doctor and patient remains a personal one. . . . By no device can the treatment be anything but the product of mutual influence, in which the whole being of the doctor as well as that of his patient plays its part."[21] It is likened to a chemical reaction in which both substances are transformed and where the patient may be influenced only if there is a "reciprocal influence" on the doctor. Willing or not, the doctor's unconscious will be influenced by the patient and by attempting to "shield himself from the influence of the patient. . . . With a smoke-screen of fatherly and professional authority . . . he only denies himself the use of a highly important organ of information."[22]

We have then a repeated and clear commitment to three theoretical points: first, that the doctor is strongly influenced and affected by the treatment process; second, that this is a necessary condition if treatment is to take place; and third, that the analyst's overt and shared reactions are an important ingredient in the treatment process.

Both Freud and Jung suggest that communications from the unconscious of the patient can be received by the unconscious of the analyst. Freud's emphasis seems to favor a more cognitive approach, which utilizes these communications to enhance

[18]Jung, "The Tavistock Lectures," CW 18, par. 321.
[19]Ibid., par. 344.
[20]"Principles of Practical Psychotherapy," CW 16, par. 2.
[21]"Problems of Modern Psychotherapy," CW 16, par. 163.

one's understanding of the patient. This understanding is subsequently employed in framing interpretations—the major therapeutic instrument. Jung, while certainly employing these communications from the patient's unconscious in a cognitive way, seems to value greatly the therapeutic effect of the overt affective responses generated in the analyst. Jung did not use the term empathy for interaction with patients. Nevertheless, his views seem much closer to his description of the empathic attitude in which "the object is assimilated to . . . and coalesces with [the subject] to such an extent that he feels himself, as it were, in the object"[22] than to his description of its opposite as "the protective antiworld composed of abstractions."[23]

Empathy in the Analytic Process: Perhaps now we can begin to evolve a "Jungian" definition of empathy as a phenomenon in the analytic process. I would initially view empathy as a way of experientially understanding a patient's (or simply another's) state of being at a given moment. It is a spontaneous event and thus a product of the activity of the unconscious. It is different from simply exercising the feeling function, which, like the other three functions, is an activity of the ego. The empathic response occurs when we are in a state of relatedness to the other person; it is therefore dependent on the presence of a feeling connection. There is in addition a connection between the unconscious of both persons involved, a communication between them, and there is the analyst's enhanced understanding of the patient's unconscious resulting from this communication. Thus empathy encompasses both a feeling and cognitive appreciation of the other person, but it is more than this. There is also, because of comparable life experiences and the activation of analogous feeling-toned memories in the analyst, a quality of sureness and a sense of correctness about the extent and depth of the understanding. This provides the analyst with simultaneous and analogous perceptions of his patient and of himself, and I would emphasize the word analogous, to differentiate it from identical. An important distinction should be made between the unconscious processes of identification and projection, which may precede the empathic response, and

---

[22]"The Type Problem in Aesthetics," CW 6, par. 486.
[23]Ibid., par. 492.

what occurs when there is a conscious appreciation of the shared experiences of a fellow human being.

This, then, provides the basis for the other side of empathic perception and understanding, what we might call the empathic response. Here I refer to those spontaneous, often non-verbal reactions which occur when we say "I know just what you mean." When Mrs. Cook tells me about the sadness she feels over the loss of a sibling soon after I, myself, have suffered a similar loss, she will doubtless perceive the sadness my own loss caused me. Dr. Dawn, a young psychotherapist, describes how upsetting it was to have a quarrel with her husband over breakfast that morning and then go off to work and attempt to concentrate on patients. My empathic understanding of her problem is accompanied by a commiserating nod or two. I've been there myself. Mr. Earl reports an extremely powerful dream which has shaken him to the core. It has brought him into a confrontation with his problem of inflation, which, until then, had been understood only in a superficial and intellectual way. His new-found respect and appreciation of the power of the unconscious are mirrored by my own open-mouthed wonderment at the process and his involvement in it. Who among us has not been awed by the unconscious?

A somewhat more unusual example is the following. I offer it with little conviction that it properly belongs, but perhaps the reader can decide. I was frequently challenged by Ms. Fremont at the beginning of an hour to explain some comment I had made during the previous hour. On this particular occasion we began the hour in a friendly way discussing a meeting she had attended. There was a pause, and then she began an angry diatribe about the critical implications of some of my questions and facial expressions during the previous hour. She ended by saying that she had left feeling very hurt and very angry. This was not an unfamiliar sequence. We had discussed it many times before, and I asked her if she had any thought about "what the process is right here, now." She replied scornfully, "I don't really care much about that." I found a slight smile coming to my face, which I realized was inappropriate to the overt content, and momentarily attempted to suppress it. My patient observed my smile and asked if I would mind telling her what I was smiling about. I offered the possibility that "we share some understanding of what's going on here at another level." She began to respond angrily "I prefer finding myself humorous first," and then abruptly broke into gales of laughter, with a complete change of affect. In a most open and undefensive way, she went on to report a dream of the previous week in which an intense image of Christ had appeared. She began exploring some extremely important, but previously unreported, religious training and experiences of childhood, as well as a recurrent preadolescent "church" dream. She related this dream to feeling exposed and without defenses while in church —"the only place I didn't have all the answers."

My smile seemed at first totally inappropriate and certainly not empathic. In retrospect, however, I realized that my patient's attack that day did not have the usual "bite" to it, that it had an almost charade-like quality. The negative projections were ready to be withdrawn, and the first realization of this, for both of us, came through the affects. It was only upon reflection that I realized the similarities between her intemperate anger and my own and the capacity it has for possessing me. My smile seemed to be an inappropriate response to the now definitely weakened complexes. Instead, it was a reaction to a desire in her to get on with the deeper analytic work.

The empathic response includes, I believe, these conditions: (1) an active, caring relationship to the other, (2) an openness on the part of the analyst to receive fully both the patient's experiences and his affects, (3) the simultaneous activation of the analyst's own analogous, affect-laden experiences and memories, (4) an awareness of the similarity between what each has experienced, and (5) a level of trust and comfort in the relationship that allows the analyst to expose and reveal the effect the process is having on him. The last point moves our understanding (definition) of empathy from the realm of an inner perceptual process, which is utilized by the analyst for a deeper understanding of the patient and perhaps as a basis for an interpretation, to an overtly manifest and shared reaction, making it consistent with Jung's practice of confronting his patient with his reaction.

This broadens Jung's earlier concept of empathy, from an inner perceptual process and one type of aesthetic experience, into an important component of the analytic interaction. During moments of empathic connection, the symmetrical nature of the relationship is a reality. "The therapist is no longer the agent of treatment but a fellow participant,"[24] and he does indeed find himself as deeply involved in the dialectic process as the patient. What we have at this moment, then, is two individuals struggling with what is perhaps the ultimate task of both in the analysis. It is expressed by Jung as "the core of the whole transference phenomenon. . . . Relationship to the self is at once relationship to our fellow man, and no one can be related to the latter until he is related to himself."[25]

[24]"Principles of Practical Psychotherapy," CW 16, par. 7.
[25]"The Psychology of the Transference," CW 16, par. 445.

The Hierarchy of Symbols

JULIUS C. TRAVIS

FREUD, JUNG, AND OTHER ESTEEMED WRITERS of psychological case histories have neglected to organize symbols into a system of quantitative values according to their sequential power and influence. This essay attempts that type of integration. Such a system would make psychological work easier for the psychotherapist and would help mankind understand himself better.

Both Freud and Jung seem to use ordering in their structures of the psyche, albeit implicitly. There is no reference to *hierarchy* in the index of Freud's *Complete Works*,[1] yet he posed a hierarchy in the superego, ego, and id arrangement. Jung's division of the psyche into persona, ego, shadow, anima, animus, and self implies a qualitative ordering at first glance, but also a quantitative one when the affects of the different levels are considered. However, he did not write of the series as a hierarchy. On the other hand, he did make it clear that symbols occur in dreams first or last according to their psychic importance, which is the clue followed here. In the general index (Vol. 20) of Jung's *Collected Works*, there is likewise no reference to "hierarchy," but the following formulation appears in *Symbols of Transformation*:

> The finest of all symbols of the libido is the human figure, conceived as a demon or hero. Here the symbolism leaves the objective, material realm of astral and meteorological images and takes on human form, changing into a figure who passes from joy to sorrow.[2]

The changing of the symbol across the time dimension is the important reference. The symbol in the dreams changes, but what it stands for does not. In several places Jung also referred to symbols as "interchangeable" or "overlapping," which makes the idea acceptable to the theory of analytical psychology.

[1] Freud, *Complete Psychological Works*, tr. and ed. James Strachey et al., Standard ed. (London), vol. XXIV (1974).
[2] CW 5, par. 251.

The idea of a hierarchy of symbols occurred to me several years ago during discussions with Mrs. Adams, a young patient, who demonstrated her contentiousness whenever she felt confused or threatened. It seemed impossible for her to believe that a dog in the dream she had just related had anything to do with a scary, ghostly figure that had been in one of her dreams a couple of months earlier, because the symbols were so unlike. The point had just been made to her that the symbols referred to the same thing, that they acted similarly, that they were different because the material was no longer quite so foreign to her as a result of our previous discussion about it, with the associations and amplifications. Her acceptance of the dog was the result of depotentiation of the underlying force. Her flat refusal to accept this idea moved me to snatch up a scratch pad and sketch out roughly a vertical list of symbols from God to the dreamer, herself. I showed her this to convince her of the relationship between the symbols in the two dreams. I told her that symbols of material which was deeply situated in the unconscious were often accompanied by very strong affects, that the symbols which produced such affects were powerful and exciting. She thus became my first audience for this idea.

Hence, the degrees of the hierarchy represent two things simultaneously, first, the remoteness of the symbol from ordinary consciousness, and, second, the degree of emotional arousal the symbol commands. Symbols which have the greatest emotional impact are apt to be the most lofty, the most distant, or the most remote, since they are deeply buried in the unconscious and foreign to conscious considerations. The more remote a complex is from consciousness, the more unusual, bizarre, mana-filled, grandiose, or grotesque a symbol is apt to be. As the dreamer becomes accustomed to the content of the complex, symbols expressing the same life situation change to more familiar places, people, things, or events, entailing diminishing affects. As the substance of a complex or archetype is repeatedly brought to consciousness in varying symbolic forms through dreams, fantasies, projections, and life experiences, it becomes more commonplace. If it is reflected upon in psychotherapy, or otherwise, it becomes less unusual, bizarre, or grotesque. This process tends to diminish the power of the substance or the force behind the symbol. As depotentiation goes on, the affect caused by such xenophobic, dangerous symbols is reduced. The symbol may then appear closer and more friendly from the viewpoint of its owner. The ultimate result is that the nearly depotentiated ideas, which in their initial symbolic expression were terrifying or repugnant in the extreme, can be viewed with a more relaxed attitude. Thus the symptoms of anxiety, fear, or anger can be psychologically relieved. This is one way of looking at the functioning of Western psychotherapies. They seem not entirely different from other systems of personality change, such as Huxley's use of drugs,[3] or episodes in the life of Casteneda's Don Juan.[4] Here repetitious discussions or experiences sometimes bring about profound and permanent alterations in the living personality, and a softening and gentling often accompany the increased understanding. There are other similar methods which I have omitted.

Another example occurred with a patient a number of years ago, Mr. Baker. He came for help because he was having the same repetitive dream four or five or six times a night: that an unknown wild beast was battering down his bedroom door. He would awaken violently in a sweat of terror, with the sound of splintering wood and wild breathing and beating in his ears. His sleep was so curtailed that he barely had reserve energy left to accomplish his managerial job. He desperately wanted sleep, yet feared going to bed. What seemed immediately apparent, that he was inadequately containing a very large amount of anger which was projected on the wild beast, turned out to be true. Associations to his own anger (at his mother) gave a different relief channel for the energy, so his dreams moved into more personal symbols of animals and people. These were less frightening channels. Eventually he could even dream of his mother directly.

Although, in my experience with patients, relief has usually been reached as a stepwise process of depotentiation of the complexes, ranging perceptibly (though by no means with perfect regularity) through the hierarchy of symbols, there are exceptions to such stepwise progress. Some should be noted here. One example is the person with an apparently weak, sick psyche (ego) who is the recipient of the *tremendum* (an example:

---

[3] Aldous Huxley, *The Doors of Perception* (New York, 1954).
[4] Carlos Casteneda, *The Teachings of Don Juan* (Berkeley, 1968).

Saint Augustine), and is never again weak or sick. He becomes utterly transformed in a nearly instantaneous process. Such a fortunate one becomes a tranquil, capable, effective person in sound health. Other techniques include ancient Oriental and modern Western methods which depend on hallucinogenic drugs or varying religious or vulgar initiation rites. All of these are directed toward circumventing or shortening the normal process of psychological growth. This article will confine itself to a description of the hierarchy as a functioning system.

It is probable that symbols of frightening questions which haunt us have a commonality across space and time. Yet the degree of remoteness of a complex varies to some extent depending upon the time and place in which one lives. For many peoples of the early Mediterranean and European cultures, the "remote" lay out in the ocean somewhere. There was an edge of the world where one fell off, and before that an ocean full of man-eating or ship-eating monsters. Today we muse about quarks and the creation of our universe (and its eventual end) in the resonant Big Bang theory. Nonetheless, despite great advances in biology, astronomy, physics, mathematics, and even religion, we are still forced to symbolize the answers to those simple questions which the psyche relentlessly poses: who am I, where did I come from, where am I going, and what is this place, among others. Once the psyche has begun symbolizing, not only can these profound, unanswerable questions be handled but also any question that arises in life. The right side of the brain would probably be used in these instances. If the left side were involved, the patient would be conscious of pain and ambiguity.

Sometimes the complex does not appear in a dream symbol, but instead in a life plan. Such was the case with Miss Cox. She was a professional young woman who was very insecure and distraught for a long time after entering treatment. Three years after treatment began, she trusted me enough to tell me the real reason she had come. She said she had had an earnest suitor, an older man who was rather wealthy. He wanted to marry her very much, but she didn't really love him. Her childhood experience included poverty, and her professional future at the time did not appear to be very rewarding, so she decided to marry her suitor and then murder him. After that decision she became terrified of herself and came to treatment demanding immediate help for "an emotional problem." Relief in such a case, where the true situation is secret, must come indirectly from the satisfaction of psychic needs by parallel routes. She worked hard in her treatment and gradually developed trust, flexibility, and self-reliance, and she was making more money by the time she was able to reveal her true reasons for wanting psychological help. She had overcome her fear of her own violence, which, although hidden from my conscious view, was apparent in early dreams. Depotentiation was partly achieved by my matter-of-fact acceptance of violent affects in everyone, and partly by her repeated experiences of it in dreams when she would be forced to look at the consequences. There were many other reasons also. And, during this period, she married another man.

Societally-derived preconceptions can be seen in many people, most of whom are trained or programmed to avoid negatively toned psychological material. Psychotherapists are accustomed to receiving new patients whose motive in psychotherapy is to rid themselves quickly of invasive, obsessive evil thoughts or dreams. Here, an example is Mrs. Denver, a handsome young woman whom I initially met in a hospital following a suicide attempt. Before therapy and during the first two years of it, she had repetitive dreams of grisly death, of seeing herself or her family members dying, dead or decomposing. The emotions that accompanied these dreams were far beyond her tolerance. It took a longer time to relieve the symptom than it did with Mr. Baker, but eventually it yielded to conscious incorporation of previously denied personal affects and ideas. What she could not believe was that the way she was conducting her life was so harmful to her; she was murdering her own psyche (as well as the psyches of those around her). The solution of her problem was very difficult, for she had a snarl of images of an erotic nature mixed up with her father's suicide, which occurred when she was quite young. With repetitious observations of her dreams, which followed her varying life behavior, she became convinced that the way of life she had been leading (and had believed to be perfectly innocuous) was in fact evil for her, no matter how many other people could live that way with happy abandon. Then the awful death figures and ghosts and devils faded away, and, instead of being an innocent victim, she saw that she could choose her own response to temptation. Ghosts became men. Irresistible forces were depotentiated to seductors, whom she learned to handle.

The pain and turmoil expressed in dreams by symbols at the nether end of the psyche—grisly death of the dreamer or loved family members, unknown beasts battering down the bedroom door, and the like—reveal projections and introjections of great power. The energy of such unconscious contents pouring into consciousness prevents people from giving proper attention to daily affairs. They conclude that such material is negative and that it should be expunged, that they themselves are evil or insane, or controlled by evil and insane forces. But the internal force of the complex, so long neglected, has built up its energy to the explosive level; it can no longer be ignored. Because such individuals are not conversant with that part of themselves, the symbols appear as distant, strange, remote, and very dangerous. These people dislike having their lives interrupted by an internal force just as much as they would dislike being ordered around by an external tyrant. If they could only realize—as great poets have—that we are all murderers, wild beasts, prostitutes, robbers, torturers, and so on (vide Hesse's *Steppenwolf*), they could avoid their painful crises.

In many cases of psychic turmoil the cure, if possible, involves familiarity with one's own negatively seen elements, just as one becomes accustomed to and familiar with a neighbor he doesn't particularly like. In such daily situations with neighbors, time and familiarity will release friendly energy for mutual help in moments of need. Any soldier who has been in battle recognizes this idea instantly, for he knows that a comrade he doesn't like may shortly be the one who saves his life. Integration, communication, and understanding are the refreshing elements which allow us to recall our common origins. Xenophobia, a general disturbance, collapses with familiarity when both sides have open minds.

A dangerously seen complex, which has been resolutely repressed, and which the subject has failed to integrate, comes to his or her attention at or near the top of the hierarchical ladder. Figure 1 outlines the general idea of a hierarchy. Other names could be given to its divisions to represent an outlook or

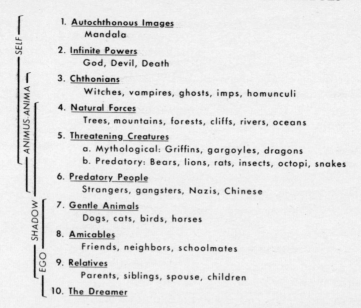

Figure 1. The hierarchy, conceived as a descending ladder of mostly negative symbols, from those bearing the most intense load of affect to those least burdened with affect.

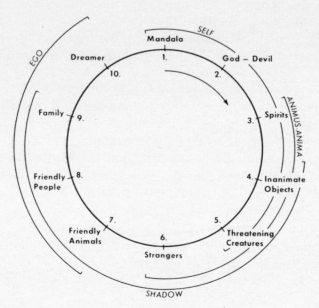

Figure 2. The hierarchy of symbols conceived as a circle suggesting clockwise or counterclockwise movement.

experience that differs from this one. After studying the idea of this staircase type of chart, one can see that it can be looped on itself to form a circle (Figure 2). The circle idea suggests the possibility of movement in either direction; expansion in a third dimension could form a helix. That makes it another possible way to view life and its products and divisions—to incorporate time, for example. In the circular chart, the usual developmental movement is clockwise, as indicated by the inner arrow. But, in the farther-out symbols 1 and 2, especially, and even 1 through 5, movement can be in either direction.

These charts, like the concept they illustrate, are a general framework rather than an exact rule. One should not be very strict in the use of such devices as these, since they may be invalid in immediate cases. In some patients, for example, the early symbol of self may be a wild animal rather than a clearly defined mandala or other unifying symbol. All numbered divisions in the charts can easily be broken down into subdivisions, but in my experience the healing process is too inexact for such detailed circumscription.

Although a hierarchy of symbols has not been previously described by others, there appears to be a tacit understanding among workers in the field that it exists. When one attends a meeting of psychotherapists of any dynamic persuasion and hears a case presentation that includes clear recounting of a patient's dreams, expressions of recognition develop on the faces of the professional audience. Mutterings of: "Aha, incest!" "Oh, oh, sounds schizophrenic!" "No fear, that patient is getting well!" and so on, are heard. We all seem to have a valuing system which can be integrated into the idea of a hierarchy.

How does the hierarchy manifest itself, and how does it function in the psyche's armamentarium against drastic disruption? Examples have been offered. Over the years of practicing psychiatry one is consulted by a number of people whose presenting problem is great anxiety and fear, stemming from their somewhat plausible belief that the world is imminently going to enter the final total war. In these patients this has been a projected fear of their own psychic disintegration, which often seems to be partly true.

This situation was demonstrated by Captain Fox, another patient of mine. He was a graduate of a naval academy and had been forced to resign from the service because he was so upset he drank heavily every day. He knew so much military and naval lore, both academic and secret, that it was impossible to dissuade him from his Third World War theory. Eventually, treatment can be made successful by turning such patients' thinking back to themselves. When confronted by a demand that they prove to the therapist their concommitant assertion— that they are going crazy immediately—they usually cannot do so. As a result of this failure, relaxation can set in, which allows the psychotherapeutic process to proceed to its proper goal. In this example, the symbol of universal destruction had erupted and taken over the cognitive elements of consciousness. Later, the projected conflict with evil was dealt with less frighteningly.

So, at times of psychic stress, people may dream of God or Jesus or Mary or the devil. Or during another period of tension, they sometimes dream of mandalas. The stress ploughs deeply into human psychic and/or physiologic root systems. The appearance of such symbols threatens the subject's sources of unity and strength and power. Because of preconceptions regarding the symbol, however, the value exposed is often considered by the subject to be negative, fearsome and dangerous, or insane. The corollary to the above must be that, without stress and tension (pain, depression, etc.), nothing of value would be exposed. When happily utilized, those awesome resources can help in the restitution of a properly functioning personality, albeit at a new level.

During the weeks before and during the early composition of this paper, young Mr. George was being interviewed. He had had repetitive dreams of being chased and attacked by gangsters (chart position 6) and wild animals (position 5). In his dreams no reason for the attacks was apparent. He could only explain their behavior by saying that he was chased because the nature of the chaser was to chase; the evil was projected to an evil person or animal. No associations of the patient opened up any avenues of personal enmity at that time; he was blank as to why all this happened. Later, however, he had a dream in which his boss (position 8) sternly confronted him with a list of his misdeeds in the office. On reflection during his interview with me, the patient was convinced that he had not in reality committed any of the transgressions he was accused of in the dream, and he knew that his boss was not at all the type of person portrayed in the dream. This is a new style of dream for him; the scenario is becoming clearer, the actors more familiar. Hence, new questions can arise as to why he sees the boss in this way, and the projections can be pulled back closer to the ego. Such questions were not clearly perceived by Mr. George when the attackers were unknown. One assumes that he is dreaming of projected personality traits of his own which one day he can swallow and digest in his growth process. With help, understanding, and encouragement he is approaching wholeness. He even grudgingly and voluntarily admits he feels better.

The change in the character of this patient's dreams satisfies the requirements of my thesis: that, as the patient gains in strength, the symbol for the same complex changes its form, and the change will follow a design which is roughly and generally uniform.

This design, when known and anticipated, helps both the therapist and the dreamer. The patient, who finds that he is following a track others have trod, becomes easier in his mind and more interested in watching the scenes which present themselves to him as he moves along. His interest in watching the inner play increases as he learns that it has a meaning. He can think of the changes in symbols, as they advance through the hierarchy, as mileposts which prove that he is not just treading water to keep from drowning but is actually making progress, though it may seem confusing and irrational.

A final note is necessary to clarify the clinical application of this thesis. The examples used above are all from patients who were relatively new in psychotherapy. As patients learn to relax in the face of their exciting symbols in further psychological development, a reversal of the process often occurs. The movement can then really be toward the more elementary and archetypal symbols, which still retain their power. At this point the patient has become an interested student who can experience the symbols with their affects without losing his balance, and can study them for meaning and application more serenely.

This thesis is offered in an early form in the hope that the idea will find resonance in others.

An Acute Schizophrenic Process Treated by Analytic Therapy

HOWARD I. LEVENE

THIS PAPER AND CASE HISTORY will present an underlying theory and approach to the out-patient analytic therapy of acute schizophrenic psychosis.

My basic training as a psychiatrist emphasized the "medical model" in the treatment of schizophrenia; namely, a heavy reliance on medication to suppress the psychotic symptomatology, rapid resocialization, and an avoidance of depth psychotherapy. In particular we were taught to avoid discussing floridly psychotic fantasy, delusion, and hallucination.

While this medically-oriented approach does, in fact, ameliorate the psychosis in an efficient manner, it is well recognized that it is no cure for the underlying process. In fact, there has been increasing concern about the so-called revolving-door syndrome—recurrent rehospitalization of patients treated in this manner, and, even more important, the possibility that such an approach leads to the adaptation of a "sick role" by such individuals, who in their acute psychosis are in fact in a highly suggestible, altered state of consciousness.

During my psychiatric residency I became so discouraged with the effects of this treatment that I thought no treatment at all might be better. My supervisors interpreted this as a "classical case" of psychiatric resident disillusionment, but I was surprised to find support for my feelings cropping up in the literature.[1] Patients discharged from hospitals with no treatment did better than those treated, and any approach which

[1] T. J. Scheff, *Being Mentally Ill* (Chicago, 1966).

emphasized prevention of hospitalization (e.g., crisis intervention, family therapy, etc.) had better results than in-patient treatment.

When I first entered private practice, one particular patient (about whom I have previously reported[2]) stubbornly refused to be cast in the sick role. She refused medication and literally forced me to listen to her inner material, which, contrary to what I had been taught, led to a rapid resolution of her psychosis within a two- to three-month period of time. Meanwhile, in a research project which I conducted at the University of California Medical Center in San Francisco on brief out-patient psychotherapy (with no medication), I found some acutely psychotic patients responding to this time-limited therapy—when the therapist was encouraged to listen to the psychotic material and try to understand what was being communicated.

Perhaps the most important factor for me in altering my therapeutic approach to schizophrenia was the course of my own analysis. As an extraverted-intuitive, I was struggling to get in touch with the reality of my inner psychic world. The archetypal material, which I fully believed would lead me to my inner sense of meaning, was not easily accessible. In listening to my acutely psychotic patients, I became aware, as Jung had become in his early studies of schizophrenia, that the material of the psychotic experience was essentially human. The fantasies, delusions, and hallucinations were the stuff of dreams—archaic, archetypal, "big dreams" to be sure—those that I could only rarely admit to my own consciousness. How could I suppress in others the very creative material that I was trying to come into contact with myself?

As my own analysis continued, I realized that for me to progress I would have to give up *my* outer reality. This led to my decision to give up my practice and my university position and enter fully into my analysis in Zurich. I was aware that I was attempting, in a controlled fashion, to descend into the same ocean of archetypal imagery which flooded the psychotic. That meant that, with the help of my analyst I must partially surrender my ego control. I had to allow the gates to open and be overwhelmed with the products of my objective psyche so that I could consciously assimilate its validity to my life.

[2]H. I. Levene, "Acute Schizophrenia," *Archives of General Psychiatry* 25 (1971), 215-22.

It seemed to me that here lay the key to a theory of therapy of acute schizophrenia. Jung clearly stated that in a psychosis, the ego is overwhelmed by the nuclei of the feeling-toned complexes—the archetypes. Is this the illness, however, or the cure? We might hypothesize that the prepsychotic ego and self-image are so distorted that such a bombardment from the unconscious is a restorative factor. In neurotics we view the unconscious as compensatory to one-sided ego consciousness. Might we not view the psychotic process as compensatory also?

The one consistent theme in the content of the acute schizophrenic psychosis seems to be death and rebirth—the theme in mythological and religious terms of radical transformation and renewal. In my experience the phenomenology of the process takes place within a variety of mythological frameworks: initiation, hero journey, kingship renewal rituals, creation myths, shamanistic rites, and alchemical transformations. Yet throughout, the theme of transformation and renewal of old, distorted ego attitudes and self-images appears.

If we communicate such a view of the psychotic process to the patient, we can establish a relationship which is not dependent on suppression (chemically or otherwise) of the archetypal material, but rather one in which each of us views the psychosis itself as ameliorative—as an opportunity for growth. This relationship could lead, therefore, not to chronicity or deviant labeling, but rather to the development of an individual with a renewed sense of meaning. He would be more creative and would have openness to the irrational and a greater sense of the *unus mundi*—a unitary world view—that the rest of us neurotics sometimes struggle for years to attain.

Initial Interview, Therapeutic Approach: Paul is a professional artist in his early thirties. He was referred by Dr. Joseph Henderson and presented himself for his first interview in an acutely psychotic state. I include some highlights of the initial interview to amplify the approach I used in treating him.

On the one hand, he was terrified that I would hospitalize him, but, on the other hand, he felt that he was dying and his body was decaying. He felt that his penis had shrunk. He was convinced that other people could tell the light had gone out of his eyes, that his eyes were hollow and sunken. He experienced the daylight as if it were somehow dimmed. He repeated over and over that he knew this was going to happen as long as three years ago, after a particularly compelling dream which had frightened him (see below). He said he had no soul—that the electricity had flown out of his body through wounds in his wrists, loins, and left side. He was afraid that he had exchanged souls with a friend, his step-daughter, his wife, and his mother. He had tried to kill himself twice in the past month or so—once by pills, and in a second, more serious episode, by going into the ocean at Devil's Slide south of San Francisco. The waves had washed him into a cave at the foot of a cliff; the fact that he failed to drown gave him hope that his death might be psychological rather than physical.

The following is a description in his own words of his psychotic experience, written at my request several weeks after we began working together:

In April began to feel strange highs, had insomnia. Thoughts were rapid, insights penetrating. In May, while painting, two flashes discharged through my mind and consumed my entire being, visually. One blue light I knew to be my Father, and a red flash, Mother. My physical reaction was an audible heart beat, pain in center of chest and neck, cold sweat and fear. Had E.K.G., blood test, x-ray; negative, but felt M.D. saw something and turned me out to die. For the next several nights I was driven down through successive psychic levels into a bottomless, dark world. Each night was accompanied with cardiac response, cold sweats, sleep broken by snorting and gasping for air. Would rush to mirror, eyes bloodshot, fact contorted. Cold chills when thought about my career destroyed. Toward end of week a loud thud crashed into the lower rear section of my head so intensely my wife grabbed for me and would not let go. She had been asleep. She said she did not know why she did it. I thought I was going totally insane; began to contemplate suicide. Drove during day, but did not trust myself. Soul escaped through wrists, left side, and loins. All electricity gone, weight dropped 15 pounds. Arms dead weight. Eyes deep in sockets. A friend's dog refused to get into my car or approach me. I felt I was the center of a great white wind. Our cat screamed when she jumped upon my chest. Finally became irresponsible. Feared straitjacket, preferred suicide. Got drunk. Sobered up next day, and took sleeping pills. Vomited after maybe 45 minutes or hour. Slept several hours. Felt better, cleaned out. Had hit psychic bottom. Was married, one reason for terminating suicide attempt.

Felt a friend who had been drawing in my studio had my soul—in fact still think he has some and I part of his and some of my wife's. During trauma there actually was a passage of white light from friend's elbow to mine and back again. I did not want his being. I have received and rejected several souls and began to remain alone fearing the transfer.

I looked so down and weight loss so extreme friends turned away or just stared. Some looked at me out of the corner of eye in horror. Others of course were rational, beautiful. Called home on Mothers Day. Mom sensed something. Left side opened again—she felt it. I received her spirit again. It filled my body with light and life. I rejected it, feeling it was phoney.

I tried to act natural. Thought my mind had become infected because of other people's actions. Events and people in my life seemed to grow worse day by day because of me. Thought things would only improve if I was dead. Thought my step-daughter had some of my mental vibrations and I could only cure her from the Domain of the Eternal. Tried to drown myself. Failed. Somehow saw hope through strength of body to resist Death, i.e., if I was not dying physically, perhaps psychologically. Then remembered rationally the premonitions from several years ago. I could not rely on the thoughts because of paranoia I have begun to experience. White Light in Dreams. Once in the belly of my wife, last night. I try to become a light within my own being and reach the upper regions of my brain for past several weeks. So far all I can "imagine" is an old, dusty attic, with trunks, chairs, etc., and a frosty window that glows but admits no light. I think I see just the light I am trying to be.

Many strange things happened in my sleep during this time. I heard bells, clearly. The familiar and beautiful but unique soft notes of a silver harp entered my mind through the base of my skull. I thought for weeks what a miserable death. Then I began to feel like Christ or a Christ. The detachment. The feeling of good will toward men. Humility, kindness, What a terrific vision, day and night, off and on. It was not quite real, rather complete. Pure white.

I intervened occasionally in the initial interview. I reflected that Paul's description of the wounds in his body reminded me of Christ's agony on the cross. I agreed that his death had a psychological meaning and asked him to reflect on what *part* of him had to die and be reborn on a higher plane—analogizing to Christ. I suggested that even Christ was unsure at the crucifixion ("My God, My God, why hast thou forsaken me?"), so I didn't blame Paul for not being sure about what was happening to him. I told him that other people had similar experiences. In response to a direct question about my own life, I shared that I had vividly experienced death and wounding in my dreams and that Jung, when deeply involved in his own analysis, had kept a gun near him for fear of being overwhelmed by the process. After Paul reported the dream which he felt predicted his experience, I said that I was interested in his dreams. I requested that he write them down, or draw or paint them, and bring them in with him to his interviews. I asked if he could contain his experiences within the therapy hours, since, just as they frightened him, they probably scared the people around him. I said I wouldn't hospitalize him, but I let him know that it was all right with me if he decided to hospitalize himself. He was immensely relieved at this and agreed to see me three times weekly.

From the brief description of the interview the main emphases in the therapeutic approach were:

(1) Establishing a relationship based on *accurate empathy* with the patient in relation to the archetypal contents. Unconditional acceptance and love are not enough. Accurate empathy depends on the willingness of the therapist to delve into his own psyche as well as into comparative literature and mythology for understanding of the patient's psychosis.

(2) Support and clarification that the experience, while frightening, is essentially psychological and basically human. It can lead to growth and renewal. This, as well as the universalization of the experience, tend to avoid the problem of inflation from archetypal contents.

(3) A request for objectification of the experience. The act of writing down what is happening, or painting the dreams, brings back the observing ego with the help of the analyst's observing ego.

(4) A recognition of the fact that this experience is as frightening to others as it is to the patient. The "dues" paid to outer reality, at least in an outpatient therapy, tend to reinforce the observing ego without necessarily suppressing archetypal contents.

Personal History: Paul was born and reared in the deep South. From an early age it became clear that he had a talent for drawing. His mother, who was an artist by avocation, found his ability intriguing and cultivated it, much to the dissatisfaction of his father, a successful businessman who felt his son should be involved in more practical pursuits. Paul's sensitivity and artistic ability alienated his father. His mother, it seems, used him and his art to solve some of her own marital problems.

As a child, his artistic abilities and sensitivities were ridiculed by his peers. At a very early age, he espoused a tough, anti-authority persona which helped protect him from inner feelings of alienation and masculine inadequacy. He was bright, but his tough style caused recurrent difficulties, particularly in school, with regard to limits imposed by external authority. He always found solace in his mother, at least until late adolescence, when he began to find her intellectually inferior to himself. By this time he had developed a power-oriented intellectual barrier in addition to his tough-guy, anti-establishment guise.

Although he could "put down" his mother intellectually, he knew that whatever force he had in his painting was coming from a center belonging to her. He was his mother's son. He could publicly hide this behind a highly developed pseudo-masculine tough intellectuality, but she was behind the screen. He resented his father for the distance between them; yet, by the time he reached adult life, painting was all he had.

Paul was unable to establish intimate relationships with women. According to one who knew him in art school, "He came on like a brawling bum—who always put me down." While he had several heterosexual affairs and displayed no overt homosexual interest, his relationships always terminated as soon as he began to feel any closeness, or when any commitment was demanded from him. He felt that allowing himself to enter into a full relationship with any woman besides his mother would destroy his painting.

After graduation from art school and study in Europe for a year, he began to fear that his inspiration to paint would run out. He felt that, if he were not painting from his own center but from one that belonged to his mother, his work was limited. He knew he would have to give up his tie to his mother but was terrified to do so. In the midst of this conscious conflict he dreamed that he would marry and, by doing so, go crazy. His dream occurred three years prior to his psychotic break and continued to haunt him.

A year before his break, he flew in the face of his fear and married a woman who he thought was different from his mother. She wouldn't control him. She had a young (11-year-old) daughter from a previous marriage, and this girl intrigued him in a way he couldn't quite understand. He tried desperately to change his painting style to a more realistic form than previously, hoping this would help accomplish the break from his mother. Again, he feared he would run out of ideas. His wife in the meantime was making demands upon him which he experienced as controlling. He began to teach a professional athlete how to paint. The man was so successful that he planned to give up his athletic career just at the time when Paul was becoming increasingly panicked about his own painting. In this context Paul became psychotic.

To formulate the problem dynamically, we can hypothesize that he was fixated in a negative mother complex. He had an undeveloped sense of his chthonic masculinity and a poor relationship to his anima. His ego was bound to the Great Mother, the source of all life and creativity. His problem was to separate the ego from the Great Mother without losing the vital connecting link.

At this point I would mention that the patient saw me three times a week from June through August of 1972 and for nine months thereafter at less frequent intervals. In addition to the regularly scheduled interviews, I was available to him by telephone at any time and told him so. In the initial three-month period during which his psychosis resolved, he presented over one hundred dreams. He literally lived his dreams day and night. He had an uncanny sense of their meaning for him, and his day-to-day state of mind varied in direct proportion to his dream life. He often hallucinated about the dream characters during the day and felt they were quite disturbing and absorbing. There was a tremendous stress on his family, and his wife needed constant support, which I offered by seeing her several times and reassuring her about the process. My role with the patient was essentially supportive and encouraging. I would help interpret where I could, but there was obviously much more material than could be handled during the hours. I found myself fascinated, frightened, and at times awed by the momentum of the process.

More than once during this period, particularly when both of us were frightened, I offered medication to bring him "down" a bit. He always refused, feeling he would "miss the train" if the process were interrupted. He tended to become inflated or deflated recurrently. I interpreted his material quite actively and shared my own feelings and dream life openly at these moments to show him that, while he was experiencing something in his unique way, the process itself was universal.

He read three books by Carlos Casteneda during this period and found in them support for the universality and fearfulness of his experience.

I will present one dream that occurred three years prior to his psychosis, and six dreams from the initial three-month period of his work with me. They represent dreams which he felt were extremely significant and which I feel demonstrate the healing process at work.

Dream 1 (occurs three years prior to his psychosis; taken as a premonition):

I was soaring above a community on Potrero Hill in San Francisco where I lived at the time. I saw myself walking and joined my body. The day was beautiful. I was married. We lived in a quaint cottage with large windows through which streamed the most brilliant sunlight one could imagine. Also I lived apart from the rest of the community, alone. My neck was usually tired from looking at the sky for ill omens which I was sure would come, and be of a political nature, and end the freedom we as artists enjoyed. One day the sky was not as brilliant. The sun began to dim and the sky took on a greenish hue. Some people began building a dwelling similar to ours on the far side of the hill. The figures wanted to look and act, even speak as we did, i.e., assume our identity. The other artists asked me about the problem. We were all beginning to experience fear. The invaders began to multiply and crawl over everything like ants—across buildings and books, pots and pans. They carried rifles, never smiled, walked stiff and erect, stooped constantly to examine stupidly, then discard. Their faces were like square plastic masks with hollow, yellow eyes burned back in their heads. They never relaxed. When we realized how helpless we were, I barged in in panic on a shaman. He was in a vivid red room sitting on a commode. I did not have to say a word. Frightened into total panic I tried to leave but saw two of the plastic soldiers guarding the front porch. They were now fully what they were: S.S.-type troopers speaking only German. They had us under military law. I felt the entire world was inundated. I ran out. It was dark. Our beautiful cottage was now turned into a high-rise hospital with bunks chained to the wall. Green sunlight came through the windows, and moss grew on everything the rays touched. The building was full of sick and wounded. I turned at full speed at the guards on the porch and shouted "Fuck you!" and gave them the finger, at which point one of them fired the rifle. The flash consumed everything visually. The bullet struck me in the back as I turned the corner of a brick building and crawled for cover in some bushes while other guards looked for me. Later I crawled to my old studio to try to organize the people to expel the enemy.

The dreamer is flying and is disconnected from his body; he lives apart from the community, and there is an emphasis on the brilliance of the sunlight. It appears that his unconscious is giving him a concise, metaphorical comment on his existential position vis-à-vis the world and himself. He is unrooted, flying, "in his head" (thinking is his major psychological function). He has no feeling connection to the community. Although he is married in the dream, the solar aspects are dominant; there is no emphasis on the lunar, feminine principle. His wife plays no role, except perhaps as a reminder to his conscious awareness that, if he were in fact to get married, something would go wrong. He stated that it was his real marriage that brought on his psychosis. The emphasis on light and sunlight is very important for the artist. He was constantly preoccupied with the light and shadow of his drawings and complained that his visual ability to create light in himself and in his works was lost during his subsequent psychotic experience.

He is aware that something is going to happen to end this situation, just as he was fearful in his waking life that he was running out of ideas in his art. The dream suggests a political struggle and the end of freedom. Frequently in a psychotic experience the battle between the opposites, particularly the battle with the shadow, is characterized as one of a political nature. The evil forces are portrayed as totalitarian governments versus the forces of freedom, or the Antichrist against the Christians.

The sky begins to dim and takes on a greenish hue. This omen represents the beginning of the descent for the dreamer. The only personal association here was that the greenish hue was sickening and nauseating. The association of these events with the death and destruction that follow lead to the image of *Sol niger* in Jung's discussion of the *nigredo*. The "*Sol niger*, a black sun, . . . coincides with the *nigredo* and *putrefactio*, the state of death"[3] towards which the dreamer is obviously heading.

Now, in the dark, greenish light of *Sol niger*, the dreamer must face the shadow invaders who want to assume his identity. The shadow figures are cold, inhuman, plastic-faced Nazi storm troopers with hollow eyes. In his subsequent psychosis his eyes became the object of his most predominant somatic delusions. He literally turned into these figures, who represent his own power orientation, his own inhumanity, and his own unrelatedness. The fact that they speak only German led us to

[3]"The Personification of the Opposites," CW 14, par. 113.

discover that his mother's father was German. This *suggests* that, on the personal level, he will be dealing with a problem quite common in the background of schizophrenics—the problem of the mother's animus. The mother, out of her own power needs, never responds to the son for whom he is or what he needs but only as an extension of herself and her own wishes. During Paul's work with me it became clear that, behind the battle with the shadow, his mother complex was being fought.

He is asked by the other artists to deal with the problem, to expel the invaders. In essence he is to be the hero in the battle with the powers of darkness. His ally in this battle is to be a shaman in a red room on a commode. This image suggests the ultimate resolution of his problem. The emphasis here is on a pair of opposites in combination—instinct and spirit. The shaman is able to go out of his body and connect with the ancestors of the spirit world. He can initiate the young boy out of the mother world into manhood by showing him his masculine heritage in the form of the totem (see below, Dream 5), yet he is also the man who can deal with something as mundane and instinctual as sitting on a commode.

This unique combination of worldliness and spirituality reminds me of Castaneda's encounters with the Yaqui Indian shaman, Don Juan.[4] During Castaneda's encounters with the spirits, Don Juan reminds him that to be caught in either the "spirit world" or the "ordinary world" is not the key to wisdom. The wise man knows that *both* "worlds" are real. This metaphor later became a central theme for the therapy. As the patient experienced, and tended to become inflated by, archetypal contents (the spirit world), he was also constantly reminded of the world of ordinary men—represented in this dream by the shaman on the commode, and he was encouraged to stay between the two worlds. In his painting during the course of his analysis, he was constantly preoccupied with this tension of opposites, and he produced a number of works in which he tried to catch their essences.

The shaman is in a red room, and here we have the next necessary element. Red, the color of emotion and feeling, is the necessary complement to the dreamer's one-sided thinking, his Logos orientation.

[4]C. Castaneda, *The Teachings of Don Juan* (Berkeley, 1968).

Finally he finds his cottage changed into a hospital, and he associates this with an insane asylum. He is wounded by the shadow figures, and the dream ends with him alive but the outcome of the battle yet to be resolved.

This dream occurred three years before his psychotic experience, and one wonders if the psychosis would have been necessary had he consciously dealt with the issues at that time.

Shortly after beginning therapy with me, he presented the following dream, in which he renews the battle with the shadow begun previously.

Dream 2 (renewed battle with the shadow):

I am in San Francisco with R., who is a super-demon, and several of his companions, who are lesser demons. He is from my home town. We go to his hotel. R. is nude on the floor. He has a torso-cadaver with gray hairs and long black thorns. He hopes I am homosexual. He changes sex, except for his torso. I discover with my hand in his vagina evidence of other human beings in layers.

I look at my penis. I find it large and glowing. R. is frightened. His companions are awed and disappear.

The patient states that R. has traits which remind him of his mother. He comes from his own home town. The thorns on the body remind him of the devil. He is afraid of homosexuality, which he relates to an unbroken maternal attachment.

The interesting feature of this dream is that we find clearer indications of the association of the shadow with the mother figure. The battle fought with the masculine representative of the mother goddess is a recurrent mythological theme. (Gilgamesh vs. Humbaba, the guardian of Ishtar's forest of cedar trees; Osiris vs. Set, the representative of Isis.) Paul, however, does not fight this battle with his wits—as he had done with his mother—but with his penis. The phallus, the symbol of essential, chthonic masculinity on the one hand, and the masculine, spiritual, creative principle on the other, will be his ally—like the shaman on the commode in the previous dream.

The bisexuality of the shadow principle in these dreams and the mythological motifs associated with them suggest that, in addition to dealing with the mother's animus on the personal level, we are facing an archetypal struggle: the ego must move out of a primitive, uroboric stage of development wherein the encompassing unconscious has not yet been discriminated clearly into the opposites.

Having confronted these monster-like representatives of the Great Mother in a number of dreams similar to the one presented, Paul then experiences an inner sense of rebirth and a deeper sense of his chthonic masculinity via a series of dreams which bring him into contact with the Father principle but which leave him with the task of redeeming the anima.

Dream 3 (rebirth, the statement of the anima problem):

People were standing around a pool or pond of crystal clear water filled on one side with some kind of ruins, like Roman columns, blocks, etc. There was the smell of death about the place. In the pool, bound, but living at the bottom, was a person who looked familiar. I took it to be myself or the person who had my soul. He or I was on the opposite side of the pool as well, where there was a high fence through which I could see a large, vicious dog. It was from the view of the dog I knew of the ramp which led down to a dungeon below. I believe the dungeon housed a woman I know. She is the wife of the person who has my soul. My feeling was to save whomever or whatever was in the dungeon. When I saw the figure in the pool, I cried, "Pull that guy out!" and someone did. It came partially to life, still wet and bound and Christ-like.

The patient stated that, when he remembered the dream, it was so vivid that he gasped for air as if he had just emerged from the water. He felt wet, and for a short time the light returned to his eyes. He was afraid of going to sleep that night for fear of losing it. But the next morning it was gone.

The smell of death and the Roman ruins and blocks of stone at the bottom of the pool suggest the humbling effects that the *putrefactio, nigredo,* and *solutio* bring to the dreamer. The one-sided power that was Rome and its subsequent fall led to the Christian concept of love. Jung suggests, in his psychological analysis of the *solutio* in alchemy, that in this phase one-sided ego-consciousness has fallen into dissolution by the avenging deluge of the objective fact of the unconscious. Only by this descent can ascent to the higher stages begin. Jung also points out that this *solutio* is the beginning of an inner psychic union that can lead to the "one stone"—the lapis, the symbol of wholeness—in contrast to our dreamer's disassembled stones, the *massa confusa,* lying in ruins at the bottom of the pool.

With the spiritual rebirth suggested by the Christ-like figure rising from the bottom of the pool, it is no accident that the light returns to the dreamer. But its presence is short-lived, for there remains the task of rescuing the woman from the dungeon. She is separated from him by a gate to a ramp guarded by a vicious dog. This symbolism suggests that he must descend into the bowels of the earth and retrieve the anima from the Great Mother. Like all men he must make conscious his own relatedness, his own inferior feeling, and Eros. The dog reminds us of Cerberus, the guardian representative of the dark mother Hecate at the gates of the underworld. Like Heracles, the dreamer must pacify the dog and bring the feminine to the light of day.

This theme, the discrimination of the anima from the Great Mother, is played out repeatedly in the patient's dreams with a variety of symbols (see especially Dreams 6 and 7 below). Even after the psychosis was resolved, much of the work of the ensuing nine months involved an effort to make this issue conscious. In the first place, it needed clarification in his marriage. He was constantly fearful that his wife was controlling him. For a long time he could view her only as a threatening mother figure. Secondly, he was fearful that his painting would suffer as he consciously gave up his ties to his mother. He had great difficulty in trusting his own inspiration (anima).

Before he could come into conscious relationship to his anima, it seemed that he needed a series of dreams in which he could find a deeper sense of his chthonic masculinity.

Dream 4 (initiation)

I was with some people in the attic of a dark old mansion occupied by an elderly lady whose painting I did not like.

I could see more art through low openings under the eaves in soft pastel rooms beyond. . . . Also dark, narrow passageways through which I descended into my past to a large room where huge, sculptured, Easter Island-type heads were being unveiled. There were many people from my past who contrasted with the way I actually experienced them in life. . . . An old friend of my father, whom I never cared for, engaged me in conversation, which surprised me. He would rephrase more articulately what I had said. I was surprised at his intelligence about art.

The dreamer stated that he had to crawl and squeeze through the dark passageways to enter the rooms where the heads were. We note that he is now separating himself from the realm of the mother. He is no longer attracted to her paintings.

The image of crawling and squeezing through dark, narrow passageways brings to mind the birth process, and the movement to a room of totemic heads gives us the flavor of a primitive initiation rite. The descent into his past allows the initiate to relearn the secret of his lineage and the cosmogony of his world. His father's friend seems more appealing than he previously felt him to be. Paul and his mother had denigrated his father and his associates for their practicality and lack of artistic sensitivity.

This encounter with the positive aspects of the father principle was immediately followed by the next dream.

Dream 5:

I am in a strange, primeval landscape. There is a beautiful, low, soft, new light. My soul soared like an eagle.

Then further on I see myself drop out of the sky, changing in a magnificent arc from the bird to an early man as I landed on my feet. I was alone in the center of the valley, bathed in the strange, beautiful light from above. I was wearing animal hide on my loins and carried a club or some sort of instrument.

We note the change in light from the previous hard brilliance to a new softness. The one-sided ego-consciousness has been compensated by its experience of the *nigredo*. The eagle, a well-known alchemical symbol, appearing after the death of the uroboric dragon, is a solar animal. While it emphasizes height, masculinity, and thinking, it is ready to come down to earth, in the body of a primitive man carrying a club (a new phallus?).

The eagle was also an early Christian symbol for Christ. Its connection with the image of the primitive man reminds us of Christ and John the Baptist—the man who wears animal hides. Only after their alliance can Christ proceed with his mission of redemption. Thus, like the image of the shaman on the commode, we find the union of spirit and instinct combined to make the whole man rather than the one-sided pseudo-masculine (mother's animus) intellectuality demonstrated by the patient prior to his psychosis.

Fortified now by his animal-spirit nature, he can proceed to the anima.

Dream 6:

I am hospitalized for a liver ailment—some pain. Elderly nurses are unconcerned about their duties. I am furious. The surgeon arrives. He is intelligent and well trained in medicine. I tell about liver. He's not worried. *We* will remove the malignant part, and replace it, and it will grow to be as good as new. He makes preparations to do surgery.

A beautiful blond nurse appears to wheel me to surgery. She feels familiar. She pushes the cart through the rear door of the hospital towards semi-demolished buildings that used to be an insane asylum.

I investigate one of the buildings, go up the stairs through rubble; a door closes behind me, and I am afraid the rubble might trap the door shut and the nurse might not hear my call. The door is not blocked. I return to the cart and see the person that was on the cart, small and dying. I help the nurse help him, knowing I am all three persons.

Next I awaken from surgery. Only the nurse and surgeon are there. I know now she is deeply in love with me, and I am falling in love with her. I do not know what surgery has been performed. The doctor lifts the sheet and I see a large, glowing penis that I must learn to use. I feel warm.

Next I am pushed out of hospital onto a lawn. I am to have my cadaverous right arm repaired or replaced. The job nonplussed the surgeon. I remove some of the dead arm myself. I want to paint. The nurse arrives again and kisses me—caresses me. Life returns to my body, a beautiful glow. I ask her name. "Aphrodite." That means I am Adonis. I feel love and loved.

The malady that the dreamer experiences is centered in his liver. This emphasizes the archetypal depth of his psychic injury. Neumann, in his discussion of the uroboric stage of consciousness, points out that, for the primitive, the liver is the seat of the vegetative, unconscious life.[5] In some cultures the liver is thought to be the seat of the soul.

The "old nurses," the mothers, are of no help. But now, with the activation of the masculine, coming both from the previous dreams and from the positive transference to the therapist, there is an alliance with a new, well-trained healer. Together, the dreamer and the surgeon will remove the malignant part of the organ. The emphasis on the surgery—the use of the knife to separate the malignancy—suggests conscious discrimination as a healing element.

A beautiful, blond anima figure appears to assist in the surgery. En route to the operating room they pass a demolished old insane asylum. The dreamer is fearful that he will be trapped in his madness, but the rubble of the insane asylum, already having gone through the process of *solutio* (see Dream 3), offers no barrier.

[5] E. Neumann, *The Origins and History of Consciousness* (B.S. XLII; 1954), p. 26.

There remains an interesting problem of interpretation at this point. Do the death-rebirth symbolism, the dismemberment symbolism, and the Aphrodite-Adonis reference point to an early stage of developing consciousness reflected in the mythology of the mother-goddess and her son-lover? Or, are we entering a later stage of archetypal development where we are dealing with a potential, psychic, transformative process which takes on even greater meaning, viz., the individuation process? Here the hero is not just a resurrected young vegetation god but an individual who is conscious of his own transcendence and relationship to immortality. The reference to Adonis, the passive role in the surgery, and the fact that life returns to his body after the anima has kissed him—all suggest the former hypothesis. But, the emphasis on the glowing penis (solar phallus?) which *he* is to use, the identification of the dream ego with the other characters, the suggestion in the dream that *we* will do the surgery, as well as the fact that *he* removes his dead arm even before the nurse kisses him—these suggest an individuation process. This hypothesis is further supported by his having experienced the battle with the masculine representative of the Great Mother, his totemic initiation, and the fact that the mother figure in this dream is of no help to him. He does not experience his rebirth through her.

The next dream may shed some light on this interesting problem.

Dream 7:

I see an old man working at a bench in a gold foundry. The old man said that here they make the best gold that has ever been produced. He is a great sort of old man that stands for something good from the past. I have much respect for him. I like him instantly.

He is pouring gold, almost white in color, into molds. I give him some gold drops that I have. They look like silver. As each batch of gold is poured into the mold, I notice that the remainder, the supply, goes on indefinitely. I feel a sense of wonder at the process.

Next I am waist deep in water trying to catch a goldfish, rather, prevent her from swimming out of the room. The fish is delicate, with beautiful flowing white fins and gold body, white belly.

I must raise her out of the water and gently blow on her so she will not drift off. She now looks like a blowfish, still beautiful, and I recognize the molds of the old man as being identical with her. She knows I want her back and says I may have her if I ask her nicely in the right way. I said, "I do, I do,

I do," and she changes into a beautiful, fair, almost pure white woman, with gold hair, sitting on the chair. As I kiss her gently between her thighs, I see the symbol that I have been trying to paint.

The dreamer meets an archetypal old man with wisdom from the past. He is an almost God-like alchemist who is in touch with endless supplies of treasure. The dreamer has gold that looks like that of the old man, silver or white. We note his (the dreamer's) active participation in the process. Solar gold and lunar white or silver are the first of several images in this dream which represent the goal of the opus—the *self*. The image of the self is also carried here by the wise old man, the endless supply of treasure, the silvery-golden fish, the white-gold anima figure, the kiss, and, at the point of this *coniunctio*, the symbol for which he has been looking. His total immersion in the process is like a baptism, which, as in early Christian ritual, takes place in a fish pond. His raising the fish out of the water and his use of his breath to balance the blowfish again emphasize his active participation with her—his conscious inspiring of her, his redemption of the anima from the unconscious.

This dream lends further evidence to the hypothesis that we were considering above: we are dealing with a true individuation process, rather than just a son-lover struggle.

Conclusions: The case history presented here lends confirmatory evidence, suggested first by Perry, that the psychotic process carries within itself a healing potential for renewal.[6] The striking finding is that the process, if nurtured and supported, does not always take years to resolve but may carry through within a short period of time. Among out-patients, I have seen several such rapid resolutions in acute, first-break schizophrenic young adults, and this has been the experience of Perry as well. The long-drawn-out affairs are seen in patients who have already been initiated into the sick role by the usual "medical model" procedures.

This history presents evidence not only for the rapid resolution of psychosis, but for the hypothesis that, in certain psychotic experiences, the individuation process presents itself in a remarkably brief period of time.

[6]J. W. Perry, *The Self in Psychotic Process* (Berkeley, 1953).

The Clinical Usefulness of an Initial Dream

RENALDO J. MADURO

THIS PAPER ILLUSTRATES THE IMPORTANCE given by Jung to the initial dream or initial dream series in either psychotherapy or analysis. Moreover, it reflects the mutual collaboration I had with Dr. Joseph Henderson, who was my principal supervising analyst for the training control case briefly presented here.

Although highlighting the possible significance of initial dreams in the analytic process is one of Jung's unique contributions to psychoanalysis as a whole,[1] surprisingly few attempts to extend or even corroborate his views are found in the literature. This is true despite the fact that a great number of Jungian analysts do ask patients for an initial dream during the first interview. For example, in assessing potential to undertake deep analysis, I generally ask, toward the end of an initial interview: "Have you had any dreams since we spoke on the phone about our appointment for today?" I was impressed by how meaningful my own initial dream in personal-training analysis was, and recently I came upon the following remark by Jung in his unpublished *Dream Analysis* seminars: "There are cases where a dream in the beginning of analysis contains the whole analytical procedure."[2]

Although I acknowledge Jung's clear implication that not all cases may fall into this category, that "beginning" may not necessarily mean the initial interview alone, and that there are crucial transference implications to be taken into account when asking patients for dreams or giving instructions, Jung's re-

---

[1]"General Aspects of Dream Psychology," CW 8; "Individual Dream Symbolism in Relation to Alchemy; The Initial Dreams," CW 12; "On the Nature of Dreams," CW 8; "The Practical Use of Dream-Analysis," CW 16.

[2]Jung, *Notes on the Seminar in Analytical Psychology; Dream Analysis*, Vol. 5, Part 2: Spring, 1930 (Zurich; privately circulated), pp. 73-4.

mark stimulated me to pursue my interest in the initial dream. I would like to share a case that illustrates the importance of the initial dream as a valuable clinical aid.

Elsewhere[3] I have discussed the initial dream itself, in more detail, as part of the beginning phase of Jungian analysis. I gave particular emphasis to the general theoretical topic in its historical perspective. I also considered what constitutes an initial dream, and how it may be handled from the point of view of technique in order to assess analyzability in relation to three analysands and brief case history materials. In this paper, I will discuss an initial dream retrospectively, first in relation to an initial interview in which it was reported, then in relation to the therapeutic process after beginning analysis, and finally in ways in which I have heard colleagues value it. Most analysts have given at least some degree of importance to its diagnostic, prognostic, prospective, compensatory, and even telepathic attributes.

It should be remembered that the following account was written up in retrospect; I have necessarily had to omit a wealth of clinical material that would help to elucidate and corroborate my initial impressions and subsequent experience with the analysand. The full clinical and theoretical details of day-to-day working-through processes in the transference-countertransference relationship are not reported at great length here.

Identification: The analysand whose initial dream I would like to comment on began analysis at the age of twenty-two while a full-time undergraduate student at a university in the San Francisco Bay Area. She is an unmarried, upper-middle-class, Anglo-Saxon Protestant who presented with the following chief complaints: (1) "fatness . . . weight problem . . . gorging or fasting"; (2) sexual inhibitions, an inability to relate to men: "a big problem with Daddy"; (3) feeling "depressed, isolated, and lonely"; and (4) the fear of "spoiling and ruining" her older sister's forthcoming wedding because of her own weight problem.

My impression of this creative young woman's psychological type was introverted-sensation-feeling, although her true type

[3]R. Maduro, "The Initial Dream in Beginning Jungian Analysis." Manuscript submitted for publication in *JAP*.

and function were masked or distorted until recently because of her eating disorder, the presence of strong schizoid features, and the role she was conditioned to play in her family.

Maya, as I shall call her, was born and reared in the American Northwest. She is the second eldest of five children and has three sisters and one younger brother. Like her other siblings, she grew up in relatively affluent surroundings: housekeepers, private schools, and vacations in Europe with Mother. Until she was thirteen, she spent every summer with her family (minus the father) in an eastern seaside resort with her maternal grandmother.

Her father is a self-made successful attorney, her mother a sensitive, creative woman and an accomplished artist. Until analysis Maya idealized her family and overrated its solidarity and cohesion. In accordance with the "family myth," everyone had what he or she wanted and needed, and was "supposed to be happy"—presenting a solid, positive front to an otherwise hostile extra-familial world. As her history was reconstructed, it became clear to us that many unresolved issues of dependency existed between her only surviving grandparent, her maternal grandmother, and her mother. The grandmother lived near Maya's home and was seen as weak, ill, and overattached to Maya's mother. The myth of the ideal family was contradicted by this relationship, which she described as "gooey, sticky . . . the family soup." She realized she had psychologically inherited a mother-daughter problem that had been passed down through generations.

In contrast to her living maternal grandmother, Maya's deceased paternal grandmother represented the spirit of independence and appropriately warm extraversion. She was somewhat iconoclastic and she had traveled a great deal. Maya often referred to this "Nanny" as a cactus and identified with her creative strength, unconventionality, and zest for life. But Nanny could also be remote, distancing, and unfeeling; Maya felt she could be "wicked . . . cruel . . . hateful . . . a bitch."

Unlike her siblings, Maya's birth and subsequent life experiences exhibited special features and kept her anxiously in bondage to her mother complex.

First, she was conceived after several miscarriages and born after her mother had been forced to lie "flat on her back for the

last five months of her pregnancy." Maya's birth was surrounded by anxiety, fear, and maternal ambivalence. Her
mother had been given several injections of diethylstilbestrol to
avert another miscarriage. This drug was later declared unsafe
and carcinogenic. Consequently, an inordinately strong attachment, based on mutual guilt and fear of uterine cancer in
Maya, aggravated an already "sticky" mother-daughter relationship in which Maya lacked initiative and a capacity to assert
her individuality creatively without experiencing profound
guilt and depressive anxieties. Mother and daughter were inseparable; they functioned as a "dynamic duo," each symbi-
otically feeding upon and nurturing the other.

Second, at age six, a congenital abnormality of Maya's eyes
was surgically corrected. The memory of this powerful and
traumatic experience was repressed, but Maya recalled it suddenly and relived it with great feeling during an analytical
hour. This experience reinforced the parental fixation, the
negative aspects of the mother-daughter fusion (*participation
mystique*). It once again singled her out from her sibs as an
"oddball," as the scapegoat or symptom-bearer within the family system. Because of her "imperfection" and illness she was
even more overprotected. It fostered an overweening dependence on her mother, who drove her to a nearby city for "eye
exercises" at least twice a week for over a year after the surgery.

Third, Maya had unfortunately been born into a family that
needed her in unnatural ways. As long as her problems could
be the center of attention and overanxious concern, her mother
and father were able to avoid making deeper feeling connections with each other. "Daddy" was rarely home because of his
business affairs, and much of the libido which might otherwise
have flowed into a close marital relationship was invested instead in Maya, who conveniently made it possible for her parents to deny and isolate hostile feelings and to avoid any healthy
contact anger.

When Maya appeared for analysis, it had been almost three
years since she had been seriously involved in a male-female
relationship. Involvements had never felt sexually satisfying to
her. She reported having had two major affairs, one with an
irresponsible, transient young puer eternus, the other with a
"safe and unavailable" married man, around whom the patient

experienced a great deal of guilt and anxiety. These experiences occurred while Maya was completed two years at a women's college near her home in the Northwest, and after she became a college drop-out. According to Maya, both men, "hated" her body. Her parents were very much against these boy friends and saw them as threats to the family myth; her father threatened to kill one of them with a gun. The gist of what Maya reported was an intense need to please these men, repeating the pattern she had developed with her parents, who, she felt, either smothered or abandoned her. She viewed her boy friends as "having all the power," and, in her over-attachments, she repeated her usual pattern of being passively overcompliant.

Subsequent to these two relationships and after she had moved to the San Francisco Bay Area, a large portion of her libidinal interests were caught and drained in a number of hypochondriacal complaints and in compulsive autoerotic masturbatory activities. These took place ritualistically in her dormitory room; she was alone and reported feeling "sealed off" and "like wanting to melt" into her sleeping bag or bed.

As the analysis unfolded, Maya sought every opportunity to gain my good wishes and to please me; this became part of the core of her new transference neurosis. Moreover, compulsive eating binges served defensive purposes against depressive anxieties related to being close, fears of penetration and of men, destructive envious feelings, but most of all: the wish for=dread of maternal engulfment, fusion (*participation mystique*). What the patient consciously reported at the beginning of analysis—"a big problem with Daddy"—turned out, upon analytical investigation, to be a defensive screen against much more frightening, underlying, oral sadistic conflicts associated with aspects of an internalized devouring breast-mother.

Finally, in the context of Maya's past history and the special features of her development and entrapment in the Demeter-Persephone myth, it is important to note the prospective function of her symptom complex: she wished to demonstrate how defiant of authority she could be. By overeating, she set herself apart from the "family soup"; all other family members are remarkably thin and trim. To some extent Maya was able to establish a kind of negative identity, which was better than feeling no separateness at all *from mother* (ego loss), since her parents and sibs consciously loathed her overweight and drew her attention to it often. "Being fat," she later told me, "means being superior, apart, different." That Maya could, because of her eating disorder, altogether avoid dealing with men (Daddy) and with the possibilities for relationship involving oedipal conflicts was of secondary importance to her fears of intimacy and ego loss.

Initial Interview: Maya appeared for her first session very elegantly dressed, attractive although overweight, intelligent-sounding, and with a detached air of confidence, sarcasm, and eagerness to please me. She spoke very rapidly. I made few attempts to direct her conversation in any way, except to ask open-ended questions occasionally and to say at the beginning that talking about why she had come to see me in the first place was a good place to start.

My main concern at this point was to gain an overall sense of Maya's ego strength and capacity to undertake analysis. I was trying to establish a warm, personal, feeling connection, a therapeutic alliance based on trust. I asked a few leading questions about her past medical history, previous psychotherapy experiences, and family dynamics.

Everything she said at first about "Mother and Daddy" seemed very pleasant; they were so wonderful and idealized. Mother was all sweetness and light, Maya's "best friend . . . very close." Most of Maya's attention focused on Daddy, and she felt much more comfortable in talking about him than about Mother. She averted her eyes, tore off leaves from the piggy-back plant near her chair, and squeezed her hands together anxiously, when the subject of how mother was experienced came up. I noted these things to myself, but said nothing to her. This is difficult for me, since I have a tendency to want to speak directly to the unconscious sometimes, without waiting. My intuition can leap out—often very therapeutically once the therapeutic process is well underway—but I have learned to be more patient over the years, and especially with Maya. Since my type is introverted-intuitive-thinking, I often have to be especially conscious of not bypassing the ego—not making premature interpretations and remarks about unconscious processes. On the other hand, my best work stems from my intuition function, especially in intensive work involving the analysis of transference and transference resistances.

Maya reported experiencing her father as "ideal, perfection, disciplined." His presence was very weak, except for wealth in the form of many cars and other cultural symbols of power. He had in fact grown up fatherless himself. When Maya would phone him, he put her "on hold." He was extremely critical of her eating disorder, hardly ever seemed to claim his own wife from the mother-daughter coalition, and was rarely demonstrative with feeling. Here again in the father transference, it has been important for me to emphasize the Eros principle in relationship to Maya, since I am a male analyst and she a female patient, and since I am intuitive-thinking and she sensation. As Maya's history unfolded in the first hour, it became clear to me that her needs to rebel, to please me, and the softening of harsh, punitive, superego demands would be important themes in the proposed analysis. With regard to internalized, perfectionist demands, Maya reported, for example: "I need to feel I do everything well, best, perfectly, or I pull away, reject, or don't do it." As she talked, I had fantasies of never being able to be quite good enough or perfect enough for her, given these expectations of herself and others.

Maya went on to describe feeling comfortable only in the mountains, where she could "escape" conflict and life's struggles by withdrawing. As she described Mother Nature and her personal mother so blissfully, I began to feel that she might prefer fusion states to real people—idealized Mother Natures who in fantasy could somehow magically and automatically understand and meet all her dependency needs without her having to take any initiative or deal with conflict at all.

I experienced Maya as a hungry patient, even though she presented initially as an overly self-sufficient person and was careful not to reveal dependent and demanding feelings until later in analysis. She wanted to be fed. Mother was only too eager to meet her needs, since this meant Maya could act out her mother's unconsciously denied neediness, which was intense. Mother needed to feed on Maya. From the very beginning of analysis she referred to two of her mother's statements very often: (1) "Maya, you are superior; it has never occurred to me that you would be anything but special," and (2) "If you ever need me, I'll be there in a flash!" These two comments were to assume great importance later in our work as the transference neurosis was allowed to flower, and as the nature of her schizoid conflicts was clarified.

As I spoke with Dr. Henderson, it was clear from the first hour that Maya presented with an elemental mother problem: an unresolved symbiotic tie, with mother and daughter feeding off each other. The patient's daily life reflected this tie. Although she was in California, she phoned home daily, usually to speak to Mother, often to Daddy. They also phoned her. She wrote to Mother at least three or four times a week—usually postcards in which they addressed each other as flowers: "Dear Petunia," and signed, "Daisy." Maya had been in the habit of phoning home for many years while away, even when she went to Europe with mother. When Mother had to return to the states, Maya phoned her at least once a week. Once Maya fell and hurt her knee in Europe after her mother had returned to the states. During the next phone call, her mother offered to be there "in a flash." When analysis began, Maya's mother was still asking her daughter to come home, to write even more often, and she wanted to visit Maya at her college. Maya experienced friendships independent of Mother as a threat to Mother, a guilt-laden experience. She refused to allow Mother a visit.

In this first hour, then, I could feel the powerful pull toward establishing states of projective identification (*participation mystique*) with me. Maya was seeking communion, not communication—fusion not dialogue.

It was my hunch that issues relating to defiance of authority, control, *handling destructive impulses* that were mainly oral and anal sadistic, separation anxiety in killing off negative ties to the great mother, and very primitive defenses (e.g., the manic defenses, idealization, denial, splitting) would probably feature prominently in her analysis.

After analysis began, the myth of Demeter and Persephone seemed most applicable. Here Persephone is in the same fix as Maya. Mother-daughter identity, rather than relationship to each other, is a central theme. My patient and her mother seemed to be, as in the myth, out in the fields picking flowers together (the postcards, their staying together, often alone in mountain cabins). As Persephone lives out this experience passively waiting, like a flower or sexual organ needing to be fertilized, the ground erupts and Hades abducts her *to initiate* her into independent womanhood. She becomes Queen of Hades for half the year; she again returns to her mother, but as an individual undergoing an experience of renewal, and this whole process symbolizes having been initiated into the mysteries. When Dr. Henderson and I discussed the transference significance of living out this myth, he reminded me that Maya would have to kill off the negative mother, and she would do this by establishing the original relationship to the mother in her transference to me. I would have to incarnate the image of her mother problem (as whole-object mother, or part-object breast-mother), but *also* I would have to be Hades (the father) for her in a significant separation rite associated with the phallic male principle. Although there were anticipatory dreams in which this deep archetypal transference was carried by me, it did not appear violently and convincingly until after nineteen months of analysis, when projecting "Daddy" not "Mommy" became the center of oedipal (Electra complex) dynamics, and an extremely eroticized transference to me developed.

Although Maya spoke glibly in the first interview about "attractions to Daddy" that worried her, contact with this attractive young woman did not feel eroticized to me. Her neurosis did not seem to be rooted in genital sexual conflicts, as she would defensively have me believe. Instead it seemed to me that something with the Eros principle had gone wrong, that fundamental issues of relationship had not been understood by the patient. Instinctually, the Eros-Phobos opposites were fundamentally unrecognized. This caused Maya to fear any real closeness; she was fearful of wishes to destroy and harm loved ones. Developmentally, the first hour felt oral (i.e., her allusions, references, etc.) and preoedipal; our encounter felt dyadic (mother-infant). It did not seem as if three or more persons could have been in the consulting room. The father tie was not being activated; only later did this occur.

At times my active listening and silence seemed to make Maya anxious. I then explained, as I usually do, that, if analysis were to take place, I would want to see her four or five times a week. I know that many analysts prefer seeing patients less frequently, but I feel more comfortable working in this way; it reflects my own personal Jungian analytical experience when I was seen frequently and used a couch. I told Maya that I would mainly listen and intervene when I felt I could be helpful, and that in fact I was talking more in the initial hour than might seem to be the case later on. My personal feeling about this involves a belief that one of the most important features of analysis, in contrast to other viable forms of psychotherapy, is that the analyst *does not* pick up on trivia to reassure, or out of his own anxieties, but sticks only to essential needs.

I told her that I would attempt to go wherever she needed me to go in any given hour, but the decision about how to use the time was up to her. I said the room and I were there for her to use. There are two chairs (one hardback and one large soft one which encloses); a couch, upon which she might find it much easier to report her positive and negative fantasies, especially as they might relate to me personally; a sandtray in one corner of the room, and figurines near; and pencils, paper, crayons—all of which were at her disposal. I was trying to impart the message that she had choices and that I was constant and would be the provider of a warm, comfortable, facilitating environment. I avoided all technical terminology.

When at one point Maya asked for reassurance, I told her I sensed her need for quick advice and explained why I didn't usually feel it was very useful in analysis. The next time it came up I was silent. She then produced a great number of fantasies and feelings about what she imagined was happening, and I used these to demonstrate or educate her to the analytic process. I did not want to be silent without first demonstrating to her that there is a good reason for being so—that something valuable is to be gained in the service of our joint effort by hearing and exploring her fantasies, not mine. It was thus possible to demonstrate in a practical yet personal and caring way how helpful this approach could be, how the analytical process would be (within broad outlines), and how the concept of a working alliance to sort out her material was crucial. I also did not fall into the trap of devouring or invading her space, as she probably expected I would do in a motherly way.

Along these lines, we began the actual work of analysis in a gentle, nonthreatening way, without activating inordinate and

unmanageable amounts of anxiety and resistance. More important, I wanted to underline the dialectical nature of the process
from the beginning, and at the same time to underline the message that Maya was to be treated as a separate individual whose
autonomy was respected. In retrospect I feel that she probably
seemed both relieved and annoyed to know I did not need to
swallow her—that I did not need to act out any of my own
neurotic needs to be a good mother, instead of really being
there as one for her to relate to in a different way. I did not
need to establish too close a bond and so act out the mother role
from which she had suffered. I feel strongly now, as I did then,
that had I been more "giving," devouring, and intrusive in
responding to her hungry, greedy feelings, she would have
anxiously fled from me and would have broken off the analysis.
Of course, I can't be certain of this.

In demonstrating the reasons why I would not always feed
on her and/or impose upon her my own answers, thoughts, and
fantasies, I was attempting to enlist her cooperation, her transference love, and a sense of me as a real person about to undertake a very difficult endeavor that would mean growth for both
of us. I asked, as I usually do, if she had had any dreams since
talking to me on the telephone.

The Initial Dream: Maya's initial dream was compensatory,
prospective, diagnostic, and prognostic in nature. She reported:

I am living in a little mountain cabin with mice in it. I am lying in bed listening
to mice. I hear a mouse running inside a garbage can. I say, "God dammit! If
they're going to have a convention, then I'm going to see what this is all
about." So, I go over to the can. I open the can and see two big rats. One is
white and one is black. I throw a brick at the black rat who becomes even
bigger. The white one runs away. I hit the black one with another brick, and it
gets twice as big. I pull out a kitchen knife, and *it* pulls one out, too. I stab it
again and again until I think it is dead. Finally, I feel exhausted and stand up
and its eyes open. It also stands up! Finally, I go back to bed and I think:
"Okay, rat, you can stay here. Just don't come too close. You keep to your
own space." Then I go back to bed and the black rat shrinks up into a little
gray mouse again.

In this portrayal of Maya's attitude toward her shadow problem, she learns that she can't deal with the problem by repression of the negative mother. The shadow problem can and
must be actively confronted. Repressed shadow aspects of her

life, when they are accepted and given some "space" to exist and are integrated, become smaller and in more realistic perspective. The rat would seem to represent her mother problem, since it is a kind of parasitic or symbiotic creature in relation to man. It may also express the Eros principle gone wrong. Rats are aggressive, can bring disease, can overrun, and be intrusive. Because they are essentially nocturnal and dirty, they symbolically represent the shadowy, negative mother problem on a level of awareness that is less than human, i.e., not developed enough through consciousness via personal relationship. One might also say that, in terms of the opposites, the rat represents the Yin principle, belonging to the feminine nocturnal; it is not totally undifferentiated unconsciousness because it can be very aware of its own needs in some ways. In another sense, the mouse/rat can be seen as a culturally patterned shadow projection for women.

At the end of the dream, the gray mouse is a unifying symbol which resolves the white-black opposites. The shadow, as a combination of these two splits, must be befriended and have some place to live; life must include some consciousness and some shadow too. I felt that the dream was a good prognosis because the gray mouse symbolized the potential resolution of the black and the white. In fact, as described below, splitting (the black and white rats) is one of Maya's major defenses against destructive impulses causing depressive anxieties.

The dream hints diagnostically at the problem of oral aggression (the rat), as well as the negative use of phallic, undifferentiated animus strength still contained or locked up in her mother (the maternal kitchen in which the knife is used), and longing for passive fusion states (lying in bed, as Maya had done very often with her mother since early childhood). In addition to splitting, Maya's other defenses operate in the dream: as denial, devaluation, isolation (the garbage can), repression, the manic defenses (she reported feeling "high" when asleep, compulsively eating at movies or when reading in bed), and idealization (the white rat who may be the cheery, happy, dreamy, light, perfect mother of spring and flower psychology). Moreover, the cabin and her passively lying in bed may reflect the mother problem—in waking life she found schizoid unrelated refuge with Mother in a mountain cabin.

The conflict between *active and passive* wishes and the need to overcome great resistances to confronting conflict with the shadow are highlighted in this dream. The cabin has no rooms —no clear boundaries, demarcations, or differentiation of the mother problem in the psyche. All of these dream elements suggested what to expect or look for in the transference-countertransference relationship, especially the lack of any inside-outside (mother as separate from daughter) quality in the dream work.

The mice (the convention) hint at a potential for extraversion, and in this way the dream is compensatory. A convention, as a social gathering, is the opposite of schizoid isolation (*con* + *vene* = come together). The dream is compensatory inasmuch as it states clearly that the black side must be given its due. Because she tries to kill the shadow rather than get acquainted with it, the mice transform into rats (more dangerous, and less easily disregarded). Because the dreamer's conscious feelings toward her mother are one-sided (she sees her as only white and positive, often split into an idealized part-object), the unconscious seems to be saying she needs to have a look at these eating, gnawing mice. That is, she's frightened by her "bad," destructive feelings about her mother, so invested with all-or-nothing power due to splitting and repression that even her good feelings go away, until she takes note of the shadow and the possibility for a new ego attitude: it is more comfortable to live with the shadow than against it.

With this dream, insight, and recognition, Maya began analysis—deciding to accept things more openly, as if gray, not as if black or white (split). The potential for symbolic unification (the transcendent function) to occur over and over again in day-to-day working-through processes during the proposed analysis struck me as a prominent theme in her dream.

Notes on the Course of Treatment: Soon after analysis began, Maya's conflict over separation from Mother became more and more clearly delineated, especially as she described and *experienced* her eating scenarios with me in vivid, remorseful detail. Her attitude toward food was an attitude toward a person, the mother.

Much of what Maya's initial dream had suggested unfolded

in subsequent interviews, especially the possibility that she would defensively avoid conflict by regression to pre-ambivalent (split) object relations.[4] The inordinate strength of her resistance to confronting and accepting the shadow, found in her initial dream, *anticipated* later developments in the analytical process, when she sought refuge in passive submission and fusion with her mother-analyst in order to avoid dialogue. The subsequent movement from fusion to dialogue meant a healthy acceptance of conflict, related to painful separation and the capacity to tolerate ambivalence. She longed for blissful union with images representing a return to the maternal uroboros.

Weekend separations, for example, were initially not handled well. She experienced "pining . . . feelings of loss . . . longing . . . wanting to be absorbed . . . like part of me will have been disappeared . . . like going to die, or like wanting to kill somebody." Outside and inside analysis she experienced schizoid withdrawal. In her dormitory room she retreated into books and masturbation while eating in bed; she had few interpersonal relationships other than classroom participation, at which she intellectually excelled. Inside the analytical *temenos* she experienced "needing to fuel up when bored," and her approaches to me were hypomanic and distraught. She wanted "to eat when feeling empty, depleted—either fasting or gorging." While "fasting" she stubbornly refused to take in any analysis at all; while "gorging" she experienced acute self-disgust at greedily wanting to get as much out of me as possible. As these feelings became stronger and more painful for Maya, I felt the necessity for transference interpretations.

During the first six to eight months of analysis, Maya gradually entered a long period of deep therapeutic regression to early infant experiences of the archetypal breast-mother which her choosing to lie on the couch facilitated. Jung has consistently emphasized, in contrast to other analytical schools until more recently, the adaptive significance of regression.[5] In *Symbols of Transformation* he wrote boldly that, "Therapy must support the regression."[6] Henderson has carefully identified

[4]R. Maduro and Joseph Wheelwright, "Analytical Psychology" in *Current Personality Theories*, ed. R. J. Corsini (Itasca, Illinois, 1977), pp. 83-123.
[5]Ibid.
[6]"The Dual Mother," CW 5, par. 508.

three major ways in which regression to the mother archetype may or may not result in symbolic rebirth experiences involving new ego identity formation processes in relation to initiation rites.[7] Following Jung and others, Henderson has furthered our understanding of the therapeutic efficacy of regression in the service of the ego and of the larger self.

In connection with this necessary regression, Jung notes in *Symbols of Transformation* that

> The question of nourishment has to be considered here because regression to the mother is bound to revive the memory of the "alma mater," the mother as the nourishing source. Incest is not the only aspect characteristic of regression: there is also the hunger that drives the child to its mother. Whoever gives up the struggle to adapt and regresses into the bosom of the family, which in the last resort is the mother's bosom, expects not only to be warmed and loved, but also to be fed. If the regression has an infantile character, it aims—without of course admitting it—at incest and nourishment.[8]

Referring to Freud's exclusive emphasis on the Oedipus complex and the sexual aims and objects of libido, Jung characteristically distinguishes himself from Freud by stressing central preoedipal issues:

> Freud's view is incorrect if we take it literally, for it would be truer to say that at a still earlier stage we knew nothing but nourishing breasts. . . . The real point is that the regression goes back to the deeper layer of the nutritive function, which is anterior to sexuality, and there clothes itself in the experiences of infancy. . . . Fear of incest turns into fear of being devoured by the mother.[9]

In her most primitive states Maya reported feeling like part of her mother-analyst. For her necessary regression to be therapeutic she had to gain insights into the defensive purpose of this "togetherness" so that the opposites and conflict between parts of herself could be experienced, integrated, and eventually become life-enhancing. This longed-for fusion state was experienced as both pain and pleasure. On one painful occasion she said, "I feel wiped out—disappeared—robbed, looted, controlled and swallowed." In another distressful fusion fantasy Maya let herself experience

> . . . the image of floating on water to the edge like Niagara Falls. Falling off. Fear. (sobs) There's no way out. It feels like I want to go unconscious. Go to

[7]J. Henderson, *Thresholds of Initiation* (Middletown, Connecticut, 1967).
[8]"The Dual Mother," CW 5, par. 519.
[9]"The Sacrifice," CW 5, pars. 652, 654.

sleep. The least painful route—to be sucked into you—like with mother's seduction. We have this special tie that goes back to the womb.

In much of her early analysis "floating on or being sucked into water," feeling "disappeared," and wanting to "go unconscious or to sleep" on the couch were prominent themes.

On other occasions the fusion feelings were experienced as pleasurable: as inflated security. For example, Maya said:

> I really want to get something out of you just like mother. So I can feel powerful, safe, and good. We work well as a pair, a package deal, a team or an act. You're now my best friend like mother. They called us "the gold dust twins," and people would ask me to tell my "mother and I" stories. She's my friendly companion who still wants to run naked with me on the beach. I'm closer to her than anybody else, except the mountains where I feel really strong—absorbed into the rocks and into the trees. It feels so natural. It's where I belong.

In order to avoid any conflict at all, the earliest regressed phase of the analysis was characterized by Maya's intense, defensive need to idealize our "togetherness."[10] She needed to maintain an illusion of analyst-analysand unity (mother-infant-togetherness) so that painful feelings relating to separation and the creative-aggressive and destructive-aggressive impulses reflected in her initial dream could be warded off in a variety of ways. When she could imagine us being "different" in any way —not a "package deal" or a "dynamic duo"—she became very anxious that we migit "affect each other in non-constructive ways." I was experienced as "so nice, good, and reliable." Maya asked, "How could I possibly be angry with you?"

But gradually Maya could, with the help of interpretations, become very active, angry, and able to confront the shadow. As the trend toward greater separation from her negative mother complex continued, the quality of her schizoid withdrawals into herself (mother-Maya unity) changed to include some *acceptance of conflict*, much less passivity (the bed in her initial dream), less "pining and longing for Mother," and fewer and less primitive defensive maneuvers such as splitting, idealization, and massive projective identification.[11] While splitting, she alter-

[10]K. Newton, "Mediation of the Image of Infant-Mother Togetherness." *JAP* 10 (1965), 151-62.
[11]R. Gordon, "The Concept of Projective Identification: An Evaluation," *JAP* 10 (1965), 127-49.

nately experienced me as black or white—as if I were *either* the all good, idealized breast-mother, the numinous source of all life to be envied, *or* the worthless, all bad, persecutory breast-mother (i.e., a part-object transference). Polarization of the love-hate opposites defined the dimensions of the problem (cf. Jung's "dual mother")[12] and reminded me often of the black and white rats in her initial dream.

After the tenth month of analysis, it was possible for Maya to see that the hungry, devouring shark-mother of a dream series was an unwanted part of her own hidden feeling life. As analysis progressed, her emotional hunger grew, although she strongly fought against it. But she would talk about her neediness and dependency, especially when these painful themes, involving wishes to attack, "murder" and devour me (especially my penis with her teeth), were reflected in the analytical relationship, free association, and dreams. My interpretations gradually helped her come to terms with her sharp, cutting, and knife-like destructive impulses toward mother in the inner world, and with painful negative transference reactions to me. By far the most crucial yet most difficult task for me was the confrontation and interpretation of transference resistances. She enviously attacked me, and ruthless devaluation was a core defense against her hostile, envious feelings. This phase of our work together was especially trying for me, but it was precisely at this point in her analysis that I found her initial dream helpful. It not only put her process and our experience into developmental perspective, but it also gave me hope. Although I did not mention the initial dream to her at this time, I believed that the potential for unification of the black and the white rats meant her psyche could, with analytical help, heal the positive-negative (passive vs. active) split in her feeling responses to both her inner and her outer worlds.

Maya needed to regress and have the archetypal experience of primary evil—to encounter the shadow archetype.[13] Her personal experience of primary evil and ego encounter with the shadow came in relation to *primary envy*, an affect first

[12]"The Dual Mother," CW 5, pp. 306-93.
[13]M. Fordham, "The Importance of Analysing Childhood for Assimilation of the Shadow," *JAP* 10 (1965), 33-47; J. Hubback, "Envy and the Shadow," *JAP* 17 (1972), 152-65.

experienced in life, as we know, from contact with the mother's breast or bottle.[14] The regression was necessary so that the split could be healed, and so that the personal shadow and its associated darkness could take on some positive life-giving meaning (have some space, as her initial dream had implied).

Later in analysis Maya had many "filthy toilet" dreams (e.g., "overflowing with shit"); in these we both worked together to clean up and repair damage or near damage. At this point I wondered about the anal, sadistic significance of the rats in her initial dream, since many of her dreams contained "rat droppings" at this time. She entered a period of deep regression to negative shadow material when she would sarcastically "hurl shit" (feces=words) at me, whom she experienced in the transference as the impinging mother. In relation to her initial dream, she then had a terrifying nightmare after a year of analysis in which a large *black and white* rat fell on her from the ceiling while she was in bed. She strangled the rat with the sheets and beat it to death in a brutal, bloody way. Although attempts to avoid shadow confrontation are still strong in this dream, where her ego-alien attitude is still basically negative and defensive, the ego complex is more active in struggling with the rat who is now at least a combination of *both* black and white (i.e., not as split as in her initial dream). It was at this point that I took the opportunity to refer back to her initial dream with therapeutic effect by remarking to her that we could talk about and struggle with both her "good" white feelings and her "bad" black feelings toward me. Her active-passive conflicts are thrown into even sharper relief by this dream than by her initial dream, where there is a greater sense of space or distance from them. There were several earthquake and storm dreams in which Maya felt secure in my presence. It was as if the unconscious were saying that, once enough trust in the therapeutic alliance had genuinely been established, Maya felt free to let loose with the shadow in personal experiences relating to me. This is precisely what her initial dream had suggested in order to compensate for her starry-eyed denial and isolation of destructive impulses, i.e., that she would have to

[14]M. Williams, "Success and Failure in Analysis: Primary Envy and the Fate of the Good," *JAP* 17 (1972), 7-16.

confront the shadow and objectify many of her dream experiences in her relationship to me so that unacceptable parts of her might feel more integrated and valuable.

Maintaining a strong healing container, the analytical *temenos*, was central to our work. I had to hold the situation over a period of time while she had, in her words, "something to push against for the first time." This is exactly what mother and the family myth had never afforded her, something to self-define herself "against" in the sense of creatively asserting her individuality. She had the kind of fairy-tale witch mother who was not so much depriving as all-giving: "Do you need anything else, dear? What is it you need? I will give it to you." Within Maya's family myth there had been no room for conflict. Her "witch" mother paralyzed will; she didn't do anything bad; she just stifled individuality and produced inertia. Maya's experiences with Mother promoted the illusory idea of absolute security and led to her never having had an important kind of contact with the real world. In this sense she felt as abandoned, rejected, and persecuted (impinged upon) as she would have with a mother who literally never gave anything. The effect on an infant of over-anxious mothering, too much feeding, feels equally rejecting, since the mother is responding only to her own needs and not the infant's rhythm. The archetype of separation[15] is not activated during a critical period of the separation-individuation process in earliest life. Maya's initiative remained unaffirmed. Although she developed many talents and ego strengths, there was an underlying area in her personality which had not emerged from a state of unconscious identity with mother. Areas of her psyche remained undifferentiated (e.g., the lack of a clear body image) although she had an organized ego structure. Her ego was obviously structured and integrated enough for her to regress within the analysis as she did, and in many ways she was a strong healthy person with an admirable sense of humor and personal warmth. It was necessary to facilitate this regression to the earliest stages of development in order to activate archetypal, maturational processes not experienced by Maya before analysis. This meant dealing

[15]R. Strauss, "The Archetype of Separation," in *Der Archetyp/The Archetype* (Proceedings of the 2nd International Congress for Analytical Psychology, 1962: Basel and New York, 1964), pp. 104-12.

with massive projective identification in the earliest phase of analysis, i.e., her needs to fuse with a satisfying mother-analyst to ward off fears of separation. Separation for Maya implied "killing off" her parents, especially mother, and in this sense corresponds to what Jung and Neumann have described as separation of the world parents.

I had to accept, affirm, and acknowledge her negativity as mother and father never could do. They were "not accessible" to her in that way. She had to learn slowly to experience me as a whole, imperfect person, a person she could simultaneously love and hate. She needed to know, in verbal and nonverbal ways, that she could "chew me out," "attack" me, "damage" and "get to" me, but that her hungry destructive wishes were not omnipotent. She came back after many hours of attacking me in and between sessions and I was still there, undestroyed, constant, and accepting (loving). She learned, slowly, over and over again, that she could "make a mess out of things" and repair it, do something about it over a period of time. We learned together during this period that her love and her hate could and did exist side by side—that "bad" feelings need not be split off and that situations can be "ironed out." In this way Maya was able to feel alive and real inside. She was able to move from intense neediness and a desire to be cared for all the time to experiencing "concern" and greater empathy for me as a separate person, rather than as an extension of her own narcissistic needs. I became a good enough mother and our experience sufficiently good. As the Eros-Phobos (love-hate) opposites[16] became more integrated, she could risk being closer to me with more consciousness and less greed and dread. Depressive anxieties had become more central than paranoid anxieties. Eventually, she no longer suffered so acutely from paranoid or depressive anxieties, i.e., the fear that her wishes to be close to me and love me ("take me in . . . give in to love") would result in irreparable harm or damage to either herself or me. She gradually experienced the inner certainty that hate does not necessarily gain the upper hand and destroy all life in the inner and outer worlds.

[16]M. Fordham, "Maturation of Ego and Self in Infancy," in *Analytical Psychology: A Modern Science* (Library of Analytical Psychology, Vol. 1; London, 1973) pp. 83-94; R. Gordon, "The Death Instinct and Its Relation to the Self," *JAP* 6 (1961), 119-35.

Conclusion: The initial dream can be a valuable diagnostic adjunct to the wide variety of other clues the analyst feels, thinks, intuits, and senses in beginning analytical therapy. The initial dream may be viewed in the same way as any other projective technique (e.g., a Rorschach card), inasmuch as the underlying premise for the construction of such tests rests on the activation of unconscious projections in response to ambiguous stimuli. *The initial interview is the ambiguous stimulus* in response to which an initial dream reflects an individual's psychic reality. As Jung constructed the very first projective test (word association) to be used routinely in mental hospitals, many Jungians have been inspired to continue his interest. Curiously, this interest has never been extended to the initial dream in relation to the initial interview(s), although Jung wrote: "Initial dreams are often amazingly lucid and clear-cut. But as the work of analysis progresses, the dreams tend to lose their clarity."[17]

The initial dream may provide otherwise unavailable information if the limitations of what we know and can say to patients about this additional piece of clinical information are kept realistically in mind. The dangers of premature conclusions, interpretations, instructions, and decisions based on the initial dream alone are real and too numerous to be discussed in any detail here. However, to cite only one example: the initial dream is not necessarily a prophecy or infallible statement. Because the initial dream is richer and more complete than conscious awareness, it may anticipate events and the activation of potentials. But if it is handled in the analytical situation as a self-fulfilling prophecy, we run the serious risk of colluding with our patients who may neurotically need to idealize the unconscious in a defensive way from the very beginning of treatment. Their expectations of us and of treatment are then unrealistically high; they make impossible demands, set up a situation in which they will inevitably be let down and disappointed, and they may ultimately flee. Or perhaps our patients feel justifiably "robbed" of having their own analytical experience and then with good reason they break off the treatment.

[17]"The Practical Use of Dream-Analysis," CW 16, par. 313.

The initial dream is in many ways similar to the initial interview. In both cases it is impossible to know everything the patient knows, but doesn't know he knows, although presumably everything important is there. Seeing the initial dream in relation to an initial interview can help us avoid losing perspective. The analyst may find—as does the clinical psychologist or anthropologist administering projective tests in the field—that this information is valuable only when considered in relation to the larger whole: the beginning of treatment altogether with the later stages, after many feeling connections have been established between parts of the patient's inner world and experiences with external reality. In holistic perspective, the initial dream often suggests areas for further clinical inquiry or mythological parallels that we analysts may have strong counterresistances to; a patient's dream evokes affects and images in us which may also be compensatory and helpful in monitoring our own countertransference reactions.

Despite the fact that we are in most cases without the benefit of lengthy free associations, amplications, genetic material, etc., by which we normally round out our clinical assessments of analytical content and processes, the initial dream may also help us to intervene more effectively at later stages of analysis or psychotherapy. One may on later occasions return and allude to such "big dreams," or one may never mention the initial dream to a patient. Whether we mention it or not, it can at least complement our more "objective" attempts at personality assessment because it sets off countertransference reactions in us.